# politics, society, self.

occasional
writings

## GEOFF GALLOP

foreword by Hugh Mackay

UWA PUBLISHING

First published in 2012 by
UWA Publishing
Crawley, Western Australia 6009
www.uwap.uwa.edu.au

UWAP is an imprint of UWA Publishing
a division of The University of Western Australia

THE UNIVERSITY OF
WESTERN AUSTRALIA
*Achieve International Excellence*

A full CIP data entry is available from the National Library of Australia.

Typeset in 12pt Bembo.

# CONTENTS

# CONTENTS

# Foreword

The clock has just chimed ten o'clock on the morning of Monday 27 February 2012. By one of those exquisite ironies, therefore, I have begun writing this Foreword at the very moment the Australian Labor Party's federal caucus is settling the leadership contest between Julia Gillard and Kevin Rudd. Rudd's bid to regain the leadership he had lost almost two years earlier offers the sharpest possible contrast with Geoff Gallop's approach to politics. For Gallop, personal popularity was never a key indicator of political prowess; nor did he ever regard a lust for power, fuelled by ego and ambition, as a suitable motive for political action.

Geoff Gallop's 1996 election as ALP leader in Western Australia happened in the way we might wish all our political leaders came to power: not by prolonged scheming followed by a challenge, but by a reluctant agreement, under pressure from colleagues, to stand for election when the job became vacant. He remained unchallenged as leader, serving as Premier from 2001-6, until a severe bout of depression caused him to quit politics altogether. He was as frank about that as he had been about everything else during his decade as Labor leader.

We always knew from observation that Gallop was an unusual politician. Now, in this collection of speeches and articles written during his time out of political life – a period characterised by the emotional turmoil not only of depression but also of bereavement and, more recently, the joy of remarriage – we glimpse the depth of his political thought.

He was, and is, a true-blue social democrat, a humanitarian and an internationalist – all of which might make him sound like a dreamy idealist, and the speeches and essays in this collection are certainly peppered with words like peace, justice, equity, fairness and tolerance. But Gallop has always retained a healthy scepticism. He has consistently acknowledged the importance of pragmatism, compromise and the need to work effectively within the constraints of a parliamentary democracy. He puts it as simply as this: "Politics is about power and in a democracy that means the support of the majority." So, like every successful modern politician, he couldn't utterly eschew populism, but he always weighed it against principle and, throughout the pieces in this book, it's easy to sense his despair – perhaps even his contempt – for those who think "whatever it takes" is a suitable basis for political action.

In Australian politics, it is rare to find a practitioner who is also a philosopher, yet Gallop managed to combine his deep sense of political theory, honed during his years at Oxford, with an enthusiasm – even an eagerness – to get things done. He has been uncompromising in his commitment to egalitarianism and all its implications for education, social welfare, employment and income distribution, and he has consistently believed that the core purpose of politics is to create a fair and harmonious society.

Geoff Gallop believes that ideas and ideals are politically compatible; that political passion should be tempered by social compassion; that policy, not populism, must be the engine of politics. He is suspicious of fundamentalism – in politics or economics as much as in religion – and he has a sense of history that brings a historical perspective to all his thinking.

He was Premier of Western Australia during something of a "golden era" for state Labor premiers. Peter Beattie in Queensland, Bob Carr in NSW, Steve Bracks in Victoria, Mike Rann in South Australia and Jim Bacon in Tasmania formed a formidable counterpoint to the dominance of the Liberal-National coalition federally, and they were widely respected in their state electorates and beyond. Indeed, this was a period when many voters were unusually impressed, perhaps even surprised, by the quality of the state premiers – Australians traditionally having had less esteem for state politicians than for their federal counterparts.

So Gallop enjoyed a period of remarkable collegiality and political security with his fellow premiers, and this may have further emboldened him in his determination to govern with conviction, rather than with one eye constantly cocked at the opinion polls.

That period now seems like a distant memory, as politicians and parties are marketed more and more like commercial brands, with a corresponding decline in public esteem for them and an electorate that is bound to become more volatile in its voting behaviour. (What's easier than switching from Brand X to Brand Y?) As a consequence of this strategic shift, the constant cry is heard: where is the vision? The integrity? The authenticity?

Had he stayed in politics, Gallop would have found himself under pressure to listen to media advisors and assorted tea-leaf readers masquerading as political strategists. But his well-known respect for the public service would perhaps have led him to resist some of the incursions of 'staffers' into the business of government and that might have made an interesting contrast with the way both state and federal politics are increasingly being conducted.

Since his premature retirement as a professional politician, he has become something of a 'public intellectual' – a term now much abused, as it broadens to include advocates and media commentators of all kinds. Yet, viewed through these papers, Gallop emerges as a thinker who is prepared to engage with issues, to explore ideas, without any concern for charisma, 'image' or personal popularity, and with a scepticism appropriate to the genuine intellectual.

Whether in politics or any other realm, the world really does seem to be divided between those who are determined to make the world a better place, and those who want to make themselves rich or famous, or perhaps both. It's the contest between those committed primarily to serving their own interests and creating their own myths, and those committed to the service of others and to the principles that might guide such service. No one observing the life and work of Geoff Gallop would be in any doubt about which camp he belongs to.

Not surprisingly, given the current political climate, he is in increasing demand as a speaker who is prepared to stimulate our political and social thinking. This collection explains why. It offers us a series of short, sharp jolts to our social, economic and political complacency, and a stimulus to our engagement with the ideas of a warm-hearted democrat.

HUGH MACKAY

# Introduction

Since retiring from active politics in 2006 I've been presented with an ideal opportunity to reflect upon a wide range of issues related to my former career. I don't think I've changed my mind on any of the big issues related to politics and government but I have been able to fine-tune some of my thinking, particularly as a result of my teaching public servants at the University of Sydney's Graduate School of Government. The teaching I have done in South East Asia and Africa has also alerted me to the assumptions that lie behind Anglo–American and European theories of the state and public administration. Indeed we can now see how financial crisis and declining economic fortunes in the industrial democracies has forced a not insignificant re-think of the role of the state in the economy.

Not surprisingly I have been asked to give my views on a range of issues related to my own experience of government, what it meant for me, and how it might be improved. If I was to summarise what it is I have been trying to achieve through my commentary it is an appreciation of the importance of the personal, practical and the idealistic elements of politics. Politics is, as they say, an "art" rather than a "science." It needs ideas to propel it and organisations to manage it but also politicians to live and breathe it – and to offer leadership.

## Politics involves power and principle

There is, of course, a degree of risk involved in this expanded freedom to think and reflect. Ideas can be attractive beyond their capacity to help and whilst it is true that politics must involve both "thinking" and "doing", when you are in the thick of it there are reasonably well-defined boundaries within which you operate. For example a serious politician will ask three questions when considering policy issues: "Is there evidence for its effectiveness?", "Can it work with the resources and capabilities available?" and "Is it politically acceptable?"

This reminds us that politics is ultimately about power and influence. In this real world of politics there are systems and rules and a wide range of actors pursuing their beliefs and interests in particular contexts and locations. Inevitably there will be winners and losers and the temptation to describe the process in these terms alone is powerful, particularly for those involved. "Whatever it takes", they say.

Politicians who think that way inevitably find themselves in trouble, even in societies without well-developed systems of accountability. The way power is gained and the ends to which it is put are equally important. Ethical thinking is part of the human condition and whilst it often finds itself lined up against powerful enemies such as the lust for power and the desire for revenge, it cannot be ignored. Caring about good process and good outcomes is a necessary if not sufficient condition for a properly strategic approach to politics. In fact, in our society the public interest is a legal obligation for all government officials, elected and non-elected.

I say they aren't sufficient because political judgement and political skills are also crucial. They make it possible for good ideas about process and policy to be successful. It's not just a question of having a strategy to back up your beliefs but also being able to handle day-to-day events. Events management as a style of politics has its attractions but can only work in a situation where there is a high degree of consensus. It is much better, however, to think of politics in broader terms — as a mix of principles, strategies and tactics, not any one without the others.

## Understanding the world of change

The capacity to develop strategies to back up convictions is particularly important. This leads me to believe that the first task of any politician is to ask the question: "What is happening in the world today and what does it mean for politics?" This is true whether your sphere of action is local, regional, national or international. The world never presents itself as a blank sheet of paper onto which you can write your own script. Ideas, technology, economics, culture, climate and even unforeseen events all play their part in providing definition for political activity. In our case, the last forty years have brought the politics of the Cold War, the politics of globalisation and, in more recent times, the politics of crisis following global warming, September 11 and the Global Financial Crisis (GFC). Each of these periods has carried its own language and produced its own leaders.

Firstly, it was a reformed capitalism versus communism, then globalisation versus nationalism and, in more recent times, a more vaguely defined crusade involving "us" versus "them". On the basis of our beliefs in reformed capitalism, globalisation and the "western way" there has been much meddling in the affairs of the post-colonial and developing world, meddling that has held progress back except in countries like China, India and Vietnam where pride and numbers were always destined to work their magic. Strongly held beliefs are one thing, but knowing how to support and defend them in a world of difference is quite another. We might compare, for example, the judgement displayed in developing the Colombo Plan as opposed to that involved in sending troops to Vietnam.

This raises the question: what attitude and approach serves us best when it comes to not just domestic politics but also to international positioning?

## Fundamentalism or pragmatism?

A fundamentalist mindset may provide a good anchor for political belief but when it comes to the peaceful resolution of conflict it is more often than not found wanting. Quite often, too, we can see fundamentalists supporting a policy without any concern for the actual and negative consequences of its implementation. The assumption behind all fundamentalist thinking is utopian — that there is just one truth and one way to imagine human society. By their very nature these "perfect" societies are highly restrictive and inevitably suffocating — too much freedom becoming license and too much control becoming tyranny.

Pragmatism, on the other hand, sees life as a work-in-progress that accepts the inevitability of difference and looks for ways to keep society moving forward on an even keel. It was the information-hungry Enlightenment of the seventeenth and eighteenth centuries which brought us to the conclusion that ways of seeing, working and living can change and are contestable. By cutting through the logic of fundamentalism with the insights of pragmatism the Enlightenment took us to our rights and responsibilities as human beings. Their practical remedies for living together in a community of difference, such as freedom of association and speech, elections and checks and balances, have generally served us well.

Today we live in a world of transition, not just because of the advances in information and communications technology, but also because of the challenge of climate change, the emergence of China as an economic powerhouse and the re-emergence of a highly political and fundamentalist current within each of the major religions. Amongst other things this has put the heat back onto the Enlightenment tradition and its support for the separation of religion and state and the politics of the open society.

## What about social democracy?

Also feeling the heat is social democracy, and its "third way" between capitalism and socialism. Is its belief in liberty sustainable in the aftermath of September 11? Is its belief in economic growth sustainable in a world of climate change? Has its embrace of free markets become too fundamentalist? Is it too reluctant to embrace the fraternity part of the French Revolution's "liberty, equality and fraternity"? Some say that social democracy has reached its use-by date and needs to be replaced by a greener and/or more populist type of politics.

There is some truth in this — green issues and the view that the system is out of touch can't be ignored. However, for social democrats to give up would be a tragedy. Social democracy has an important agenda-setting role that can produce long-term gains, as we saw in the 1940s and 1950s when it took up the cause of working-class welfare and the economics of Keynesianism. By focusing on economic stability and fairness it gave the market system a much-needed moral and political boost that was essential in the battle against the extremes of right and left.

When it comes to the contemporary scene, think of it this way: improved productivity will not only come from more investment and entrepreneurialism, but also from human capital and a healthy community, and a low-carbon economy requires not just pricing and policy initiatives but also support for those affected by the transition. This is social democratic territory.

However, it is not enough to see fairness as no more than a means to the ends of economics and the environment. Do we want to live in a society where those with high and middle incomes can set the agenda for taxation, health and education policies? Is it one where the health and education systems lock in inequality and social disadvantage rather than challenge them? The only hope for social democracy is to make these questions *its* questions and to *campaign* on the policy implications that follow.

Modern social democracy has been well served by common sense on economics and a genuine commitment to the environment but has become too complacent on equality, particularly as it relates to the all-important areas of health and education.

## Politics and leadership

In a very important sense, politics and leadership are inextricably linked. Politics is an activity that opens us up to the future. However, where short-term thinking and vested interests hold sway politics guts itself of the potential to make a difference — it becomes a self-reproducing system rather than a creative force. More to the point, populism and events management may have worked in the 1990s when the future seemed secured, but that is not the case for a world in transition. It follows that we need leadership for change to complete the picture.

Leadership for change today means more than just being smarter than your opponent. It means a better integration of principles, strategies and tactics and engaging the electorate around a story that deals with the past, present and future. It means being willing to take on vested interests in the public interest. It means planning for the future and being seriously concerned about policy and its outcomes and evaluation. Leaders need their tacticians, spin doctors and pollsters to keep their feet on the ground but not to set the agenda.

Secondly, it means taking seriously the power of government and the role of the public service. When government regulation of commerce fails we all suffer. When government services are less than adequate we inevitably fall short of our aspirations. Markets need good government just as much as communities need markets to generate change. It is true that the introduction of market principles to government administration has brought its benefits but it doesn't always work.

Thirdly, it means harnessing the potential of federalism and the energy of decentralisation to promote innovation. Over the years our commonwealth government has been expanding the scope of its work. To a large extent this is the result of its financial power but it's not only that. The restlessness of its politicians and the nationwide aspirations of its public servants have also played a role. All too often the states and territories have also been willing participants in the process by putting money first and federalism second. Put simply, the commonwealth has spread itself too thin to be effective. This has been recognised in the *Intergovernmental Agreement on Federal Financial Relations (2009)* but whether or not there are the attitudinal changes needed to complement the agreement is a moot point.

Fourthly, it means taking our rights and responsibilities more seriously. To enact the principle in law that we have rights and responsibilities is never easy but always important. By taking up the cause of human rights, a viable form of multiculturalism becomes possible, as does an approach to governing which seeks to include all, minorities as well as majorities. The view that this is an ill-fated enterprise that simply gives power to the judiciary breeds contempt for the principle of a 'fair go' and diminishes us as a community. However, what supporters of a rights and responsibilities agenda need to understand is that it doesn't take away the need for judgement — rights often clash in any situation and the exercise of executive power is not to be undervalued as a force for good.

## The challenge from within

Just as much as democracies like ours are being challenged by external events like 9/11, climate change and the GFC, so too is there a challenge from within. Do the measured outcomes from the market system provide us with the right signals for community well-being or do we need alternative indicators of progress? Are the feelings people have about their lifestyle just as important as the products and services they enjoy? Is economic progress enough? In societies like ours, mental health has become a major political and policy issue, particularly, but not only, as it affects the young. Although the focus of much debate has been on the effectiveness of various forms of individualised treatment regimes, the question has been asked: is our society conducive to our health and well-being as much as it is to our liberty and property?

The fact that these questions are being asked at the same time as we recognise the depth of the new challenges to our economy from competition and climate change, and to our open and respectful society from religious fundamentalists, makes them all that much harder to answer. It's as if we have re-entered a material world but haven't lost our post-material concerns. Is this really a time for re-evaluating the importance of an economic mindset? Shouldn't productivity and climate change be our sole concerns? Isn't psychological and social malaise simply a result of the decline of traditional religion? More pointedly, some say it is nothing more than Western self-indulgence.

Thinking and acting in this way would be a mistake. It's not that life without contradiction and anxiety is possible but that we complicate these realities with unrealisable aims and dysfunctional social relationships. We prefer the illusion of freedom to the complexities that come with self-awareness — both as individuals and as communities. All too often happiness is seen as a pre-packaged consumer item rather than an outcome of a well-lived life in a well-balanced and well-managed society.

Nor is it going to be possible to run away from the larger questions of meaning and purpose in a constrained world. Rigid rules based on ideology or religion may give meaning, but at the cost of autonomy. Growth that undermines the environment is self-defeating. Growth courtesy of colonialism is dead and its successor, imperialism, should join it at the cemetery. Protectionism will only bring frustration and tears. So too will tears follow if life and economics are reduced to a "free-for-all" in which the "winner takes all". Finding a better balance between work and leisure, incentive and obligation and the material and the spiritual, both as individuals and as a community, may just be not only the best way but the *only* way to deal with the challenges of our times that is acceptable and sustainable.

## Self-awareness

Can we expect to find that level of collective self-awareness and good leadership to make all these things happen? Consider how difficult it is for individuals to escape the embrace of their own illusions and prejudices, let alone for communities to do it. Even when they come to an intellectual understanding they soon find that is only half the battle — old habits die hard!

Indeed, it's one thing for political leaders to be across all the issues of the day and to have a strategy for addressing them and quite another for them to be effective in delivery. They too are individuals with strengths and weaknesses and doubts and uncertainties. They may be intellectually smart but politically inept. They may have an abundance of emotional intelligence or very little. Some may relish a fight whilst others shudder at the very thought of conflict. Some may even be predisposed to anxiety or depression.

These things do matter and in this sense the personal is the political. "Knowing about yourself" is as important as "knowing what you stand for". Beliefs are important but they aren't everything. Being comfortable in your position and with what is expected of you is also important. Sometimes we learn these things the hard way with our commitment running ahead of our capacity to cope, emotionally as well as politically.

It might seem strange that a discussion of politics which started with a discussion of a world in transition should find itself going beyond ideas and interests and focusing on the person in this way. This reflects my own experience, and that of many others, that we take too much for granted about ourselves. We learn that skating over the surface and ignoring what is happening below has its benefits but can be costly and is more often than not unsustainable.

I'd like to think, then, that the essays and lectures I've reproduced here will encourage all of us to think more carefully, not just about politics and what is needed to address contemporary issues, but also about ourselves, our strengths and weakness and how we can best contribute to the community. What I've called leadership in politics is in fact needed in all areas of life. We need leaders as much as we need Leaders!

# 1.

# The World Today

# Globalisation, the State and Social Justice

Speech delivered at
the Policy Network/Australian Fabian Society
Symposium

Melbourne, 12 April 2007

The contemporary interest in globalisation is enormous. Rarely is politics discussed without the 'g' word being mentioned. Sometimes it presents itself as a benchmark around which the politics of different governments can be compared and contrasted. Sometimes it presents itself as a description of the way the contemporary world is moving under the influence of modern technology. Sometimes it is presented as a good thing and sometimes as a bad thing. Supporters say it should be promoted and opponents say it should be controlled.

Globalisation emerged as a comprehensive ideology when the Soviet Union collapsed and previously controlled economies were integrated into the world market. To complete this liberating moment, governments were urged to break down the barriers to international trade and investment, promote the exchange of information and ideas, and support increased international migration. Here was a chance to harness difference and creativity in the interests of more wealth and opportunity for all. It was everything the pioneers of the eighteenth-century Enlightenment had dreamed of.

In looking at the public policy questions raised by globalisation it is important to focus on the facts as well as the theories. They tell us a story that is more sobering but not discouraging if one wants to promote peace and justice for those who inhabit the globe.

Certainly modern information and communication technologies have facilitated greater and easier exchange between people and businesses and the falling costs of international transport and communications have assisted trade in goods and services. This being said, the extent to which this has led to the internationalisation of trade, commerce, and experience has been exaggerated.

Writing in *Foreign Policy*[1] Pankaj Ghemawat speaks of a "semi-globalised world" with geography, language and distance still playing a limiting role. His analysis of the levels of internationalisation associated with cross-border migration, telephone calls, management research and education, private charitable giving, patenting, stock investment and trade as a fraction of G.D.P. produces figures of around ten per cent, with trade higher at around twenty per cent.

Most fixed investment is still domestically based and cross-border exchanges are still limited, despite the potentiality that comes with modern technology. The number of long-term international migrants as a proportion of the world's population is still lower than it was at the end of the nineteenth-century.

Both overseas investment and immigration are contentious issues. There is widespread scepticism about the ability of developed countries to receive and integrate immigrants, particularly those from a Muslim background or from Africa. New restrictions around concepts of "culture" are being developed to appease these public concerns.

Nor is the move to freer trade a foregone conclusion with divisions between the developed and developing world holding up world trade talks and growing protectionist sentiment influencing governments in Europe and North America, particularly since the emergence of China and India as major players in the world economy. "We have to entertain the possibility", says Ghemawat, "that deep international economic integration may be inherently incompatible with national sovereignty".

Feeding a good deal of the anti-globalisation agenda is not only the imbalances in power and wealth between the developed and developing countries, but also the undue influence exerted by the United States. It's not just a case of the enormous power of the United States but also of the sceptical attitude it has taken to global rules and institutions, preferring bilateral arrangements and coalitions. This certainly contrasts with the attitude taken by the United States in the years following the end of the Second World War even though, of course, the Cold War provided an ever-present incentive for many of these arrangements.

As a matter of fact, this summary tells me the following:

(1) That the nation state is still an important player to whom citizens generally and special interests in particular turn, and

(2) that international co-operation based on respected rules and institutions is as important as ever.

Let me turn to the nation state first and indeed to all governments, local, state and national. There is a logic to the relationship between democracy and globalisation. Governments that work on the basis that there are trends and constraints but no inevitabilities can succeed. Those that submit to the short-term thinking associated with economic rationalism always battle for political legitimacy and simply create space for neo-populism.

In other words, if leadership is to be given on behalf of a more open economy and a multicultural society — and I think it ought as a matter of priority, given the significant benefits involved — it needs to be coupled with strong support for capacity-building infrastructure and public policies that promote social justice.

Globalisation needs to be approached from a 'strategic' rather than an 'ideological' point of view. The role of government is to facilitate and manage from the political left of centre, avoiding the extremes of economic rationalism and neo-populism.

Only by securing a base at home can the all-important work of supporting international rules and institutions proceed. This is important, not just for "idealistic" reasons but for "practical" reasons. Only through genuinely global strategies, institutions and rules, backed up by a sense of collective responsibility, will it be possible to fashion some sort of global consensus on issues like trade, investment and intellectual property.

Just as important, we need to note that issues like global warming, global terrorism and global crime cannot be tackled by nations acting alone. They require not just co-operation between governments but capacity-building within nations. Ashraf Ghani and Clare Lockhart have recently reminded us that 40 to 60 countries in the world have governments which are failing to perform the basic functions of statehood. Along with developing nations generally, they need to be better integrated into the world economy:

> If the largest injustice to the poor is their exclusion from the market, finding market-based solutions to the problem of inequality is urgent. The visible hand of the market, through instruments such as risk insurance, venture funds, microfinance and management training could do much more than the aid system.[2]

Add to this the challenge of the rising powers of Brazil, China, India and Russia, let alone significant countries like Indonesia, Mexico and South Africa. We have already seen the political and human consequences of not properly managing changes in the balance of power throughout the course of the twentieth century. An internationalist agenda is not just important, it is essential if we are to provide a framework for peace and development.

Contemporary governments, then, remain at the centre of things, facing pressures from below and from above. Opening up the economy and society to more of the market *and* more of a global agenda in the aftermath of the Cold War was never going to be as easy as the ideologists implied, and this has proved to be the case. What is clear, however, is that the democratic left is once again well placed to offer leadership within communities that are uncertain of their futures and within a world that is divided by power, wealth and religion. Globalisation makes the case for rather than against politics and political management.

### Notes

1. See "The Myth of Globalisation", reproduced in *Australian Financial Review*, 16 March 2007.
2. "An Agenda for Harnessing Globalisation", *The Washington Quarterly*, Autumn 2006, pp. 75–76.

# Financial Instability, Religious Fanaticism and Climate Change

## Some reflections on the world today

In the years following the Second World War the battlelines were clear. Fascism had been defeated and democracy was hard at work containing capitalism. Peace and freedom seemed so close but remained so remote as a new Cold War divided the world into left and right. What should have been an orderly end to colonialism became complicated, as did the long-held dream of peace in the Middle East.

In such a world a truly progressive liberalism never found it hard to breathe easily. Compromised by Cold War realism and haunted by colonialism, it sought refuge in the power to produce and consume, not a bad aspiration given the trials and tribulations of depression and war. However, time marches on and it was little wonder that the Baby Boomers took up the cause of personal authenticity in the 1960s and 1970s. Unlike communism, post-war capitalism may have had a heart, but it certainly lacked a soul. It was, as Herbert Marcuse observed, one dimensional in its thinking and its practice. Its creativity was restricted to the production of things rather than the development of people.

In the battles that followed it was capitalism, albeit a reformed capitalism, that was victorious over both its own counter-culture and its external enemies to the left. Communism collapsed under the weight of its own injustices and inefficiencies. Even the former colonies, many of which had taken up the ideology of socialist planning, began to move in a capitalist direction. Indeed, so triumphant was capitalism that some spoke of an end to history.

For its part, the counter culture gradually lost its critical edge and became a part of the one-dimensional society it had once criticised. Indeed, alternative thinking and practice were legitimised and marketed as part-and-parcel of capitalism. Crucial social reforms followed, which further strengthened democratic capitalism's grip on the public imagination.

It seemed we had created a world without borders and a world without enemies. China had embraced the market. Left and right had merged to create a "third way". Science and religion combined in the interests of a new pragmatism. Developed and developing nations joined together under the umbrella of aid and assistance to create new markets and new opportunities. Imperfections there were many, but it was a world with a future worth believing in.

It couldn't last and it didn't last. September 11, climate change and the Global Financial Crisis saw to that. Once again, democratic capitalism has acquired enemies — the religious fanatics, the greens and the regulators. However, unlike the twentieth century, the capitalist states have no colonies to exploit, their economic base is no longer dominant and the sources for new productivity improvements are not so easy to find. No longer is economic progress guaranteed.

At the same time, the wars they fight can't be won with military might alone and the ideological prejudices that hold sway in the minds of many of their leaders, particularly about the Islamic world and China, make it hard for them to develop effective and sustainable strategies. It is a new world in which power is being redefined and redistributed. Democrats will need to be sensibly tough rather than recklessly aggressive.

For a number of years now we have seen how a future based on global peace and security could be crafted, but the moves in that direction have been half-hearted in effort and compromised by misguided beliefs. In the first category I would place moves to tackle world poverty and climate change. We need to risk more in the interests of social justice and a low-carbon economy. As hard as it is, and as politically dangerous as it is, it has to be done. Sharing the burdens and benefits of the future is not just socially desirable, it is economically necessary, as we saw in the 1930s when capitalism was challenged by depression.

In the second category I would put the War on Terror and the emergence of a populist version of fundamentalism. The historical and cultural factors that saw firstly tolerance, then politics, and, finally, democracy emerge in Britain and Europe over two centuries can't be replicated at the point of a gun, particularly a gun held by the infidel. Defending ourselves against the terrorist threat should be that and no more. This is good economics as much as it is good politics.

The democratic capitalist world doesn't just feel threatened by economic competition, Islamic extremism, financial instability and climate-change environmentalism, but also by social and psychological dysfunction. Why is it the case, many ask, that unparalleled wealth has not brought universal happiness? Why is it that we see such high levels of mental distress and illness, particularly amongst the young? What happened to the anchors that seemed to secure the individual and give purpose to their endeavours? Or, as a former Prime Minister might have put it: Why are so many in our prosperous society of today not "relaxed and comfortable"?

Good evidence-based public policy offers a lot when it comes to answers for these questions, but just as individuals don't always react in a rational way when they feel anxious and threatened, so too is it the case with communities and nations.

The battles of our times are being played out at a very basic and emotional level. It has become us versus them, self interest today versus the environment tomorrow, and the people versus the elite. We can see this populist current vibrating through Europe, North America and Australasia. It denies and it resists, it reduces and it narrows, and it searches for simplicity in a world of complexity. It knows the world is changing but, not surprisingly, looks to government for protection rather than advice.

Of course, there is nothing in all of this that should surprise. Politics is about power and in a democracy that means the support of the majority of the electorate. It follows that there are few if any governments in the world today that eschew all forms of populism. The task is to meet the challenges of the future and keep the people on side. In many circumstances of required reform this mix proved feasible, particularly where there is relative freedom from powerful vested interests and a step-by-step approach is possible, as it has been for the extension of rights to previously excluded segments of society. So too was competition reform easier to implement in an optimistic world with a surplus to share.

In today's more explosive world of financial instability, religious fanaticism and climate-change politics, it's not so easy. Indeed, it's much easier for politicians to respond to fear and emotion than it is to seek fundamental change on climate, promote mutual respect across cultures and religions and keep the microeconomic reform ball rolling. This is an approach that works. Not only is it the bible for many in the political class but also for many of those who write and commentate about politics.

# 2.

# Politics or Fundamentalism?

# On Fundamentalism

Speech delivered at
The Fourth Global Conference on Buddhism

Perth, 10 June 2006

Fundamentalism was first used in our theological discourse to refer to that tendency in early twentieth-century Protestantism that rebelled against science and secularism. For the fundamentalists the Bible was to be read literally (it meant what it said despite the contradictions) and what it said was the truth without qualification.[1]

Today, however, the term has a much broader application and refers to similar tendencies in all religions. Sometimes the term "Strong Religion" is used as a substitute.[2]

This broadening of the application of the term makes sense as we observe the same commitment to a literal reading of the texts, their inerrancy and their uses as the basis for a radical critique of modernisation in some if not all of its features.

In recent decades we have seen fundamentalism make a dramatic comeback as a theological, social and political force.

In working out how to address the questions it poses we need to look at three elements.

- fundamentalism as belief
- fundamentalism as a way of life
- fundamentalism as politics.

## Belief

The beliefs associated with fundamentalism represent a full-scale attack on the Enlightenment and the commitment to science and human welfare that went with it.[3]

After being liberated from dogma, science has again been reduced to the handmaiden of theology by the new fundamentalists. Human self-expression has again been straitjacketed. Fallibility has been replaced with certainty and pragmatism with dogmatism. Just as there is no dialogue with their texts over what is the truth, there is very little dialogue with others. That would be to assume doubt, and doubt has no place in fundamentalism.

For those of us who believe that "living with difference" represents one of the major challenges and "dialogue" is one of the imperatives in the modern world, the hard edge of fundamentalism creates inevitable tension, if not conflict, in our social existence.

In dealing with the challenge of fundamentalism, then, our first task is to activate all of those faith traditions for whom a critical attitude and a belief in the need for evidence is central.

At the same time, we need to go beneath the surface and seek an understanding of fundamentalism for human beings who seek salvation in the face of suffering and mortality. This may create the space necessary for a dialogue across the boundaries set by fundamentalism.

## Way of Life

I now turn to fundamentalism as a way of life.

For fundamentalists, spreading and applying the truths contained in the religious texts is an obligation. There is no surprise or controversy in this. After all, we all have beliefs that we propagate and would like to see in practice. Nor should it concern us that fundamentalists may wish to practice an alternative life-style based on the strict application of their religious principles. That is part and parcel of what it means to live in a multicultural society.

However, there is an issue that emerges when the law clashes with one of these practices. Should a commitment to difference allow for a different application of the law or should the law itself allow for exceptions?

Whilst our laws allow for some compromises in respect of religious practice, this should be a qualification that always requires strong justification and good argument before being accepted.[4]

Our first and foremost commitment must be to human rights. If our commitment means challenging certain practices that infringe those rights, so be it. This has been a controversial issue in respect to the position of young people and the rights of women, for example, in respect of female genital mutilation. Our aim ought to be to protect our children, expand the horizons for women and reduce cruelty generally throughout society.[5]

Yes, we have a right to religious expression and practice but that lies alongside our obligation to protect the rights of all. Sometimes we need to call on the state to back up such an obligation.

## Politics

Finally, we come to the question of politics.

For fundamentalists, politics is directed and unidimensional, the means by which the truth is established in law. Liberal distinctions between the law and society and law and morality have no place in a fundamentalist mindset.

They believe they have the truth and it is their responsibility to bring it to all of us. Such a politics means bad news for those committed to different beliefs. It's also bad news for the negotiation and compromise necessary for a democracy to work.

And all too often we forget that democracy works if there is trust and good will within the community. Fundamentalism has brought a hard edge to politics that makes consensus difficult to achieve.

There is a world of difference, however, between the fundamentalists who seek to establish their hegemony within a democracy and those who seek to establish it through fear, intimidation and violence.

It is at this juncture in the development of fundamentalism that it often rears its ugly head as religious barbarism. What are tendencies at work within all fundamentalist thinking become the foundation stones and justifications for terror. It is when religion becomes evil.[6]

## Tackling Evil

It's one thing to campaign for intellectual freedom and to stand up for human rights against religious malpractice but quite another to defend ourselves against religious barbarism.

Just as we need a strong state to combat racism and prejudice, so too do we need a strong state to defend us from terrorism.[7] But just how far do we take that principle? It is all too easy to fall into the trap of absolutism, even in the defence of its opposite.[8]

There are no absolutes in politics. Values often come into conflict and difficult choices have to be made. It is the management of the intersections between our values that requires judgement preceded by dialogue and deliberation.

However, while strictly speaking there can be no absolutes, there ought to be biases:

- A bias to freedom
- A bias to engagement
- A bias to rights
- A bias to compassion
- A bias to peace.

This means that if freedoms are to be restricted, engagement limited, rights undermined, compassion thwarted and peace replaced with force, there needs to be good and powerful reasons and a proper dialogue.

## To summarise:

We need to take up the challenge of fundamentalism as a set of ideas.

We need to ensure that the state and the law protect those whose rights are infringed by a fundamentalist way of life.

We need to defend ourselves against fundamentalism when it takes the form of religious barbarism, but be very careful that we don't throw out the baby with the bathwater in the process.

### Notes

1    On the history of the word and of the reality of "fundamentalism", see Richard J. Bernstein *The Abuse of Evil: The Corruption of Politics and Religion since 9/11* (2005), pp. 109–119 and James Barr, "The Dynamics of Fundamentalism", *St George's Cathedral Perth Lecture* (2000).

2    A. Almond, R. Scott Appleby and Emmanuel Sivan, *Strong Religion: The Rise of Fundamentalism Around the World* (2003). They list five ideological and four organisational characteristics of fundamentalism. The ideological characteristics are:

     1.   Fundamentalists are concerned "first" with the erosion of religion and its proper role in society

     2.   Fundamentalism is selective of their tradition and what part of modernity they accept or choose to react against

     3.   They embrace some form of Manicheanism (dualism)

     4.   Fundamentalists stress absolutism and inerrancy in their sources of revelation

     5.   They opt for some form of Millennialism or Messianism.

   The organisational characteristics include:

     1.   An elected or chosen membership

     2.   Sharp group boundaries

     3.   Charismatic, authoritarian leaders

     4.   Mandated behavioural requirements

3    See Francis Wheen, *How Mumbo Jumbo Conquered The World* (2003).

4    For example, in Western Australia, in religious education institutions and in the ordination of priests or ministers of religion, it is not unlawful to discriminate against someone because of their sex.

5    Geoff Gallop, "Living with Difference: Does Multiculturalism have a future", *Walter Murdoch Lecture* (2003), and "Interactions Between Cultural Diversity

and the Law", *Onyx: Journal of the Blackstone Society UWA*, October 2004, pp. 22–29.

6   Roger Kimball, *When Religion Becomes Evil* (2002).

7   This view is forcibly argued by Sam Harris in *The End of Faith: Religion, Terror and the Future of Reason* (2004), pp. 199–203.

8   See Bernstein, *The Abuse of Evil*.

# Religion and Politics: Trusted Friends or Sworn Enemies?

Speech delivered at
the Institute of Advanced Studies,
University of Western Australia

Perth, 3 July 2008

One thing is certain, it is impossible to ignore religion. That, of course, wasn't always the case. Indeed for a large part of the twentieth century it was believed that religion — or at least, the view that there was a God over and above and in charge of our destiny — would wither away in the face of a science-produced prosperity. Inasmuch as matters spiritual needed to be catered for, the marketplace for self-help and self-improvement would do the job, embellished, perhaps, with some of the less-confronting insights from the religions of the East.

This theory of inevitable secularisation was always going to fail, just as all theories based on "laws of human history" come unstuck. It was very much an Anglo–European point of view that struggled to make sense of the rest of the world, including the United States where a faith-based radicalism was playing such an important role in the Civil Rights Movement. However, the real turning point came with the Iranian Revolution and Islamic radicalism generally. The fact that secularisation was not just put to the blowtorch by an Islamic Jihad but also by a rejuvenated Christian fundamentalism led some to conclude that the great Age of Enlightenment had come to an end.[1]

In our own society we have seen a decidedly religious perspective brought to bear in debates over abortion, euthanasia, stem-cell research and the position of gays and lesbians in our society. It would be wrong, however, to limit the list in this way. We also see faith-based political commitment at work in campaigns in support of the rights of refugees, Indigenous communities and marginalised groups generally, as well as in debates over labour-market regulation, free trade and globalisation. In the Christian world the question of whether Jesus is on the right or the left of the political spectrum has enlivened many a theology seminar!

That all of this has been happening at the same time as we see the emergence of climate-change politics and a shift in the balance of economic power away from the United States and Europe makes it all the more complicated. It is the first time since the advance of communism in the twentieth century that the United States and Europe have faced such competition and constraint. It is a period of global change and uncertainty where very little can be taken for granted, including the living standards that have been enjoyed. Uncertainty breeds doubt, and doubt seeks a solution. Inevitably, religious-type considerations have entered the political debate about these issues.[2]

One person who has recognised this is Pope Benedict XVI. He speaks of the process of "encounter and mutual penetration of cultures", which is a feature of the modern global community. In this process, "ethical certainties that had hitherto provided solid foundations have largely disintegrated". He draws out the implications of this as follows:

> This lends great urgency to the question of how cultures that encounter one another can find ethical bases to guide their relationship along the right path, thus permitting them to build

up a common structure that tames power and imposes a legally responsible order on the exercise of power.[3]

This takes us straight to the world of politics.

## In Defence of Politics

Politics, of course, is the process by which we attempt to sort all of this out, including the issues thrown up by contemporary globalisation. It helps guide us along the right path by sorting out our problems without violence. It is a way of guiding us along the right path. Its enemies are tyranny on the one side and anarchy on the other. The establishing of political order, as Bernard Crick notes in his classic *In Defence of Politics*, is "not just any order at all; it marks the birth, or the recognition of freedom". It represents "at least some tolerance of differing truths" and some recognition that government is best conducted "amid the open canvassing of rival interests". Crick goes even further.

> ... *politics is a bold prudence, a diverse unity, an armed conciliation, a natural artifice, a creative compromise and a serious game on which free civilization depends.*

In it is found "the creative dialectic of opposites".[4]

What Crick has done is remind us that freedom requires not only political and civil liberty, but also a range of political virtues — prudence, conciliation, compromise, variety, adaptability and liveliness. He sees politics as a complex activity designed to settle differences in a peaceful way. In other words, politics is not just about systems of representation and the freedom to think, advocate and associate, it is a way of dealing with the inevitable differences that emerge in society. It is deserving of praise as "the master-science" because it is the only social activity "which aims at the good of all other 'sciences' or activities, destroying none, cultivating all, so far as they themselves allow". Its very essence is in its practice.[5]

In Crick's world of politics there are no ideological, institutional or technological fixes. It is a world requiring judgement and creativity, a world that is open to change as well as being mindful of the past. It is a world that requires order as well as freedom, and sometimes it has to be protected from its friends as well as defended from its enemies. Amongst those friends, Crick lists the non-political conservative, the apolitical liberal and the anti-political socialist. He may well have observed "you cannot have politics without politicians".

There are a number of reasons I think Crick's activity-based definition of politics is a solid foundation on which to build an argument. In the first place, it accepts difference. As Jonathan Sacks has written in *The Dignity of Difference*:

> *The glory of the created world is its astonishing multiplicity: the thousands of different languages, the hundreds of faiths, the proliferation of cultures, the sheer variety of the imaginative expressions of the human spirit...*[6]

In the second place, it grasps the importance of trust and mutual respect, and all that follows from them in the preservation of a free and civilised society. This is not just a matter for noting, we need also to draw the political education implications, as Veit Bader has done:

> *...we should focus on civilised and decent ways of living with disagreement: liberal-democratic culture, attitudes or habits, virtues and traditions of good judgement, and good practice are crucial.*[7]

It is important that we "develop the duties of civility, such as the duty to explain positions in publicly understandable language, the willingness to listen to others, fair-mindedness, and readiness to accept reasonable accommodations or alterations in one's own view".

## The Meaning of Religion

It is interesting to note, however, that at least in one important respect *In Defence of Politics* is a product of its times — there is no chapter on religion. Should religion be classified as an enemy, along with ideology and nationalism? Or, as Pope Benedict asks, is religion a "healing and saving force" or "an archaic and dangerous force that builds up false universalisms"?[8]

The first problem we face in coming to a conclusion about this issue is definitional. After all, religion is a vast ocean from which many fish can be trawled. However, for the purpose of our discussion I will use the following:

> Beliefs, actions and institutions that assume (a) the existence of supernatural entities with powers of judgement or action, or (b) impersonal powers or processes possessed of moral purpose.[9]

For some believers, such assumptions are matters of faith and beyond our ordinary understanding of the nature of things. For some they are more like commitments that compel action rather than particular claims requiring verification. For others they are views that can be reasonably held as reflecting reality, even if it is a deeper and more profound reality than that revealed by human experience and scientific investigation. For some, again they are just matters of fact, as indeed are miracles and other supernatural phenomena.

For my own part, I remain an agnostic but one who is keen to learn as much as is possible from the religions.[10] Ours is a human condition that involves suffering, uncertainty in the face of death and the contradiction in the journey of life. Attempts to force unity onto all our thinking and practice inevitably fail. It is a pluralistic world and one in which our needs always seem to be more complex than our capacity to understand and manage them. However, we have no choice but to live with the consequences of what we do.

In such a world, religion offers consolation and hope. It provides a story that has a beginning, a middle and an end. Quite properly, it takes us to the mystery of the universe, but all too often it completes the picture by pushing aside reason and experience. I find agnosticism a more appealing option. It is based, as Stephen Batchelor has argued in his challenging tract *Buddhism Without Beliefs*, "on a passionate recognition that *I do not know*. It confronts the enormity of having been born instead of reaching for the consolation of belief". He continues:

> *Agnosticism is no excuse for indecision. If anything, it is a catalyst for action; for in shifting concern away from a future life and back to the present, it demands an ethics of empathy rather than a metaphysics of fear and hope.*[11]

What is lacking in the traditional "does God exist?" debates between believers and non-believers is an agreed verification principle. I prefer to work within the world of history and experience. It provides us with a common language. We learn as we go along — as individuals and as communities. Insofar as there are truths, they are like signposts along the way rather than individual pieces of a story that explains everything. Some might call it a commitment to an open mind.

Religions have been — and are — part of that process. That there are important truths that can be learnt from religion does not have to be a matter of blind faith, but can be demonstrated from reasoning and investigation. They need to be defended, but to say they will not be capable of defence without belief in God is special pleading from those of a religious disposition. Truths about the centrality of freedom, for example, need to be defended by all people of good will, be they fundamentalists or sceptics, agnostics or atheists, believers or non-believers.[12]

## Religion and Politics — Separate Worlds?

What then, are some of these truths as they relate to the worlds of religion and politics? Is it true, for example, that religion is best kept out of politics? In other words, should religion be a private affair, separate from the world of politics and collective responsibility?

Certainly it is important to recognise the right of all to freedom of conscience. Indeed, in civilised countries, the concept of conscientious objection has been given a degree of legal recognition. So too do we in Australia accept the doctrine of the separation of church and state, at least in the sense that there ought not be an established religion or national church. As Paul Kelly argued in his Acton Lecture in 2006, "There is no basis for compromise on this point. The secular state is non-negotiable and this principle is fundamental to our pluralistic society."[13]

This being said, we are still left with the question: Is there no room for interaction between church and state?

It is unrealistic, but more importantly, inappropriate to say religion should always stay out of politics. After all, religion has always had plenty to say about how we ought to govern our affairs. Religious commentary on public policy is no better or worse than all other forms of commentary. However, the fact that it is commentary by religious figures does not give it any special or privileged status, and should politicians agree or disagree with it, for that reason alone, they could very well be opening the gates to the curse of sectarianism. It is always best to start and finish with the public interest test.[14]

Nor can religions demand a complete and unqualified freedom, even though some of our laws have made compromises in the interests of religious freedom and difference, for example, in our Equal Opportunity Acts. The Western Australian Act states that nothing in this Act "affects [...] any other act or practice of a body established for religious purposes, being an act or practice that conforms to the doctrine, tenets or beliefs of that religion or is necessary to avoid injury to the religious susceptibilities of adherents of that religion". On the other hand, there may be certain practices common to particular groups, such as female genital mutilation, that are offensive to our values and cannot be defended by reference to freedom of religion. So too may particular communities find themselves the target of surveillance in a world where religious sanction is given to acts of terror such as we have seen in recent years. There is no easy way around this challenging issue which always emerges when peace and order are threatened.[15]

We are left with the conclusion that politics cannot expect to be completely free of religion, nor can religion expect to be completely free of politics. We live with one of the great compromises of modern history, a compromise which works, even if unsatisfactory to the radical secularists on the one side and radical religionists on the other. It is a political solution to a political problem, non-doctrinaire but always mindful of the needs of freedom. It is what I had in mind when referring to "learning from history".

## Religion, Dialogue and Violence

This leads me to a second argument about religion and politics, one that is associated with the new breed of militant atheists. Religion, so the argument goes, is in and of itself a source of violence. Sam Harris explains it this way:

> Why is religion such a potent source of violence? There is no other sphere of discourse in which human beings so fully articulate their differences from one another, or cast their differences in terms of everlasting rewards and punishments. Religion is one endeavour in which us–them thinking achieves a transcendent significance. If you really believe that calling God by the right name can spell the difference between external happiness and external suffering, then it becomes quite reasonable to treat heretics and unbelievers rather badly. The stakes of our religious differences are immeasurably higher than those born of mere tribalism, racism, or politics.

Harris goes further in noting that religion doesn't allow for dialogue because it is "the only area of our discourse in which people are systematically protected from the demand to give evidence in defence of their strongly held beliefs". What we need, he concludes, is "an utterly non-sectarian way of talking about the full spectrum of human experience and human aspiration".[16]

On this last point I fully agree. Indeed it echoes the Crick view of politics which I endorsed earlier in my paper. "A free government", said Crick, "is one which makes decisions politically, not ideologically".[17] This means thinking through the consequences of one's decisions. It brings a healthy dose of empiricism to our considerations.

However, on his first point — that religion is especially divisive — Harris pushes his case beyond that which is reasonable. Religious views are one of many ways by which human beings create difference and division. Race, class and nationality are others. Each carries its potential for conflict and violence. Indeed, quite often religion is linked with one of the other three in ways that add flavour and force to the divisiveness. What makes religion distinctive in this line-up of divisions is the contradictory nature of the claims it makes. Indeed, the truth it proclaims is often a plea to go beyond tribe, nation, race, class and even religion itself to create a truly human community. To quote Jonathan Sacks again: "The supreme religious challenge is to see God's image in one who is not in our image. That is the converse of tribalism".[18]

Fundamentalism does not have to be a fundamentalism of difference, it may be a fundamentalism of unity. Think, for example, of the prominent position pacifism has or the role that utopia plays in many religions. Indeed, some would argue that religion can be best defined by the transcendence beyond self that it promotes, not just for individuals but also for communities and nations.

Harris won't allow for a distinction between the truth claims made by a religion and the beliefs inherent within the religion itself. The former may be implausible but the latter credible and constructive. The transcendence it seeks may be deeply personal or radically political, or both. It may be about this world or the next. Unswerving faith in the existence of God has been linked to a whole range of political doctrines and tendencies.

This being said, we have seen how faith linked to certainty linked to power can distort our reasoning and poison our body politic. Religion can tempt its adherents into the world of evil.[19] In relation to ideology this tendency was aptly called "the totalitarian temptation". We see it in attempts to establish by force a heaven on earth or through the acts of suicide bombers seeking martyrdom. Such tyranny and such terrorism is the antithesis of politics. The "passionate quest for certainty" in government is, as Crick observes, "the death of politics".[20] The world of politics is the world of diversity and contested ideas. This doesn't rule out improvement, but should we approach perfectibility, it will be via the hard slog of individual enlightenment (you might say salvation) coupled with social reform.

In reality, all doctrines have the potential to overwhelm their adherents. This can lead to irrelevance just as it may lead to dangerous fanaticism. It is true that the certainties of faith can drive such fanaticism and give it a particularly ugly form, but so too can humanistic creeds like socialism. Fanaticism is the issue not religion.

## Religion and the Prophetic Voice

There is, however, one more aspect of the relationship that needs recognition — religion as social critique.

This takes me back to Crick's definition of politics which has been the building block of my argument. Crick was rightly defending politics against all attempts to straitjacket it. It is always more than the systems that give it shape and can never be reduced to the doctrines that seek its attention. Some form of compromise will always be at its core — there is never a "perfect political packet".[21]

However, it is also important that social change is possible so that "groups can come to feel that they have an equitable stake in the prosperity and survival of the community". This is why he lists socialism — along with liberalism and conservatism — as important in the sustainability of a political order. Quite correctly he notes that "indifference to human suffering" and the failure "to extend the habits and possibility of freedom from the few to the many" are, along with the search for certainty, a threat to politics.[22]

Just as religion can be tempted by the politics of certainty, so too can politics be tempted by the machinery of power. Indeed modern politics is full of it — opinion surveys and marketing techniques designed to find the "will of the majority". It is politics as technique, a means to an end that has become an end in itself. It narrows the range of possibilities and shields those in power from the needs and interests of the marginalised, both here and abroad.

From these and other influences, such as "the reduction of the citizen's field of action to the private realm", Jurgen Habermas has concluded that "the democratic formation of a common opinion" is losing its "functional relevance". Action based on "values, norms and a vocabulary intended to promote mutual understanding" is being expelled from more and more spheres of life. The nourishment of social solidarity has become a necessity.[23]

Amongst the friends of politics are the social critics who look to the bigger picture in the interests of justice and community. In many ways this has been the historical role of religion — and remains so today. It means speaking truth to power without seeking power itself. It is probably impossible to imagine a politics that completely focuses its attention on the poor and marginalised as is recommended in the doctrine of a "Preferential Option for the Poor", but it is important that we be continually reminded of its implications.[24] Imagine political debate without the Parable of the Good Samaritan calling us to a better world.

Put simply, I think politics needs its prophets as well as its practitioners and sometimes the boundaries need to be pushed. A study of history and human nature tells us that hope is not an illusion and change is possible. However, it also tells us that the battles between good and evil will be settled not just by objective factors like economic power and military strength but also by subjective factors like the extent and depth of political commitment. In this context ideas matter, so do values. Both are central to the concerns of religion.

## Conclusion

My argument has centred around a particular definition of politics, "the thing which enables us to enjoy variety without suffering either anarchy or the tyranny of single truths".[25] It's not just about a system of political and civil liberty, it's also about trust, mutual respect and judgement. Politics is too important for there to be indifference about its role or contempt for its processes.

Religion can be a friend or foe of politics. By its very nature it is neither. Its certainties about God are just that and no more. They can generate furious fanaticism or a gentlemanly moderation. From religion can come policy advice about particular issues or substantial criticism of the state of society. The prophetic voice of religion can help turn the wheels of politics in an otherwise indifferent world.

For its part, politics is a friend of religion — but not without limits. It defends freedom and promotes sensible compromises. However, one does not have to be Sir Thomas More to understand that there are tensions in the relationship with "conscience" and "religious integrity" on the one hand and "the rule of law" and "political order" on the other.

On this fundamental point, politics may bend but it should not yield. It is the fulcrum on which freedom is balanced.

## Notes

1   See Francis Wheen, *How Mumbo-Jumbo Conquered the World* (Harper Perennial, London, 2004).

2   See Tony Blair, "Faith and Globalisation", *The Cardinal's Lectures*, Westminster Cathedral, London, 3 April 2008.

3   Joseph Cardinal Ratzinger and Jurgen Habermas, *Dialectics of Secularization: On Reason and Religion* (Ignatius Press, San Francisco, 2005), pp. 56.

4   Bernard Crick, *In Defence of Politics* (Penguin, Harmondsworth, 1964), pp. 18, 160–161.

5   ibid., p. 140.

6   Jonathan Sacks, *The Dignity of Difference: How to Avoid the Clash of Civilizations* (Continuum, London and New York, 2002), p. 21.

7   Veit Bader, "Religious Pluralism: Secularism or Priority for Democracy", *Political Theory*, vol. 27, no. 5, October 1999, pp. 614, 618.

8   *Dialectics of Secularization*, p. 64.

9   Steve Bruce, *Politics and Religion* (Polity, Cambridge, 2003), pp. 9–10.

10   See Geoff Gallop, "The Experience of Knowledge", *The Australian: Higher Education*, 7 March 2007, p. 39.

11   Stephen Batchelor, *Buddhism Without Beliefs: A Contemporary Guide to Awakening* (Bloomsbury, London, 1997), pp. 19, 38.

12   This very point has been made by Bernard Crick in a newspaper article calling on people of all creeds to combat fanaticism: "This age of fanaticism is no time for non-believers to make enemies", *The Guardian*, 22 October 2005.

13   Paul Kelly, "Religion and Politics — Contemporary Tensions", *Acton Lecture*, Centre for Independent Studies, 11 December 2006.

14   See Geoff Gallop, "What is the Public Interest?", *Public Administration Today*, July–September 2007, pp. 44–48.

15   As I have written in the debate about multiculturalism: "Mutual respect goes beyond positive tolerance in asking for styles of conduct and speech consistent with co-existing in a world of difference". See 2003 Walter Murdoch Lecture, *Living with Difference: Does Multiculturalism have a future?* (Murdoch University, Perth, 2003), p. 19.

16   Sam Harris, "Killing the Buddha", *Shambhala Sun*, March 2006, pp. 74, 75.

17   *In Defence of Politics*, p. 160.

18   *In Dignity of Difference*, p. 60.

19   For a comprehensive analysis of this process, see Charles Kimball, *When Religion Becomes Evil* (Harper, San Francisco, 2002).

20   *In Defence of Politics*, p. 160.

21   ibid., p. 139.

22   ibid., p. 160.

23   *Dialectics of Secularisation*, pp. 36, 45–46.

24   See Gerald A. Arbuckle, *A 'Preferential Option for the Poor': Application to Catholic Health and Aged Care Ministries in Australia* (Catholic Health Australia, 2007).

25   *In Defence of Politics*, p. 26.

# Why Does Politics Matter?

Speech delivered at
the Inaugural Gough Whitlam Lecture,
Sydney University Fabian Society

Sydney, 13 March 2007

In tonight's lecture I will be seeking answers to the following questions:

- What is meant by politics and political commitment?
- Why is political commitment important?
- How does politics differ from other forms of commitment?
- What does political commitment mean for the individual?

In exploring these questions I will refer to the career of Gough Whitlam and other prominent Labor leaders from the last century. I begin, however, with an account of what I mean by "politics" and "political commitment".

By "politics" I mean electoral politics and all that is associated with it — organising, campaigning, and planning both in respect of the over-arching issues like policy and strategy, and the more mundane issues like fundraising and candidate selection. You can't have one without the other and no one should ever underestimate the intellectual and practical commitment required to undertake these tasks efficiently and effectively. It is, as Ken Turner and Michael Hogan put it so well, a "worldly art".[1]

Politics, of course, deserves a broader definition than this. Indeed, it could be argued that electoral politics is only one way of looking at it. We engage in politics by the way we live, the choices we make about consumption, travel and energy use and by the decisions we make about our health care and education. As individuals we can make a difference by the signals we send to government and register in the marketplace.

We also engage in politics by taking up issues in our community, be they local environmental controversies or broader national or international matters related to peace and war. We may attend meetings, distribute leaflets and sign petitions. In this case, we seek to put pressure on governments by moral and political force.

Both forms of activity are to be encouraged and are important in building a better world. However, they are limited in what they can achieve. The politics of personal choice can work, but is all too often thwarted by collective decisions that push society in a different direction. Pressure from without can work too, but usually only with respect to single issues or local causes.

Whichever way we look at it, elections and the politics that surrounds them are absolutely vital. It is the way we have structured and defined politics in our own Antipodean version of parliamentary democracy and representative government.

Approaching politics in this way has its critics on the revolutionary left and the populist right. To the former, electoral politics is limited by capitalist reality, whilst to the latter it is constrained by inbuilt checks and balances that constrain the popular will. The best reply to both has always been that of Winston Churchill:

Many forms of government have been tried, and will be tried in this world of sin and woe. No one pretends the democracy is perfect or all-wise. Indeed, it has been said that democracy is the worst form of government except all those forms that have been tried from time to time.[2]

Secondly, let me make it clear that I approach the issue from a left-of-centre perspective. You might say that is not surprising given my occupation of the last twenty years. I say it tonight, however, to emphasise the point that if you are on the left and committed to a more democratic, just and peaceful world, it is my considered view that involvement in electoral politics and acceptance of all the compromises that this entails is the best way to move from theory to practice. We simply can't afford to be self-indulgent about our political commitments when there is so much that needs to be done.

All too often the left has worked with the assumption that history is on its side and that somehow events will turn out in its favour. That there is an unhealthy level of arrogance in this view is clear to see, but what is not so clearly seen is the disabling effect it can have. History should teach us that power is always contested and that those to the right will do so vigorously. Indeed, those on the right have an advantage in that they tend to see 'power' and 'power relations' not as problems to be analysed and addressed but as normal and inevitable parts of the human condition. For them, concerns relating to the tension between means and ends are less pressing and therefore less restricting when it comes to the development of political strategy and tactics. It is a world of dog-eat-dog, of winners and losers, and what is important is to make sure you are on the winning side.

What both left and right often fail to see, however, is that change is a constant. How often do we find that what is necessity today becomes unnecessary tomorrow. How often do we find that what has currency today loses value tomorrow? Our democracy is designed to facilitate and manage this process of change. To this end we have politics and the politicians who make it all happen.

However, politics is not only influenced by change, it influences change. Political leadership is a major factor in setting the terms and conditions of change. What is involved here is not just a set of relationships between government and people, but also interaction between governments and oppositions. By their strength or weakness, oppositions can influence what governments do and the way they do it. From time to time you can see a strong opposition setting the agenda for a government that has become tired and out of touch.

The end-point of politics is leadership. Just as political leaders lose authority when they fail to recognise change, they gain authority when they understand change and offer credible solutions for its management.

This takes me to the person after whom my address is named — Gough Whitlam. He was a leader who applied his intellect and exercised his will in the cause of changing the Labor Party. He challenged Labor's White Australia Policy and its opposition to state aid for non-government schools. Not only did he win these battles, he was successful in opening up and making more representative Labor's National Conference, with both federal and state parliamentary leaders being given automatic membership.

Just as importantly, he saw how Australian politics was being affected by new social movements and aspirations, and how the question of urban infrastructure had become vital for those living in our newly created post-war suburbs.

He was a student of modern society and the forces that were influencing its development, and he understood that Labor's traditional method of looking at policy through the prism of public ownership of the means of production was limited and limiting, both constitutionally and politically. In this respect he challenged his colleagues to take up the causes of social research and pubic policy.

Even though the Whitlam Government was only in power from 1972 to 1975, its effect on national life was explosive and its achievements many. Australia would never be the same again as a result of the Whitlam years. "Whitlamism" became a benchmark for political comparison and those on the left and the right defined themselves in relation to it. Criticisms of Gough and his politics are many, and in many cases they are valid, but no one can dispute the enormous personal and political effort he put in on behalf of Australia, democratic politics and the Labor Party. His is a case study of the marriage of intellect and political will.

His career is a perfect illustration of the importance of electoral politics and what can be achieved by involvement in it. Note also, however, that he needed supporters for his cause of party and policy reform. The foot soldiers for the Whitlam Revolution were many and varied in background and temperament, but they all played their role.

Whitlam's story also reminds us of how far his opponents on the right were willing to go to defeat him. Not satisfied with the regular process of accountability via election they manoeuvred within Parliament to bring a premature end to his government with the assistance of State Premiers, a Chief Justice and a Governor-General. As never before in our history, the consensus that underpins our political system was put to the test. It survived, but the memory lived on only to be revived as a nightmare when the Australian government refused the Norwegian freighter *MS Tampa* (and its 438 refugees on board) access to Christmas Island. For the Australian right, the task of gaining and keeping power is a serious and uncompromising business.

There have always been two responses from within the democratic left to the dilemmas posed by the militancy of the Australian right. There are those of the "whatever it takes" school of thought who see politics as Machiavellianism.

On the other hand, there are those who preach the politics of patience, hard work and democratic principle. They argue that Machiavellianism creates more problems than it does benefits, particularly in respect to the politics of duplicity and unscrupulousness.

All too often, those of a left-wing disposition despair of these complications and either drop out or limit their politics to community-based activism. With them go huge resources of intellect, energy and enthusiasm.

Max Weber has offered us a way through this problem in his lecture "Politics as a Vocation".[3] He distinguishes between the "saint", who always turns the other cheek as instructed to in the Sermon on the Mount, and the "politician", who is both passionate about his objectives and responsible in their pursuit. The politician will take account of the "average deficiencies of people" and accept responsibility for the foreseeable consequences of his or her actions. We should, says Weber, feel the responsibility of our actions with "heart and soul". Politicians must be able to say "in spite of it all!" when faced with the reality of an unreceptive or untutored people. Weber put it this way:

> Only he has the calling for politics who is sure that he shall not crumble when the world from his point of view is too stupid or too base for what he wants to offer.

This argument holds for those who become involved in politics generally as much as it does for those who seek leading positions in political parties. In the modern world this is complicated by the fact that all politics is subject to comprehensive scrutiny by the media and increasing regulation by the state. There are guiding principles to assist in decision but no over-arching framework that removes ambiguity and uncertainty. This means that criticism after the event will always be possible, not just in relation to the political judgements involved, but also in relation to the moral calculations implicit within them.

Weber understood this very clearly and outlined the nature of the qualities that were necessary if one was to take up politics. "Even those who are neither leaders nor heroes", he wrote, "must arm themselves with that steadfastness of heart which can brave even the crumbling of all hopes".

These are not just philosophical arguments produced by academic philosophers, they are day-to-day realities for those involved in politics. What distinguishes the Machiavellian from the non-Machiavellian is that the former all too often, and as a matter of acceptable practice, overlooks the moral tensions at the heart of the political project. Politics involves collective decision in a world of individual interest and aspiration. Politics involves distribution of burdens and benefits in a world of scarcity. Politics involves decisions involving peace and war.

Politics is about gaining power as well as using power. It involves that which separates us (gender, class, age ethnicity etc) as well as that which unites us as human beings. Reason often battles emotion just as minorities battle majorities and the future competes with the present. It involves loyalty and tribalism as well as objectivity and rationality.

Good politicians understand all of this but are not swept aside by it. It is when each of the tensions is ignored and politics reduced to a technique that we enter troubled waters. There is an important distinction to be made between the techniques that can assist politicians and politics as a technique. Politics requires research into both its ends and its means, but above all else it requires the capacity to judge and the will to decide in an imperfect world.

Let me illustrate this by reference to another great Labor leader, John Curtin, Prime Minister of Australia from 1941 to 1945. Curtin came to the Labor leadership in difficult times. The party had split in response to the Great Depression, and it was unsure of itself and divided on foreign policy. He held the party together and developed his own views on a defence policy of self-reliance and a stronger Air Force.

What particularly interests me about Curtin was his rejection of the idea of a national government of all parties which, of course, became a reality in the United Kingdom. He was put under enormous pressure to enter a national government but his belief in Labor as a force for good ran deep. His was a fight for social reform *and* national sovereignty, not one *or* the other.

It was in a similar vein that he countermanded Churchill's order to divert Australian troops returning from the Middle East to fight in Burma. Curtin wanted them home to defend Australia against the Japanese. His was a fight for national integrity *as well as* a fight against Fascism. This also took him to the American Alliance and support for new international institutions like the United Nations.

Curtin was certainly a pragmatist, but underneath it all he had not just a strength of character, but a clear sense of Labor purpose. He recognised (and felt) the tensions involved in the circumstances he faced but was not afraid of decision. As Paul Hasluck said of his Prime Ministership, "His own dedication was complete. He held back nothing from his service to the nation".[4]

What marked out Curtin and Whitlam was not only their strength of purpose but also their comprehensive account of the world and Australia's place within it. They understood that political commitment required the big picture as well as the day-to-day tactics. Sometimes it means challenge, sometimes it means response; sometimes attack and sometimes defence. In other words, politics needs heart as well as intellect.

In more recent times, the Hawke/Keating governments also had a clear view of the national interest. They were governments of globalisation supportive of the free movement of capital as well as goods and services. They saw competition within and without as the key to growth and prosperity. This required a new balance between capital and labour to be achieved by an enabling state rather than a protective state, and by the social wage rather than the living wage. They, too, challenged established interests and redefined social democratic priorities so that they were relevant to the circumstances in which they found themselves.

When Labor's domination of federal politics came to an end in 1996 it began to gain ground in the states and territories.

These governments have been pragmatic in style and reformist in content. They have brought ideas associated with strategic planning, sustainability and democratic engagement to their administrations. Some have embraced radical policies for the environment, incorporated charters of human rights into their legal framework and introduced many overdue changes to their political systems. Most recently, Western Australia achieved one vote value for its Legislative Assembly, and Victoria proportional representation for its Legislative Council. State and territory governments have been tough on crime but also keen to find new solutions to the causes of crime. They have governed from the centre and left little room for their opponents.

It was Don Dunstan, the Labor Premier from South Australia from 1967 to 1968 and 1970 to 1979, who laid the foundations for progressive state government. Don Dunstan had a similar agenda to Gough Whitlam — Aboriginal land rights, sex and gender equality, urban amenity, electoral equality, multiculturalism — but applied it at state level. Similar reforms were introduced by the many state Labor governments that followed in the last quarter of the twentieth century. These governments were part of a world-wide movement for devolution and regional and state innovation in governance and service delivery.

Bob Hawke understood what was happening with improved government at state level and developed the concept of "co-operative federalism", with support from both Labor and Liberal Premiers. Through this model the states preserved their autonomy but agreed to pursue issues deemed central to the national interest, such as competition reform. Ironically, it is John Howard who has been pushing for more commonwealth control to facilitate his agenda of Australian values and labour market deregulation. His is not an agenda that is comfortable with the diversity that comes with federalism and pluralism. Nor is he comfortable with the Labor policies and priorities that have pursued by the states and territories. One thing is for certain — he has never been able to convince the voters in the Labor states and territories to vote out their governments.

This takes me back to the beginning and my definition of politics as electoral politics. There is, of course, a more general definition of politics as the process by which we peacefully resolve conflict. It's all about negotiation and compromise and, in a democracy, it is underpinned by civil and political liberty and regular elections.

It is a messy business that allows for the expression and management of interests. Consensus is never assumed but is an objective towards which politicians need to direct their efforts. It is a worrying feature of much political commentary today that such processes are seen as inefficient and divisive. Impatience with politics and pluralism needs to be understood but ought to be carefully monitored by those committed to a free and creative nation.

To conclude. We need politics as a guiding principle for the way we govern our affairs. This is the definition to which I have just referred. It's essentially creative and open to the future. It encourages debate and dialogue, and promotes participation to the end of politically desirable outcomes. However, you can't have politics without politicians, and this takes us to the main point of my lecture.

The very decision to become involved in politics is an act of leadership and certainly an expression of citizenship. Politics can't just be an ongoing process. At regular intervals we need collective decision and political closure. Those of us to the left of centre would like to see those decisions favouring social justice, sustainability and peace. That won't happen without political commitment and responsible leadership based on intellect and imagination, or as Max Weber put it so well:

> ...all historical experience confirms the truth — that man would not have attained the possible unless time and again he had reached out for the impossible.

## Notes

1    Ken Turner and Michael Hogan (eds), *The Worldly Art of Politics*, (Federation Press, Sydney, 2006)

2    Speech in the House of Commons, 11 November 1974 in *Oxford Dictionary of Quotations*, (OUP, Oxford, 2004), p. 221.

3    For a copy of the lecture see http://www.ne.jp/asahi/moriyuki/abukuma/weber/lecture/politics_vocation.html

4    Quoted in David Black and Lesley Wallace, *John Curtin: Guide to the Archives of Australia's Prime Ministers*, (National Archives of Australia and John Curtin Prime Ministerial Library), p. 14.

# 3.

# Rights and Responsibilities

# Rights and Responsibilities: Towards a Genuinely Australian Understanding

Speech delivered at
the Sambell Oration, Brotherhood of St Laurence

Melbourne, 30 August 2006

I feel privileged to be delivering the Geoffrey Sambell oration at the Brotherhood of St Laurence.

The Brotherhood has been at the forefront of tackling poverty and researching its causes and consequences. Under the influence of pioneers like Father Tucker and then Archbishop Geoffrey Sambell, it has raised the standard of debate about our nation and how it should imagine and organise its affairs.

It has brought together the prophetic and the practical in a way that would be appreciated by its founders. Indeed, one of Geoffrey Sambell's successors at the Brotherhood, Michael Challen, has pointed out to me that he saw the need for a holistic, creative and effective response to the Gospels.

Today's proceedings could do well to follow that advice. Let's start then with the Old Testament.

## The Gift of Freedom
To use concepts like rights and responsibilities is to enter the world of the Old Testament and the invitation its God sends to

human beings to become His partners in the world of creation. As Jonathan Sacks puts it:

> *The God who gave us the gift of freedom asks us to use it to honour and enhance the freedom of others.*[1]

God's gift of freedom to which he refers is the freedom to choose. With that freedom is born responsibility and a call to justice.

How we choose determines the type of society in which we live. Decisions — even non-decisions — will all have their consequences. We can never escape from freedom — it is inherent within the human condition.

We live in a society whose declared intention is to uphold the human rights of its citizens. What does that mean and how does it relate to our personal and collective responsibilities in today's society?

In order to answer this question I intend to pursue three lines of inquiry.

Firstly, I will look at the concepts of rights and responsibilities and see what a preliminary analysis of them tells us.

Secondly, I will examine the concept of social rights from the point of view of the English liberal and radical tradition as it expressed itself in early capitalism, mature capitalism and post-industrial capitalism.

Thirdly, with the insights gained from this conceptual and historical overview I will move on to look at mutual obligation and the Welfare State in the contemporary Australian context.

## Human Rights

Rights are inalienable and possessed by *all* human beings. They signify a particular commitment to the dignity and the autonomy of the human person. They also signify the *equality* of all, whatever the race, religion, nationality or background.

Talking about rights takes us into the territory of human relations. It is a relational concept. The context may be relations between people generally or it may be relations between a government and the people.

It is our responsibility to respect the rights of others and it is the responsibility of government to protect the rights of its citizens.

Although obviously pertinent to any discussion of rights the role and special character of the right to national self-determination will not be addressed today.

Back, then, to a society underpinned by a doctrine of human rights.

What are our rights?

The earliest proponents of a rights-based philosophy spoke of the rights to "life, liberty and property". As time progressed and the concept was clarified in practice, a distinction was drawn between civil rights, political rights and social and economic rights.

In a sense, the first were our liberal freedoms, the second our democratic freedoms and the third a mixture of property rights and welfare entitlements. The latter are usually referred to as our social rights and were woven into the fabric of public policy throughout the twentieth century.

When put together, these rights give us a concept of "community". Indeed, to talk of community without reference to "liberty", "citizenship" and "solidarity" all at once ought to leave a feeling of incompleteness. It is because we live in a rights-based society that there is so much debate about restrictions on freedom, limitations on participation, gaps in accountability and conditions on welfare. However, the unfortunate reality is that the incorporation of rights into law and the application of these laws to specific situations do not happen without complication.

Rights have to be defined and their boundaries marked if they are to provide the basis for law. What are the limits of free speech? How is the right to vote institutionalised and voting organised? What are the range and type of benefits available to a citizen? Just how free is health and education?

At the same time, we know that rights can come into conflict. In concept there ought to be no hierarchy of rights but in practice decisions have to be made that may mean the setting of priorities and the creation of compromise.

Both of these issues — the definition of rights and the application of rights in the real world — are matters for intense debate in a society such as ours where terrorism has emerged as a challenge, Australian traditions of labour market regulation are being undermined, and mutual obligation is being applied to our welfare system. The question we must never forget to ask is: How do any restrictions and compromises affect our community and its declared belief in freedom, democracy and solidarity?

Now to responsibilities and their connection to rights.

## Responsibilities

Rights without responsibilities are pure abstractions. Responsibilities without rights are empty. My right is your responsibility to respect it. My right is the government's responsibility to protect it.

There are, however, other connections. My right is my responsibility to *care for* and *exercise* it. It is not just a case of freedom *from* but also a case of freedom *to*. If this wasn't the case what would be the point of saying we have rights?

This is what we might call our personal responsibilities not only to ourselves (and, I would say, our families) but also to the wider society. Sometimes we make these personal responsibilities *legal* responsibilities. For example, in Australia we not only have the right to vote we have a *legal duty* to enrol and vote.

More generally, our responsibility to respect the rights of others is captured in law and various punishments follow from any transgressions.

Responsibilities, then, are well and truly part of the rights equation. They personalise and socialise human rights.

What does this account of the concepts of rights and responsibilities tell us?

Firstly, each needs the other. Without responsibility, freedom is either inactive or in danger of becoming license. Without rights, responsibility is emptied of the ballast it needs to promote human welfare and it is unleashed on a journey that has seen it take up residence in the provinces of nationalism, authoritarianism and fundamentalism.

Secondly, there is no simple formula available to define our rights and provide boundaries for their application. This requires a dialogue within the community that will involve not just general principles but particular circumstances and real people. Such a dialogue has produced contention in all areas, but today I am going to focus on our social rights. To do this I am going to refer to the English liberal and radical tradition of thinking which has taken these rights seriously and which argues for their proper place in a true community. They were the first to aspire to a system of welfare capitalism, they helped bring about such a system and they have been arguing for its reform in more recent years.

## Thomas Paine: Security and Opportunity

In this theory they start with an imaginary state of nature without society and government. In such a state, all have access to subsistence and that which they access is theirs as long as they leave plenty for others.

Even though the context changes with a division of labour and the formation of civil society, the principle of natural rights remains the same. In the state of nature all were given access to the means of subsistence. In civil society, all should have access to the capacities required to earn a living in what had become a complex society. Nature had provided humans with equal opportunities and society should ensure that this principle was maintained.

Note that in this theory work is both a right and a responsibility. It was acknowledged, however, that there would be those who would be unable to work through age, illness, injury or incapacity. They too should be provided for in order that no one falls into misery and destitution.

This theory of welfare capitalism took shape throughout the seventeenth and eighteenth centuries, starting with the Levellers and reaching its high point with Tom Paine's *Rights of Man: Part 2* (1792) and *Agrarian Justice* (1797).

Paine made it clear that individuals had not just a claim to relief but also to mobility and opportunity. This meant making the tax system fair by removing the burdens it was placing on artisans and labourers and distributing the revenue so that distress was relieved and opportunities provided. Paine aimed to tackle the want associated with being blind, lame or poor and to "furnish the rising generation with means to prevent their becoming poor".[2]

In *The Rights of Man*, Paine proposed child allowances, old age pensions, birth and funeral benefits, workshops for the unemployed and child education from the savings coming from the abolition of the monarchy and the revenue from a progressive tax on landed estates.

In *Agrarian Justice* he proposes to give everyone a lump sum payment on reaching 21 years of age and an annual pension on reaching 55. This was to be paid for by death duties of ten per cent on land values.

Paine and his radical colleagues from this era of early capitalism saw the connections between liberty, democracy and solidarity. Their enemy was monopoly power — in the economy, society and polity. They were the friends of liberty and opportunity for all.

They believed that the real solution to what became known as the "social question" was a move beyond the Poor Law approach to welfare to an equal-opportunity approach based on economic and social rights. However, without reform of both the revenue raising and expenditure sides of government such equality could not be achieved.

They understood that rights could not be properly exercised without good health, literacy and numeracy, a decent income with provision for old age and death and, importantly, the capital and skills necessary for work.

In other words, for rights to be exercised individuals needed capacities and these could not be assumed beyond a basic human aspiration for happiness. Individual rights came with personal responsibilities and the obligation on the part of the government to ensure that its citizens had the capacities necessary to exercise those rights.

## T.H. Marshall and the Welfare State

Although many of the principles underneath Paine's thinking were realised throughout the next one-hundred-and-fifty years, they did so in the context of an industrial form of capitalism.

When he wrote his famous essay "Citizenship and Social Class" in 1950, T.H. Marshall was able to reflect upon the changes that had occurred largely as a result of the democratisation of politics and the influence of trade unions and reformist political parties. The ideas and policies for change came from thinkers such as John Maynard Keynes and William Beveridge. Indeed, it was Beveridge who spoke of the five "Giant Evils" of Want, Disease, Ignorance, Squalor and Idleness.

Marshall takes us on a journey from civil rights to political rights to social rights. He writes:

*Citizenship requires a bond of a different kind, a direct sense of community membership based on loyalty to a civilisation which is a common possession.*[3]

Like Paine, Marshall believed that "status differences can receive the stamp of legitimacy in terms of democratic citizenship provided they do not cut too deep, but occur within a population united in a single civilisation, and provided they are not an expression of hereditary privilege".[4]

Marshall spoke passionately of the need not just to abate "the obvious nuisance of destitution" but also to modify "the whole pattern of social inequality". He continues:

*What matters is that there is a general enrichment of the concrete substance of civilised life, a general reduction of risk and insecurity, an equalisation between the more and the less fortunate at all levels — between the healthy and the sick, the employed and the unemployed, the old and the active, the bachelor and the father of a large family.*[5]

This is the doctrine of the Welfare State at its best, emerging as it did after a war that saw social classes united in a common effort and after a depression into which no one wished to descend again. The development of an economic theory which produced strategies for full employment was also an essential element in this post-war version of welfare capitalism.

Inasmuch as there was a development of this model from the 1960s and 1970s, it was in the area of active labour market initiatives to guarantee the continual upgrading of skills so that the challenges of structural and technological change could be met. As the pace of change gathered momentum the status of these initiatives took a significant leap forward.

What, then, do we learn from these pioneers of the system of social rights which developed last century?

They understood that rights were only meaningful if the people had the capacity to develop them and it was important for the state to facilitate this development. They understood that there were times when people needed support because of age, incapacity, illness, or some other circumstance. In the case of the Keynesians, they also understood that there was a link between macroeconomic policy and social rights. Unemployment was seen as a condition that could only be tackled in a capitalist economy with a mixture of demand management, industry and job-training initiatives.

## Anthony Giddens and the New Radicals

Over time, of course, the range and type of benefits associated with the Welfare State changed as society and the expectations people held about standards of living changed. Not only were there changes but there was an expansion in the range of benefits made available to people deemed in need of support at various stages of their life and in the different family circumstances they may find themselves.

As is the case with all human institutions, the system itself took on a life of its own and serious questions began to be asked about its functioning, if not its relevance for the era of globalisation and post-industrial capitalism in which it now found itself.

For social democrats looking for solutions to problems, elements of the neo-liberal critique which followed the questioning process had a distinctive but not decisive influence. As Anthony Giddens remarked:

> ... *third way politics sees these problems not as a signal to dismantle the Welfare State, but as part of a reason to reconstruct it.*[6]

The role of welfare, Giddens said, was not to take society beyond the market but to work with the market to expand opportunities. He called this "positive welfare" in a "social investment state".

In language that echoes Paine more than Marshall, he spoke of the need for an "entrepreneurial culture", with those currently excluded given the chance to enter the mainstream. Policy ought to involve initiatives to help those without skills acquire them, those with outdated skills to update them and those with a lack of confidence to be encouraged.

Giddens recognised the significant changes that had come to the economy due to the influence of information technology, the growth of the service sector and changes in family patterns. Entrepreneurship associated with small business emerged as a key capacity along with traditional job skills.

The transcendence required was not beyond the market but beyond the narrow income-based supports that were showing every sign of defeating the very purposes for which they were established:

*Benefit systems should be reformed where they induce moral hazard, and a more active risk-taking attitude encouraged, wherever possible through incentives, but where necessary by legal obligation.*[7]

It should be noted, however, that such a legal obligation was seen as only one part of a strategy to lift people out of disadvantage.

Addressing family supports and family dysfunction, social capital and social networks, education and training, emotional and psychological development and employment opportunities all had to be brought to bear on what came to be seen as "welfare dependency".

What the current issues associated with welfare are revealing is the assumptions that lay behind the proposals of reformers like Paine, Beveridge and Keynes. They assumed functioning families, social order, a desire for self-improvement and an acceptance of personal responsibility. By providing security and opportunity, the state would allow all to share to the full in the "social heritage" of the times.

Today we can point to sections of our nation where such assumptions no longer apply and where "law and order" within and "law and order" without have crumbled in the face of a range of pressures, temptations and moral hazards to the degree to which they are now "the issue". As has so often been the case in recent years, Noel Pearson has come up with the words to describe our predicament: "It's now a question of personal responsibility as well as legacy".[8]

Let me put it in these terms. For the advocates of welfare, from Paine to Marshall, personal responsibility was assumed and the role of government was to allow it to work by guaranteeing rights and helping develop individual capacities. For the new radicals like Giddens and Pearson, responsibility cannot be assumed and the role of government is to recover it where it has been lost.

Hopefully, then, this analytical and historical overview provides a context for the discussion of mutual obligation in

Australia today:

- Our rights and responsibilities are linked
- Exercising our rights requires capacities
- Social rights developed to equalise opportunities and to look after those in need
- All too often, personal responsibility was assumed rather than being made the subject for attention.

Less said but equally important in this more sophisticated analysis of modern welfare was the recognition that the *way* the state operated with respect to its service delivery. Giddens speaks of a "top-down" approach that gave insufficient attention to "personal liberty".[9] Pat Dodson was even more to the point when he noted that "mutual obligation" should be "a real negotiation" involving not just changed behaviour in Aboriginal communities but changed "public sector behaviour" too.[10]

Also noted in the approach of Giddens and Pearson is the recognition that the *overall* approach of a community to its individual and collective responsibilities will have an impact on "inclusion" and "exclusion". Giddens talks of the "revolt of the elites" manifested by fortress communities and a pull out from public education and public health systems.[11]

Pearson has not only emphasised the way the system of income supports worked in the specific context of Aboriginal communities to trap many in poverty, he understands that many of the attitudes of mainstream Australia about history and dispossession, Aboriginal culture and languages, and autonomy and self-determination are part of the problem.[12]

They are both making a profoundly spiritual point — we are all in this together and assumptions and attitudes are part of the fabric that help define who we are and what type of society we create. It is not just about "them", it is also about "us".

## Mutual Obligation

Mutual obligation has been the catchword for addressing social disadvantage for two decades now.

Why shouldn't those who receive benefits meet certain conditions? Isn't this just a reflection of the fact that we all have responsibilities as well as rights? In particular, why should those who receive benefits that enable them to avoid work be supported? Isn't it only fair that they seek work or undertake the training necessary to find it? If they are not willing to act in this way, why shouldn't they lose the benefits?

These are the sorts of questions that are behind mutual obligation policies. The lines of reasoning they have been used to back this up are as follows.

Firstly, we see the view that social and economic rights are "negotiable claims that balance not only the freedom and autonomy of the claimant, but also the concerns and voices of other members of society".[13] This leads to the conclusion that obligations should be imposed on welfare recipients on behalf of the taxpayers.

Secondly, we see the view that social and economic rights are undermining personal initiative and the desire to work. Obligations should be imposed on recipients in their own interest, even if they did not recognise it immediately. It is called "compassion with a hard edge".

Like all policy proposals of the "social engineering" variety, mutual obligation carries a high degree of risk — particularly for the recipients.

As the Report by the Brotherhood of St Laurence and St Vincent de Paul in 2003 showed, those with social, intellectual, mental health, addiction, education or communication difficulties — particularly in Indigenous, recent-migrant or refugee communities — were the victims of strictly and narrowly applied mutual-obligation policies.[14]

Rather than being uplifted into the mainstream, many find themselves displaced and looking for support from family, state government or charitable organisations. Such displacement has also been the experience in the United States of an estimated 10–15 per cent of former welfare recipients.[15]

Pat Dodson and Noel Pearson hit the nail on the head when commenting on the application of mutual obligation principles to Aboriginal communities:

> *Aboriginal people and those community leaders who are charged with engagement between the community and governments have a responsibility ... to obtain the resources needed to sustain their culture, language, physical wellbeing and other aspects of their lives to the future of our people — but not at the expense of the basic human rights of those whom they represent.*[16]

They point out that in many Aboriginal communities there is "a legacy that has ruptured the natural reciprocity and responsibility that underpinned their traditional society".[17] Exactly the same point could be made about those for whom drug and alcohol abuse has undermined the basic elements of personal responsibility.

In assessing any mutual obligation regime we should look beyond the theory to the actual consequences. This means situating it in the real-world context of individual capacities and circumstances and labour-market conditions.

For many, the process of capacity development and the recovery of responsibility can only happen within a timeframe much longer than that imposed by the government or required by the labour market. Whether or not they will be better off will be determined by the nature of the job they gain and the wages and conditions attached to it. Indeed, they are usually being pushed into low-wage labour markets.

In the United States, an evaluation of the "workfare" measures by *The Economist* magazine concluded that a good deal of "idleness" and "dependency" was overcome but not poverty. "America's second challenge", they say, "now that so many former welfare mothers have ended up in low-paying jobs, is to raise the incomes of the working poor".[18] In Australia this would be less of an issue, but with the changes now occurring in the labour market one cannot expect this to stay that way.

Once rights are seen to be negotiable — either in the labour market or in the context of welfare provision — such problems are bound to emerge. So too they are bound to emerge if majorities forget their responsibilities to minorities.

History and experience tells us that once the balance between collective support and individual initiative is upset, life can quickly become "solitary, poor, nasty and brutish" for too many."[19] Mutual obligation policies can become, as the *Much Obliged* report of 2003 put it, not so much a case of "welfare to work" as "welfare as work".

We are still left, however, with the conundrum that personal responsibility is necessary if our rights-based society is to work. All too often our policies and our implementation of them ignores the *personal* (and indeed the *locational*) elements of poverty and disadvantage.

Talking of the personal is challenging but necessary. Dealing with the personal is even more challenging but still necessary. We need government and non-government agencies to be responsive and we need individuals and communities to accept responsibility. However, this can't simply be assumed, as it needs to be developed along with, and in concert with, initiatives to develop the skills and capacities needed for people to participate in the modern economy and for communities to properly organise their affairs.

## An Enabling State

My view is that the problem with the modern Welfare State is not that it is a *welfare* state but that it has yet to become a truly *enabling* state. In the first place, we see regular outbursts of ideological overkill from left or right which set the clock back. In the second place, there are timelines and resource implications here that are much longer than the regular election and budget cycles of modern government. All too often, then, the difficult areas of government are put into the "too hard basket" to wait for another day and another idealist.

The fact is, however, that we now have a range of policies and initiatives that we know can work, including strong law enforcement with respect to domestic violence and child abuse, new models of delivering health, education and training, linking individuals and communities to job opportunities, support for leadership development, measures to improve parental and community responsibility, and the use of place and case management.

For all of these measures to work there needs to be a focus on the longer term. This means a re-prioritisation of government activity towards:

- Early childhood development
- Capacity building and lifelong learning
- Family-friendly work places
- Localised and personalised service delivery
- Developing community leaders.

Such an approach takes us back to where we started with the early radicals — social rights as a platform for participation and a support in times of need. In this context, I commend the Brotherhood of St Laurence for its own strategy of working not just to alleviate, but to prevent, poverty.[20]

None of this will work without an understanding of the personal, the historical, and the circumstantial. Nor will it work without a substantial commitment by government, business and community.

However, more than anything else, connections need to be established between individuals, communities and the real economy. It is partly the responsibility of the business community to develop such connections and we have seen how it can be done in the mining industry throughout regional Australia. These initiatives need to be directly supported by government and also backed up by education and training programs. All too often we have postponed economic development in favour of income support because, as Noel Pearson has observed, "it is just too hard to figure out how to assist disadvantaged people, especially if they are Indigenous".[21]

Put into this broader context of social and economic supports, mutual obligation can have a place. It may complement the sorts of measures outlined above but could not replace them and it can only work if it is genuinely mutual with obligations being accepted by service providers. It involves responsiveness as well as responsibility.

There are no shortcuts when it comes to our individual and collective responsibilities. We have to be purposeful, patient and realistic. Indeed, in this whole debate we all too often see bold assumptions and narrow categorisations of human nature to the extent that it is sometimes hard to recognise real people living in real communities.

What we ought to have learnt is that human welfare requires rights, capacities and responsibilities. Rights need capacities, and capacities need to be exercised. Both context and commitment are required, as are individual and collective responsibilities.

What we know is that when our nation's commitment to equal opportunity is effectively discharged and combines with a desire for change and improvement on the part of individuals and communities, significant results follow.

Indeed, I would call it liberation.

Jonathan Sacks puts it this way: "When light is joined to light, mine to yours and yours to others, the dance of flames, each so small, yet together so intricately beautiful, begins to show that hope is not an illusion".[22]

**Notes**

1    *To Heal a Fractured World: The Ethics of Responsibility* (2005), p. 3.
2    http://www.thomaspaine.org/Archives/agjst.htm.
3    *Citizenship and Social Class and Other Essays* (1950), pp. 40–1.
4    ibid., pp. 75–6.
5    ibid., p. 56.
6    *The Third Way: The Renewal of Social Democracy* (1998), p. 113.
7    ibid., p. 122.
8    "The Cape York Agenda", Address to the National Press Club, Canberra, 30 November 2005, p. 10.

9   *The Third Way*, pp. 112–13.

10  "Dodson backs mutual obligation", http://www.abc.net.au/insiders/content/2004/s1258245.htm.

11  *The Third Way*, pp. 102–3.

12  For recent expressions of this view see "Don't listen to those who despise us", *The Age*, 26 June 2006, and "Big Government hurts Aboriginal population", *The Australian*, 26 June 2006.

13  Robert Henry Cox, "The Consequences of Welfare Reform: How Conceptions of Social Rights are changing", *Journal of Social Policy*, vol. 27, no. 1, 1998, p. 12.

14  *Much obliged: Disadvantaged job seekers' experiences of the mutual obligation regime* (May 2003).

15  See "From Welfare to Workfare", *The Economist*, 29 July 2006, p. 35.

16  "The Dangers of Mutual Obligation", *The Age*, 15 December 2004.

17  ibid.

18  "From Welfare to Workfare", p. 35.

19  With apologies to Thomas Hobbes.

20  "Studying the map and plotting a course", *Brotherhood Comment*, November 2005, p. 1.

21  "The Cape York Agenda" p. 1.

22  *To Heal a Fractured World*, p. 271.

# In Defence of Left Liberalism

Speech delivered at
the 2007 Don Aitkin Lecture,
University of Canberra

Canberra, 3 December 2007

I feel very privileged to deliver the 2007 Don Aitkin Lecture.

Professor Aitkin has made and continues to make a significant contribution to our public life. His store of experience is enormous and he accepts the obligation to draw upon it when participating in current debates about history, politics and education. I am particularly fond of the reflective style and approach he adopts in his recently published books and articles. In *What was it all for? The Reshaping of Australia*[1] he charts the changes that have come to Australia in the second half of the twentieth century. In particular, he notes that we have become more tolerant, curious and progressive. So too are we more diverse and individualist and, perhaps, more selfish and less compassionate.

Like many here tonight, I have witnessed or experienced many of these changes myself. As a state parliamentarian for twenty years I was a participant (and decision-maker) in many of the debates that led to change in the way the economy was organised, society was imagined and politics was practised.

Sometimes the desired changes didn't come, most notably the republic. Sometimes change came, but as the result of external events rather than internal pressure, most notably the counter-terrorism legislation.

Since retiring from politics I have had the chance to reflect upon these issues and, like Don Aitkin, have been asking what was it all for? What were the driving forces for change?

In seeking answers to these questions I find myself examining the ideas that lay behind and which justify the changes. More importantly, I find myself re-entering the debates that occurred at the time. After all, the changes that occurred were all contested and are still being contested. My oversimplified summary goes like this: within the left, the move to market economics was opposed and, on the right, moves to a freer and more diverse society were opposed. Interestingly, though, it was the latter contest rather than the former which was more bitter and sustained. My conclusion is that the most important battles haven't been between liberals and socialists, rather they have been between left liberals and conservative liberals. This is as true for the modern Labor Party as it is for the Liberal Party.

In my lecture tonight I will enter this debate on the side of the left liberals. I don't pretend that the application of such principles in the real world is ever easy or uncomplicated. However, I would hold, firstly, that many of the criticisms of its logic and applicability are self-serving and, secondly, that left liberalism has strong credentials when it comes to offering leadership in a world of difference. What is at stake in this battle is the way we understand and support our democratic institutions and the society and economy that underpins them.

However, let me begin with a summary of the criticisms of left liberalism developed in recent times but situated in the wider context of history and ideology.

## What do the critics say?

How many times have we seen it written or heard it said in recent years that left liberalism is to blame for the problems we face today? The use of the term "politically correct" is a useful indicator that you are about to be exposed to such an argument.

Sometimes it is put in terms of generations ("the baby-boomers and their New Left fantasies"). Sometimes it is put in terms of sociology ("the Chardonnay socialists and their elitist prejudices"). Sometimes it is put in terms of the psychology of self-indulgence, sometimes in terms of the philosophy of scepticism and relativism.

The sins that have been said to result are many and significant — a culture of "anything goes", a society without guiding principles and a polity gutted by the demands of minorities.

The end of the Cold War may have brought an end to international hostility between "East" and "West", but it opened the door to the culture wars between left and right. Even the threat posed by Islamic terrorists became a battleground in the culture wars, with sections of the right pointing to the culture of human rights and the policies of multiculturalism as part of the problem when it comes to the defence of democracy. We've even been told that left liberalism helps create "civilisational weakness". Politics, so the argument goes, shouldn't be about universal values, rather it should be about our national values. The formula was simple — too much humanity and not enough society leads to national weakness.

However, when it comes to economics the argument was reversed. In that case, too much society and not enough economy leads to reduced initiative and lower growth and productivity. Here we see the focus on personal responsibility and self-help as opposed to the left's emphasis on structural disadvantage and inequality.

In taking up the challenge of responding to these criticisms it is important that we clarify the definitions and provide some context for the discussion.

## The Liberal Tradition

In many ways, liberalism is the defining philosophy of our times. Certainly it is the most resilient.

It makes the case for freedom against tyranny and opportunity against restriction, and emerged in the battles against religious intolerance, Mercantilism and political authoritarianism in the seventeenth and eighteenth centuries.

However, history is always complicated and liberalism has never been given a free ride. From the right it has always been challenged by conservatism and nationalism, and from the left by socialism and collectivism.

What, then, became of liberalism as a result of these encounters with right and left?

Like all ideologies that find themselves in the marketplace of politics and history, it splintered. Some kept the focus on the idea of freedom from government interference not just in the economy but also in society generally. Their theme was simple — distrust of government and support for market exchange and voluntary association.

Whilst such libertarianism has survived as an important tendency of thought, the most common result, at least in the world of politics, has been a marriage between liberalism and the right, and between liberalism and the left. The conservative liberals, or neo-conservatives as we now like to call them, advocate a mix of strong government, traditional social values and market economics. Left liberals, on the other hand, support the widest possible application of the principles of freedom and equality. They seek a form of community underpinned by civil and political rights, social freedom and an enabling state.

Left liberals accept that a civilised world will involve necessary restrictions on freedom and inevitable inequalities in standards of living. However, when looking at the issues facing government, left liberals will always ask tough questions about any restrictions proposed for human expression and activity. So too will they be concerned with the pressures on individuals associated with cultural and social conformity. This libertarian streak is coupled with support for equal opportunity against the restrictions which flow from caste, tradition and class.

## John Stuart Mill

In many ways the case for left liberalism is embodied in the thought and politics of John Stuart Mill. Indeed, for my generation the battle between the liberal ideas of Mill and the socialist ideas of Karl Marx was central. Whilst the Marxist idea of revolution had enormous intellectual and emotional attraction it was Mill's ideas of freedom and opportunity that had most impact. The myth of revolution was replaced by the practicalities of reform under the banner of human rights and opportunities.

Freedoms were extended and discrimination outlawed. At the same time, the principles of multiculturalism replaced the ideas associated with cultural nationalism. Indigenous rights were recognised and significant resources devoted to tackling educational disadvantage in society generally. New social movements and new ways of thinking and living became part of the social furniture and a demonstration of the variety which lies at the heart of the human condition. Just as important was the left's acceptance of the liberal argument against the centrally planned and regulated economy. The state's role was to support macroeconomic stability, promote competition and tackle inequality.

All of this was consistent with Mill's thinking. However, it is worth noting that Mill's left liberalism also involved a substantial critique of modern commercial society with its "trampling, crushing, elbowing, and treading on each other's heels". He envisaged a future society that would respect individuality and diversity, and one that allowed for a market economy. With the "moral and mental cultivation" that came with labour-based co-operatives and the spread of political participation throughout society the hard edges would be removed from trade and commerce. Assisting in this process would be government initiatives in areas like education, factory reform and land ownership.[2]

Mill believed that the "manifold unlikenesses", the "diversity of tastes and talents" and the "variety of intellectual points of view" were "the mainspring of mental and moral progression". As Geraint Parry has observed of Mill's thinking: "Liberty was not so much the supreme good in itself. It was a necessary condition if men were to develop their very varied capacities to the full. The result would be a rich and differentiated society in which every man — even the greatest eccentric — could find his home provided the achievement of his desires did not hinder the interests of others".[3] Mill's was a case for individuality, independence and self-cultivation as opposed to paternalism and conformity.

Having made these preliminary comments I now turn to my defence of left liberalism as a primary pole of attraction for those keen to promote and build a better way of life.

That left liberalism has had a significant impact on public policy is there for all to see. Not only have the boundaries of personal freedom been expanded but measures to promote equal opportunity have become incorporated into our political architecture. However, just as the twentieth century came to a close, questions began to be asked about the sustainability of this project linking freedom and equality. It wasn't just that some of the achievements were questioned but also that the very premises underpinning the project were seen to be wanting. In particular, concerns were raised about philosophical scepticism, the human capacity for rationality and the relationship between unity and diversity in a democratic society. It is to this issue of unity and diversity that I would now like to turn.[4]

## Multiculturalism and Democracy

It is acknowledged that we live in a multicultural society. However, multiculturalism as a guiding principle for governments working in a world of difference has been subject to significant criticism. According to the critics, multiculturalism is based on relativism and the compartmentalisation of cultures. Rather than promote unity through mutual respect it is said to provide a protective wall for social separation and fundamentalist and extremist thinking and practice.

I note the irony in the fact that criticism of multiculturalism has come at the very time when its benefits are clearly visible. It was — and is — all about learning to live with difference in an increasingly globalised world. This opened up Australia to new people and new influences and has without doubt been a factor in our contemporary success.

What, then, of the criticism? In the first place, we need to note that multiculturalism wasn't just about learning to live with difference, it was also a much-needed and direct attack on racism, discrimination and other forms of social isolation and exclusion. It was all about respect for Indigenous culture, equal opportunity in a new country and the education of people to live peacefully and co-operatively with their neighbours. Indeed, there is an eerily theoretical and other-worldly quality to much that has been said against multiculturalism and its strong support for a fair go. It is as if the critics are in denial about the continuing presence and threat of racism and discrimination in our society.

In the second place, we need to remind ourselves of the central tenets of multiculturalism. It is not a doctrine empty of unifying content. Indeed, it has always relied on a commitment to democracy and human rights as the foundation for unity, with culture and religion being matters for personal reflection, healthy dialogue and political advocacy but not requirements for citizenship.

Multiculturalism occupies that heavily contested territory at the intersection of a democratic polity and a pluralistic society. It accepts that religion and cultural difference is a reality and that without a degree of negotiation and compromise democracy couldn't work. For example, the mainstream Christian

Churches have successfully incorporated some exceptions into anti-discrimination legislation to accommodate their views. In a real rather than a theoretical democracy there will always be accommodations of this sort. They don't mean the end of western civilisation but rather they are a sign of our moral maturity in a world of difference.

This takes us to the heart of the difference between conservatives and left liberals. Conservatives are unable to imagine unity based on liberty, democracy and the politics they produce. For them, the social contract has never been enough. To bring people together, conservatives see a need for a pre-liberal sense of shared identity based on religion, culture and national values. Take away the socialisation and social control related to these national values and the worse-case scenario is a "war of all against all". At best, then, differences can be tolerated but certainly not embraced.

Let me illustrate this point by referring to the Pledge of Commitment used at Australian Citizenship ceremonies. When people from overseas join us we don't ask them to give up their religion or culture but we ask them to commit to a democratic way of life:

> *From this time forward, I pledge my loyalty to Australia and its people, whose democratic beliefs I share, whose rights and liberties I respect, and whose laws I will uphold and obey.*

Having attended many citizenship ceremonies, I have always been struck by the elegance and simplicity of this Pledge of Commitment. It is apolitical language that can speak to all, not just some; and it goes to the heart of our most basic commitment as a citizen in a democracy.

What we can socialise around is our ideology and system of civil and political liberty. This also allows us to draw a line in the sand when cultural or religious practices and behaviour undermine civility and infringe rights. Finding that line is not easy, as we have found with our anti-discrimination laws and their potential impact on some religious institutions. In a free society the different traditions and religions are always battling for respect on the one hand and seeking privileges on the other. Politics is about managing this process. It is not a mathematical exercise; indeed, it requires leadership and judgement. Should leaders ditch multiculturalism in the name of a narrower band of national values they risk losing the ability to speak to the community as a whole. They also disarm themselves in the important battle with the extremist currents that exist in all the traditions. Indeed, they risk creating the very tensions which they claim to reject. This is one of the many ironies of contemporary political practice in an age of terror and uncertainty.

## Freedom and Democracy

I trust I have been able to establish that left liberalism is not silent on the question of core values. They understand that you can't have freedom without a free society and that free societies need to be defended from their enemies. Conservative criticism on the point has always been self-serving. Perhaps the problem is a different one — that left liberals are too rigid and absolutist in their commitment to freedom; so much so, in fact, that they give too much space to the enemies of freedom. This was certainly a position taken during the Cold War years and it is one which has re-surfaced as part of the War on Terror. It is an argument that requires both a methodological and political response. Let me start with methodology.

The left-liberal way of thinking has always grounded the idea of freedom in its social, economic and political context. This means considering the "freedom from" and "freedom to" agenda as part of one whole. It also meant considering them in the context of history. John Stuart Mill, for example, exempted the application of his principle of liberty from any nation "anterior to the time when mankind have become capable of being improved by free and equal discussion". Despotic government may be justified in societies lacking civilisation provided that the powers of government were being used to promote and develop civilised values and institutions such as the rule of law. When such a society made progress the need for government intervention would reduce.[5] As Jonathon Ree has observed when reviewing a recent biography of Mill:

> *He was a disciple of progress before he was a disciple of liberty, and he valued liberty not for its own sake or for the sake of short-term human happiness, but as a contribution to what he called 'the permanent interests of man as a progressive being.*[6]

In Mill's writings, then, we can see a healthy degree of pragmatism. Freedom is not seen as an absolute. We also saw pragmatic tendencies at work in the accommodation of the sorts of differences which are part of a multicultural and multi-religious society. It is not a philosophy based on absolutes and understands the need for political judgement when applying principles like freedom and democracy. In fact, the view that strong and decisive action by the state may be necessary to defend freedom isn't anathema to a left-liberal position. Nor should it be. However, for a left liberal, such developments would always be contentious, and even more so if associated with restrictions on freedom of expression or if part of an attempt to impose cultural and political conformity. A left liberal would look at the question itself (to increase or not to increase state's power?) and at the way it is being handled politically, and what this means for the health of our community life.

This last point is important, particularly in the context of the development and administration of laws to counter terrorism. Such laws take us into new and potentially dangerous territory and need to be administered carefully by the police and other agencies. The type of political leadership given to these agencies and the vigour of the scrutiny applied to them has special significance. How easy is it to politicise that process and, as Noel Pearson put it recently, conflate cultural war with the war on terror? The use of wedge politics, racism and xenophobia for domestic electoral gain is not only dangerous but, as Pearson notes, it also undermines the unity of purpose needed to successfully prosecute the war on terror.[7] This is understood by a politics informed by left-liberal thinking but not or too little by those for whom "national values" should be pre-eminent.

## The Human Rights Agenda

This being the case, the question is asked: should our democracy provide for extra checks and balances? Left liberals say "yes" and point to bills or charters of rights as that check. There has already been momentum in this area with charters established in the A.C.T. and Victoria.

However, it's not just another check and balance. Committing to human rights signifies a belief in the dignity of all human beings, no matter what their race, religion, nationality or background. Once again we are in the territory that allows for education and socialisation around values that make sense for the whole community and not just parts of it, most usually the dominant part. It formulates an individual responsibility to respect the rights of others and a collective, political responsibility to protect the rights of all.

The debate about the charter of rights tells us a good deal about contemporary conservatism. Sometimes the critics focus on the restrictions that a rights-based regime places around the process of designing legislation and public policy. Politics and not judicial decision, so the argument goes, should have the capacity to find the balance between liberty and order that best suits the circumstances that prevail. This is another version of the argument that left liberalism is too absolutist in its approach.

Is it true, of course, that the establishment of a charter of rights is intended to exercise a limiting function on the exercise of power. That's why charters are attractive to liberals in the first place. The question remains as to whether they provide too many limits on the exercise of power. The answer to this question is no. In Victoria, for example, the Charter of Rights and Responsibilities makes it clear that rights can be limited under law to an extent that can be "demonstrably justified in a free and democratic society".[8]

This is not the end of the story as far as the critics are concerned. The major complaint seems to be the shift in power towards the judiciary. For some it is the very fact that the judiciary is given a role that is the problem. Why is this? Because many of the judges are thought to be out of touch with the community on questions of law and order.

This may or may not be true. The key point, however, is that it is irrelevant to the argument. Judges are given the responsibility to adjudicate without fear or favour. Should we have a charter it will be the result of political judgement and parliamentary decision. Any role being played by the judiciary will be there because of legislation. The more important question is whether the Parliament should relieve itself of some of its sovereignty.

Such a question is appropriate when talking about a constitutionally entrenched bill of rights that allows judges to overturn legislation. I note in passing that judicial review doesn't seem to be a problem when it comes to rulings on the powers of the commonwealth and the states in our federation. I agree that, should we extend this role by incorporating rights into our constitution, there would be plenty to argue about. However, the fact remains that the charters established in the A.C.T. and Victoria preserve the sovereignty of Parliament. What they do is ensure that the human–rights implications of any proposed law is fully considered and that existing laws are interpreted "as far as is possible in a way that is compatible with human rights".[9] At the same time, all public authorities are obliged to act in ways that are compatible with human rights.

In other words, the whole charter movement is more about debate and more scrutiny, but not at the expense of parliamentary sovereignty. What the critics seem to be saying is that such debate and scrutiny is unnecessary or, probably more accurately, that should such debate occur it should be through the normal channels of parliamentary and extra-parliamentary politics and would not be assisted by a charter and judicial commentary on it.

This takes me back to Mill and his deep concerns about conformity in modern democracies. He wished to see "virtue" and "intellect" and not just "numbers" and "interests" playing a role in the political process. He also wished to see minorities protected, and to this end favoured a system of checks and balances for popularly elected assemblies. In contemporary Australia we have seen these ideas take shape in many ways. An example is proportional representation for a majority of our Upper Houses, most recently Victoria. So too have we seen new institutions established to scrutinise the executive and promote wider debate about public policy. All of these developments can be seen in the light of left-liberal political agitation, most of it emanating from the much-maligned ferment of the 1960s.

## Rights and Responsibilities

Talk of the 1960s takes me to the last argument I want to address tonight — that concerning rights and responsibilities. It is all very well to acknowledge the role of left liberalism in improving our political system. Indeed, this is a role it continues to play in the campaign for a charter of rights. The problem is, so the argument goes, that individuals have been encouraged to see themselves as separate from the community. Choice has become an unattached principle and our responsibility to each other lost in the search for an illusory autonomy. In particular, the whole notion of lifestyle diversity has been the subject of extensive criticism, particularly because of its assumed impact on the moral fabric of the community.

There are, of course, variations on a theme here. Some of the critics argue from a religious position, others from a position of secular concern. With respect to religious critics, it is easy to see the discomfort felt at recognition of gay and lesbian lifestyles and many of the achievements of the women's movement. There is little room here for compromise between the religious conservatives and left liberals. It is a clear clash of values.

That our society has — and continues to — widen the scope for personal freedom is one of our strengths. It is a recognition that diversity lies at the heart of the human condition and helps secure rather than weaken our bonds of community. That we have improved our community life by removing discriminatory laws and tackling prejudice is clearly demonstrated by noting what happens in countries that have not moved in this way.

This takes me to the secular critics of modern society. There is no shortage of writers, many in fact who we would classify as left liberal, who have pointed to the values vacuum at the heart of our modern commercial and consumer society. Indeed, it was the central player in the story I have been telling, John Stuart Mill, who was very clear on this point. "I am not charmed", he said, "with the ideal of life held out by those who think that the normal state of human beings is that of struggling to get on".[10] The conclusions he reached are as relevant today as they were in the nineteenth century. R.J. Halliday put it this way: "As a radical Mill assumed the interdependence of reform by individual exertion and reform by public agency. To him, self-culture and social reform were inseparable; an intelligent and active character presumed a responsible society".[11]

It is in this area that we see a radical switch in the critique of left liberalism. From being insufficiently concerned with the public consequences of so-called private behaviour, left liberals are accused of being social engineers in their desire to reshape human society. For conservative liberals, rights and responsibilities are understood in the context of consolidating traditional social values and a market economy. Being responsible means upholding those values.

Left liberals, on the other hand, have always been restless in the face of commercialism and inequality. Whilst markets are accepted as necessary to freedom and progress, the way they operate can be influenced by government and community. Values like fairness translate into policies for equal opportunity. However, not all action should come from government. For left liberals, civil society is just as important as the home for free association and the development of alternative modes of production and consumption, such as those we associate with the co-operative movement. Left liberals are concerned with the tendency to uniformity and a one-size-fits-all approach to economic organisation that comes with both socialism and unfettered capitalism.

Just as you can't straitjacket human society within *one* culture or *one* religion, so too you can't straitjacket the economy within *one* system of ownership and control. A healthy economy will involve government and private-sector enterprises as well as other economic forms such as co-operatives and mutual societies. This is good for reasons of choice and efficiency as well as for reasons of balance. As Henry Mintzberg has put it: "Above all, we need balance among the different sectors of society. This applies to attitudes no less to institutions. Private sector values are now pervading all of society. But government and other sectors should be careful about what they take from business."[12]

## Social Inclusion and Exclusion

Left liberals have always understood that to exercise rights, capacities are needed, for example, a general education, work and life skills. It is seen as the responsibility of the democratic state to guarantee the capacities to participate in social and economic life and provide support for those incapacitated by age, illness or disability. In more recent times it has been recognised that personal responsibility could not be assumed as a given, particularly in a welfare system highly focused on income support. Reform of the Welfare State itself has become a left-liberal objective. This is seen in the strong emphasis given to capacity building alongside the traditional income supports. The role of welfare, explained the English sociologist and reformer,

Anthony Giddens, was not to take society beyond the market but to work with the market to expand opportunities.[13]

However, what is understood by this social inclusion/exclusion agenda is that rights and responsibilities go both ways and include all. If poverty is to be tackled and society improved, business and community, as well as government, have a role to play. Indeed, the social values of mainstream society, whether reflected in withdrawal of elites from public education, the creation of walled suburbs or the inability to confront the facts about Australian history and Aboriginal dispossession, are as much a part of the rights and responsibilities mix as is the attitude of welfare recipients to the benefits they receive. So too are the broader issues associated with work/life balance and well-being generally.

What is at stake here is not individualism versus mutual obligation but the terms and conditions of mutual obligation. Two questions stand out. Firstly, are our motivations solely economic? Are monetary incentives or sanctions the only way to change behaviour? Secondly, do wider social attitudes and practices matter? If we answer "no" to the first and "yes" to the second, we are on the way to developing strategies and policies that have the potential to work. If we answer "yes" to the first and "no" to the second, our strategies and policies are bound to fail. I reach these conclusions because policy has to deal with real people living in real communities with real histories and individual needs.

Human well-being, as Mill outlined so clearly, requires rights, capacities and responsibilities. Rights need capacities and capacities need to be exercised. Both context and commitment and individual and collective responsibilities are important. Yes, we need liberty and democracy, but so too do we need solidarity, but free of the constraints of race, religion or culture that can pollute its purpose and undermine it liberating power.[14]

## Conclusion

The time has come to summarise the arguments and reach some conclusions. In particular, we need to ask whether there are consistent themes at play in the battle between the left liberals and their conservative-liberal challengers.

On the conservative side we see elements of fear and suspicion. They fear the disunity that can come from difference and are suspicious of attempts to build unity on the basis of civil and political liberty alone. They fear freedom and point to its habit of becoming licence. They are suspicious of a rights-based individualism and the case it makes for gender and sexual equality. They fear the loss of incentive in a supportive society and are suspicious of government attempts to promote equality of opportunity. A good deal of their politics is built on these fears and suspicions.

The left-liberal reply to all of this is very straightforward — give everyone a stake in the society by guaranteeing their civil, political and social rights. It is uniformity, conformity and inequality that undermines society and holds back the progressive instincts of humankind. They assume diversity in human nature and advocate diversity in the economy, society and polity. It is this assumption rather than opposite that guarantees unity and provides a basis for political education. Indeed, it is the suspicion of diversity that all too often degenerates into prejudice, the suspicion of rights that all too often facilitates oppression, and the suspicion of freedom that all too often leads to paternalism.

I cannot emphasise enough the importance of diversity in the left-liberal world view: diversity in political institutions in order to provide balance in political representation and checks on political power, diversity in ways of thinking and living in order to inspire change and learn more about the human condition, and diversity in the economy in order to encourage innovation and provide different options in work and organisation.

Diversity is not just a means to an end, but it is a reflection of humanity's restless and inquiring nature. Best to build a theory on the basis of this diversity than to start with assumptions that fail the test of time and experience. That was, of course, the fate of socialism and is the Achilles heel of conservatism.

Left liberals are the sceptics of modern politics. For them there is no overpowering "Truth" that encompasses all of reality. There are truths such as the link between freedom and progress but even that is conditional. Rather than advocate for a particular religion they prefer to advocate dialogue across religions. They are the gatekeepers for reason and tolerance. Their enemies are not those with faith or strong beliefs but those who propagate their views with an unhealthy and dangerous fanaticism. Providing for checks and balances, building bridges between people of different backgrounds and encouraging inter-faith co-operation are not optional extras but essential ingredients of a free society, as is balance between the public, private and community sectors.

The challenge for government, then, is to provide context for diversity. That means a system based on liberty, democracy and solidarity, and political leaders committed to the expansive and embracing ethos required to make such a system work. It is the case, of course, that offering leadership around these principles is not easy. Nationalism and prejudice creates an "us" and "them". Religion creates "believers" and "heathens". Commerce creates "winners" and "losers". All of these divisions create the basis for political mobilisation. Indeed, the tyranny of the majority, or what Mill called the tyranny of collective opinion, is an ever-present danger. Charting a course through this minefield can be a nightmare and the best of left liberals often fall at the first hurdle.

Still, it has to be acknowledged that politics involves compromise and a degree of give-and-take is part of what it takes to hold society together. However, what we also know is that a politics built around human rights, multiculturalism, a wide range of checks and balances, and an enabling state has the best chance of delivering the common good. The reasons for this are simple. Firstly, it accepts the reality and understands the benefits of diversity; secondly, it understands that political power, economic power and the power of collective opinion all matter; and thirdly, it seeks to give all a stake in the future.

It is a challenging agenda but so are the times in which we live.

### Notes

1    Allen and Unwin, 2005.
2    This account of Mill's thinking and the quotes come from Gregory Claeys, "Justice, Independence and Industrial Democracy: The Development of John Stuart Mill's Views on Socialism", *The Journal of Politics*, vol. 49, 1987, pp. 122–47.
3    "The Idea of Political Participation" in Geraint Parry (ed.) *Participation in Politics* (Manchester University Press, 1972), pp. 27–8.
4    See also Geoff Gallop, "Living with Difference: Does Multiculturalism have a future?", Walter Murdoch Lecture 2003 (Murdoch University, 17 September 2003), and Geoff Gallop, "Freedom based on tolerance", *Australian Higher Education*, 4 April 2007, p. 36.
5    See "Justice, Independence and Industrial Democracy", pp. 138–9.
6    "The Advanced Liberal", *Prospect Magazine*, Issue 141, December 2007. http://www.prospect-magazine.co.uk/printarticle.php?id=9896
7    "All enemies aren't equal", *Weekend Australian* http://www.theaustralian.news.com.au/story/0,25197,22731563-5013477,00.html
8    See *Charter of Human Rights and Responsibilities Act 2006*, 5.7 (2)
9    ibid, 5.1 (2) (6)
10   Quoted in R.J. Halliday, *John Stuart Mill* (George Allen and Unwin, 1976), p. 108.
11   ibid, p. 94.
12   "Managing Government Governing Management", *Harvard Business Review*, May–June 1996, p. 83. I have developed this argument on the need for balance in politics, society and economics in "Essential Ingredients of a Healthy Community", Keynote Address Western Australian Community Foundation Annual Summit, 9 June 2006.
13   *The Third Way: The Renewal of Social Democracy* (Polity Press, 1998), Ch. 4.
14   I have outlined these ideas more fully in "Rights and Responsibilities — Towards a Genuinely Australian Understanding", The Sambell Oration 2006 (Brotherhood of St Laurence, 30 August 2006).

# The Case for a Charter of Rights

### Speech delivered at
### Human Rights Arts & Film Festival

### 18 March 2010

There is little doubt that one of the most powerful ideas in the modern era is human rights. It has been a clarion call to revolution as well as an impetus to reform. Its universality has seen it applied in many circumstances and on behalf of all those who are oppressed or discriminated against on the basis of their race, colour, sex, language, religion, disability or background.

For those of a religious disposition, the call to protect and promote rights is part of God's "gift of freedom" (as Jonathan Sacks has put it in his theological and political tract *To Heal a Fractured World: The Ethics of Responsibility* (2005).[1] For humanists, rights are a "form of protection of what it is to be human — of our capacity to act consciously and deliberately in the formulation of our life's journey".[2]

In this morning's talk I wish to address the question — should Australia back up its stated commitment to a politics and culture of human rights by legislating for a Charter of Rights as other nations have done and, indeed, as the Australian Capital Territory and Victoria have done? In order to do this I propose to undertake the following tasks: firstly, to discuss the concept of human rights itself and how it relates to responsibility; secondly, to provide a brief overview of the Australian experience in this territory; and thirdly, to examine what has been said about the Charter proposed for Australia, with a view to reaching my own conclusion.

## Rights and Responsibilities

Let me begin by talking a little more about the concept of human rights.

Human rights are inalienable and possessed by *all*, no matter what their race, religion, gender or background. The very idea of a human right is closely linked to two other powerful ideas developed in the modern era — liberty and equality.

Linking rights to liberty and equality created a political and social program for both radicals and reformers in the eighteenth century. It was the Enlightenment at work in the world of politics, with America and France choosing the revolutionary path and Britain the reformist path.

The earliest proponents of a rights-based philosophy spoke of the rights to "life, liberty and property". As time progressed and the idea was clarified in practice and a distinction was drawn between civil rights, political rights and social and economic rights. In a sense, the first were our liberal freedoms, the second our democratic freedoms and the third a mixture of property rights and entitlements to education, health and, in the case of misfortune, welfare. It was about opportunity as well as freedom.

Think of it this way. When we put together these rights we are presented with the powerful idea of "community". Indeed, to talk to community without reference to each of "liberty", "citizenship" and "solidarity" leaves us with a feeling of incompleteness. We might have freedom but do we have equal opportunity. We might have democracy but do we have freedom? Each requires the other and each supports the other.

However, the unfortunate reality is that the incorporation

of rights into law and the application of these laws to specific situations do not happen without complication. Rights have to be defined and their boundaries marked. What are the limits of free speech? How do we institutionalise the right to vote? What are the range and type of entitlements that should be made available to a citizen?

At the same time, we know that rights can come into conflict, for example, between freedom and entitlement. In theory there ought to be no hierarchy of rights, but in practice decisions have to be made that mean the setting of priorities and the acceptance of compromise. Such compromises, like those which are associated with wartime, can take us to the very edge of the boundary between a free and an authoritarian society.

This leads me to say something about the relationship between rights and responsibilities. Rights without responsibilities are pure abstractions. Responsibilities without rights are empty. Not only is my right the responsibility of others (and the government) to protect, it is also my responsibility to care for and exercise it. As the political philosophers might put it — it is a case of freedom to, as well as freedom from! If this wasn't the case, what would be the point of saying we have rights?

Responsibilities, then, are well and truly part of the rights equation. Without responsibility, freedom is either inactive or in danger of becoming license. Without rights, responsibility is emptied of the ballast it needs to promote human welfare and it is unleashed on a journey that has seen it take up residence in the provinces of nationalism, authoritarianism and fundamentalism.

I believe there is a clear understanding of the importance of civil, political and social rights to the well-being of our society. The question becomes — just how far are we willing to take that understanding when we know there is no single or simple formula available for their application to the real world, and when we fear (if only secretly) that support for such rights will challenge some of the assumptions we have about the way society should be ordered.

Let me now turn to the Australian experience. What does this story tell us about the way we have handled these dilemmas?

## Historical Overview

Australia is now the last of the great democratic nations to have a Bill or Charter of Rights built into its legal system. The drafters of the Constitution only included a small number of limited civil and political rights — trial by jury (S80), freedom of religion (S116) and interstate residence (S117). To do otherwise would have been surprising given the blatantly racist and discriminatory attitudes and laws prevailing at that time. There was, of course, some reference to economic rights, with one of the key drivers of Federation being the desire to create a unified national market. Thus followed section 92 of the Constitution which provides for trade, commerce and intercourse between the states to be absolutely free. Property rights also found a place in the Constitution by way of a requirement on the commonwealth to provide fair compensation for the compulsory acquisition of property (S51xxxi). We were left, then, as George Williams has observed, with "some checks and balances but few express rights, set within a framework of responsible government".[3]

Attempts to change this state of affairs have met with little success. Proposals to include human rights in the Constitution failed in 1944 and 1988. In 1944, two states voted yes (South Australia and Western Australia). In 1988, no states recorded a yes majority in relation to the questions on fair elections and rights and freedoms. In both cases, "States' Rights" won out over "Human Rights".

This has also been a major issue with respect to failures by the commonwealth government to institutionalise human rights through legislation in 1973, 1983 and 1988. The one bill that passed into law — Malcolm Fraser's Human Rights Commission Act (1981) — was much more limited in scope and did not impact on the states. This is precisely the limitation that had been placed on the trial by jury and freedom of religion clauses in the Constitution itself.

It is true that Anti-Discrimination legislation has been passed by Commonwealth and State Parliaments. They cover sex, race, disability and age. However, as Zifcak and King have observed, they are not "a comprehensive guarantee of equal treatment in Australia. They are at best legislative compromises that have attempted to balance the interests of different groups and have been deliberately confined to particular fields and particular activities within those fields".[4] What this means is that the Anti-Discrimination Acts, as good as they are, do not fully meet Australia's international obligations under the International Covenant on Civil and Political Rights or the International Covenant on Economic, Social and Cultural Rights.

Some progress was made in the 1990s, when the High Court determined that sections 7 and 24 of the Constitution guaranteed a system of representative democracy through their requirement that the House of Representatives and the Senate "be directly chosen by the people". What follows from this, the Court concluded, was the freedom of political communication. Such a freedom needed to be distinguished from the freedom of speech generally and could not be seen as absolute as a legitimate public purpose could justify its restriction.

A similar logic has been applied in *Roach v Electoral Commissioner*. In this 2007 judgement, the High Court upheld an implied right to vote, although it, too, is not absolute. To quote the Court: "Voting in elections for the Parliament lies at the very heart of the system of government for which the Constitution provides".[5]

It is true, then, that our rights receive some recognition at the national level through the Constitution, legislation and judicial interpretation by the High Court. It is, however, a very limited recognition that doesn't provide the basis for building a political culture that respects and promotes human rights. Fortunately, however, we have been presented with a ready-made model to achieve this objective through the Australian Capital Territory's Human Rights Act (2004) and Victoria's Charter of Human Rights and Responsibilities Act (2006). It has been this model which has largely formed the basis for the recommendations of the National Human Rights Consultation chaired by Father Frank Brennan.

The major features of this so-called "dialogue model" that are relevant to my speech today are as follows:

Firstly, the rights protected are civil and political rights which, in the Victorian case, includes the cultural rights of Indigenous people.

Secondly, there is a general limitation clause allowing all the listed rights to be limited in particular circumstances.

Thirdly, any Bills introduced to Parliament must explain how the Bill is compatible with human rights.

Fourthly, Committees of the Parliament have been established to examine Bills for their compatibility with human rights.

Fifthly, and so far as it is possible, laws must be interpreted in a way that is compatible with human rights and the Supreme Court can issue a Declaration of Incompatibility if that is not possible.

Sixthly, the public sector is required to act in ways that are compatible with human rights. The legislation seeks to ensure that human rights are observed in policy development and administrative practice.

Seventhly, in the case of the ACT, an individual who feels he or she has had their rights violated by a public authority can bring a claim and, with the exception of damages, the Supreme Court may grant the relief it considers appropriate.

The aim of such Charters is to facilitate a dialogue between the Legislature, the Executive and the Judiciary. It does this without undermining the pre-eminence of Parliament and with full recognition of the need to balance rights against each other and against other competing public interests. The

Brennan Committee went further in arguing that some civil and political rights should be without limitation — the right to life, protection from torture and cruel, inhuman or degrading treatment, freedom from slavery or servitude, avoidance of retrospectivity in criminal trials, freedom from imprisonment for inability to fulfil a contractual obligation, freedom from coercion or restraint in relation to religion and belief, and the right to a fair trial.

What this overview tells us is that those seeking constitutional or statutory protection of human rights in Australia have encountered significant opposition. Australia is the only democratic nation without a national bill or charter of rights. In the first instance, opposition was based on the majority view that discrimination based on race was necessary and acceptable, that the legislative freedom of the states could be undermined at the expense of the federal balance, and that the English mixture of parliamentary government and the Common Law was sufficient to protect our rights. In more recent times, the argument about race has left the scene only to be replaced by a view that the need for the executive government and legislature to act "in the public interest" would be unduly thwarted by a charter or bill. Balancing our rights and interests is said to be a "policy" decision that should be left to the political process and kept out of the courts. Some go further and argue that the Westminster system itself would be undermined as power shifts from the Parliament (and the governments it produces) to the Judiciary.

Underneath all of the argument, however, is a continuation of the view that we do not need to go beyond our current constitutional and legislative arrangements to protect rights. As Bob Carr put it so clearly: "A bill of rights is an admission of the failure of parliaments, governments and the people to behave in a reasonable, responsible and respectful manner. I do not believe we have failed".[6]

In essence these are now the arguments against — it places an unnecessary constraint on government, it undermines parliamentary democracy and is not needed anyway if rights are to be promoted and protected. Certainly the federalist argument is still lurking in the shadows but is more difficult to sustain given the Brennan Committee's conclusion that a national Human Rights Act should only apply to the commonwealth and its institutions and agencies. "It would be counter-productive and unwise", they say, "to have the Federal Parliament impose on the states and territories a catalogue of human rights and a process for determining the regular limitation of those rights".[7] What happens in the states and territories is best left to the political processes there. This is an important recommendation by Brennan and his colleagues because it recognises the role local innovation can play to progress reform in a federal nation. This is exactly what the ACT and Victoria have contributed to the national debate about human rights.

One other more general point needs to be made and that relates to the Common Law. I find it somewhat strange that the Common Law is often invoked in defence of the status quo. The former Chief Justice Murray Gleeson put it this way:

> There is an inconsistency between an assertion that the Common Law makes legislative protection of human rights unnecessary and a complaint that legislative protection of human rights will empower judges who apply the legislation to make decisions about matters that are inappropriate for judicial decision making.[8]

Such an inconsistency exists, of course, because it is the judiciary, not the elected parliamentarians, that establish and develop the Common Law.

The fact is the judiciary plays a significant role in our political system — the Common Law, the Constitution and interpretation of Parliament's laws and regulations. Our founding fathers built judicial review into the fabric of Constitution and our Parliaments regularly incorporate judicial review mechanisms into their legislation. As Zifcak and King have pointed out, "the courts are everyday required to give meaning and effect to legislative criteria such as whether the executive actions are 'unreasonable' or 'improper' or 'procedurally unfair' or 'contrary to the public interest'. It is hardly possible to get legislative criteria that are broader".[9] Years and years of judicial interpretation have seen definitions developed and refined as new circumstances emerge. It is part of our valued system of "checks and balances", why, we might ask, could they not be trusted to play a similar role in relation to a Charter of Rights?

One would hope that all of us agree that the answer to this question is in the affirmative. However, in fairness to the opponents of a charter I think what most are really saying is that the Courts should not be given this role in the first place, not that they can't be trusted. They present an image of the Courts being clogged up with silly or trivial cases, most of which require a balancing of rights with each other or with the broader public interest. It is the whole enterprise of institutionalising our rights in this way that offends them.

Why, then, do I support such legislation?

## The Case for a Charter

There are a lot of good things about Australia but one of them isn't the re-emergence of a form of political and cultural nationalism, backed up at times by a particularly crude and nasty form of populism. The temptations faced by politicians as a result of this "tyranny of collective opinion" (as John Stuart Mill put it) are many and varied. Sometimes our governments go close to crossing the line between right and wrong, sometimes they cross that line. I'm talking here not just about the laws and regulations they pass but also about the messages and instructions they send to the bureaucracy about how they are to relate to the individual and communities they are required to serve.

We describe ourselves as an egalitarian and tolerant nation, but significant and unjustified inequalities remain as do not-insignificant pockets of racism. Just to give one example reported on by the National Health and Hospitals Reform Commission: in Australia, less than 30 per cent of those with disability due to mental illness participate in the workforce. This is less than half the rate of comparable OECD countries. This is part of a more general story in which Australia's public institutions have not been able to produce the same equalising efforts in education and health as other similarly democratic nations.

We need always to remember that the public interest involves minorities, the marginalised and the vulnerable as well as majorities. Ensuring that this is the case is never easy but would be greatly assisted if a Charter of Rights could be given a role in the legislative process, the administration of policy and the interpretation of our law.

Requiring Ministers to table statements of compatibility when introducing legislation to Parliament and involving MPs in the process via a Joint Committee has been shown to increase attention to the human rights implications of new laws. Parliamentary debate will improve and the issue of human rights is given the status it deserves in our free and democratic society.

Requiring public sector agencies to incorporate human-rights compliance in its Codes of Conduct, to report on its human-rights compliance and to act in a manner compatible with the Charter will send a powerful message to our public servants about their responsibilities. In saying this I note the comments of the British Institute of Human Rights when reviewing the day-to-day functioning of UK's Human Rights Act:

> Too often the Human Rights Act is associated with technical legal arguments or perceived to be limited to high profile — and sometimes spurious — claims by celebrities and criminals. These case studies reveal a very different picture. They show how groups and people themselves are using not only human rights law, but also the language and ideas of human rights to challenge poor treatment and negotiate improvements to services provided by public bodies.[10]

We are reminded by the UK experience that the Human Rights Act benefits ordinary people and, in particular, the all-too-often marginalised and vulnerable in our society such as the elderly, the disabled, the mentally ill, the victims of domestic violence and asylum seekers. Indeed, the Institute reminds us that the Act has helped plug gaps in the anti-discrimination framework and is increasingly being used to assist public-sector agencies consider the needs of individual service users.

It is true that many of our public-sector agencies understand and act on their obligations to citizens and clients, but it is a different matter when they are legally obliged to and individuals are granted the right to institute an independent course of action for any breach of human rights by a federal authority. With the Court being able to provide the usual suite of remedies — including damages, as is the case in the UK — a strong onus is placed on the public sector to think and act responsibility and respectfully.

In making this point I note that the Brennan Committee did not believe that social and economic rights ought to be amongst those for which public agencies had a requirement to uphold and for which they would be accountable through the courts. It was concluded that primary economic and social rights such as the rights to education, housing and the highest standard of healthcare were not matters for the Courts because they usually involved decisions about resource allocation "which courts do not have the expertise or information to make".[11] Rather, complaints in this arena could be heard by the Australian Human Rights Commission. At the same time, the proposed Joint Committee on Human Rights could examine whether proposed legislation is "reasonably tailored to progressive realisation of these rights".[12]

Requiring the High Court to interpret legislation in a way that is compatible with the human rights expressed in the Act and to issue declarations of incompatibility is equally important. This obliges the executive arm of the government to respond, review and explain. Importantly, however, it remains the privilege of Parliament to conclude that legislation breaching rights is in the public interest and should be left in place.

In defending this role for the High Court (and for the courts in the ACT and Victoria), we should note the case for a "limitation clause" in respect of a range of civil and political rights listed. This is commonsense and recognition that we are not dealing with absolutes.

Such a model has been well described as a "dialogue model", with Parliament at the centre of and in ultimate control of proceedings. Parliament not only has the role of debating and passing the Human Rights Act, it remains in charge of its width and breadth, no matter what the courts say. Through such legislation it places constraints on the exercise of executive power in a way that is consistent with the many reforms that have supported the equality and dignity of people, no matter what their background, race, gender, religion or sexuality. Indeed, it gives extra bite to these longer standing commitments.

Perhaps this takes us to the heart of the matter. Human rights have proved to be a pest to tradition, to religious fundamentalism, to political authoritarianism, to prejudice and bigotry and to administrative intolerance. Belief in human rights has generated important movements for reform and the universality of the idea guarantees it will continue to play that role, not only within politics but also within civil society, where many institutions have traditions and rules that restrict rights and liberties. The campaign for equality of the sexes within the Christian Churches comes to mind as an important example. Our laws have tolerated such discrimination as part of the grand historic compromise between freedom and tradition. Traditionalists, however, often express concern that under a Charter their "rights" are at risk of being trampled on by the onward march of progress.

More to the point today, however, is the deep suspicion within elements of the political elite that a Human Rights Act will make it too hard for them to govern when faced with challenges such as terrorism and crime generally. We have even seen immigration policy linked to border protection in ways that would have been shunned thirty years ago. The political elite has also expressed concern at the improbability that reference to a range of rights can help solve the decision-making dilemmas faced by politicians and public servants when dealing with complex matters involving individuals, the community and resource allocation.

I believe these two sets of criticism miss the point. Firstly, it is clear that a rights-based society in law as well as ideology throws a light, if not a legal sanction, on remaining pockets of discrimination, intolerance and barbarity. In some cases, such as female genital mutilation, this has prompted state intervention to ban the practice. In others, the historical compromise about which I spoke earlier is maintained and progress or otherwise left to the internal process of the voluntary association. This tension between what our legal system aspires to and what our social system sanctions is healthy and necessary. On the other hand, not having a Charter of Rights legitimised by the Parliament sends a message to the community that the government itself is fearful of subjecting itself to serious human rights scrutiny. It all comes down to what sort of society you wish to live in and how far you are prepared to go in tolerating cultural relativism. The Charter model is sensitive to difference but supportive of progress. This is a good balance to have.

Secondly, it is clear that a Charter of Rights doesn't undermine decision making in government and parliament, but it does make it a requirement that human rights always form part of the discussion. It helps avoid the tunnel vision that all too often operates within government. Indeed, the British case studies show that the existence of a human-rights protection has encouraged public authorities to search for solutions in situations they had previously been viewed as unavoidable and unalterable. However, without the back-up of a legal sanction one wonders how far such creativity would be possible, let alone encouraged within public sector decision-making.

What has been happening in our political system in recent years is that the checks and balances on the executive and the scrutiny placed on the practices associated with tradition have been caught up in the so-called Culture Wars. Opposing a Charter of Rights has become more than a policy issue. Rather, it has become a battleground with "moral truth" and "tradition" on one side and "progress" and "human equality" on the other. What it demonstrates is that the progress which was assumed for the world at the end of the Second World War when the Universal Declaration of Rights was adopted by the United Nations in 1948 cannot be taken for granted. It has to be argued for and fought for every inch of the way, whether the question relates to high-profile issues like capital punishment and torture or more mundane matters like the rights of the elderly in nursing homes or transport access for the disabled.

What the Brennan Committee has proposed for Australia is measured and consistent with our parliamentary system of government, but at the same time it places the rights and liberties of our people at the centre of our political equation. It is a check and a balance that won't guarantee their full realisation but it will certainly help fill in the legislative and procedural gaps that currently exist in Australia. Just as importantly, it will help focus the energies and priorities of the nation around the rights and liberties of the people. It gives us a philosophy of unity and hope rather than a culture of division and despair.

**Notes**

1    Schoken Books, 2005, p. 3.
2    Spencer Zifcak and Alison King, *Wrongs, Rights and Remedies: An Australian Charter* (Australian Collaboration, Albert Park, 2009), p. 15.
3    George Williams, *Human Rights under the Australian Constitution* (Oxford University Press, Melbourne, 1999), p. 45.
4    *Wrongs, Rights and Remedies*, p. 25.

5    *Roach v Electoral Commissioner* (2007) 233 Commonwealth Law Reports, 162 @ 198.

6    Bob Carr, "The Rights Trap", *Policy*, vol. 17, no. 2, Winter 2001, p. 21.

7    *National Human Rights Consultation Report* (Commonwealth of Australia, 2009), p. 364.

8    Quoted in *National Human Rights Consultation Report*, p. 350.

9    *Wrongs, Rights and Remedies*, p. 55.

10   *British Institute of Human Rights, The Human Rights Act — Changing Lives* (Second Edition) (London, 2008), p. 5.

11   Tom Campbell and Nicholas Barry quoted in *National Human Rights Consultation Report*, p. 366.

12   *National Human Rights Consultation Report*, p. 366.

# 4.

# Left-of-Centre Politics

# Does Social Democracy Have a Future?

Speech delivered at
Ideas and Society Program, La Trobe University

Melbourne, 7 December 2010

In order to address the question before us tonight we might begin by reminding ourselves of what can be meant by "the future". It could mean that which we need to manage, like the inevitable scientific and technological changes that come with human ingenuity. It could mean that which we seek to avoid such as financial chaos, nuclear catastrophe or destructive climate change. However, it could also mean that which we seek to create. In other words, there is a future to be made as well as one to manage and avoid. Politics is as much about will as it is about analysis. We need both to examine and to propose.

This being said, I turn to the question before us tonight, namely the future of social democracy. In order to design a future for social democracy we need to understand its past and present condition as a political and social movement.

## The Grand Era of Social Democracy
It began as a movement that initiated and managed change of its own making. It was a leader in the community and in politics.

It regulated and reformed capitalism in the aftermath of the Great Depression and in the face of the challenges of fascism and communism. It brought social justice to the table of public policy by taming the market and influencing the means of production, distribution and exchange. It extended the Welfare State and broadened it to ensure that health and education were available to all.

By the 1960s its interests had moved from the economy to society. Its conception of social justice linked it with new movements for change — equality for women, anti-racism, multiculturalism, law reform and rights for gays and lesbians. Once again it played a leading role in promoting and institutionalising change, with many social democrats outflanking the right with their commitment to liberal reform. In saying this, I think of people such as Don Dunstan and Gough Whitlam in the Australian context, and Tony Crosland and Roy Jenkins in the British context.

Here was the grand era of social democracy from the 1940s to the 1970s. Even when not in power, social democrats were setting the agenda in the interests of a freer and fairer society. We could accurately describe it as a hegemonic force.

## Globalisation and Social Order

However, as the world around it changed, so too did social democracy. Communism collapsed under the weight of its own injustices and inefficiencies, and the idea of economic freedom, within and between nations, made a dramatic comeback. It came to be seen as an imperative for all governments — national, regional and local — if good living standards were to be sustained.

From being a leading force for change of its own making, social democracy used its support in the community to become an effective supporter and manager of globalisation and the microeconomic reforms it required. This meant changing or dismantling some of the public institutions it had itself established in the aftermath of the Second World War. Although there were important variations on a theme, the overall trend from market sceptic to market advocate was clear.

From an appeal based on the immediate material and social interests of people it made its case on the basis of the national interest against vested interests in an increasingly competitive world. Not surprisingly, some of its working-class base began to have doubts about this drive for efficiency, even when steps were taken to assist them in the transition to a more market-based economy.

Society, too, was changing. The long period of economic expansion had brought material success but not, it would seem, happiness. Thus began the values debate and its culture wars. A revived fundamentalism questioned the liberal reforms from the 1960s and gave new life to the social conservatives, who had been on the back foot within social democratic parties. The "freedom to" question became as important as the "freedom from" question. A new "tough on crime" agenda, mutual obligation policies and a zero-tolerance approach to a range of questions exposed divisions that many thought had died peacefully twenty years earlier.

Not surprisingly, some of the civil-libertarian base of social democracy began to have doubts as this law-and-order phenomenon from the right came to exercise influence over the parties of the centre left.

From being a leading force for change with a clearly defined ideology and constituency, social democracy had become a manager of competing forces within the body politic — right and left, economics and the environment, and liberty and order. This managing in the middle was not without its political and policy achievements, but it did take a chunk off its membership and electoral base, with some going to the green left and others to the populist right.

Even the style and demeanour of its leaders changed. Off went the radical edges and on came the focus groups and marketing. From being a mission, politics had become a method. It looked and sounded a little like the end of history, a third and final way, as Francis Fukuyama had predicted in a book with the same title.

## The Challenge of Climate Change

Meanwhile, a new issue had emerged demanding attention — climate change. Social democrats had taken the environment on board as an important issue, but there was a vast chasm between the politics of nature conservation and environmental amenity and the politics of moving to a low-carbon economy. It involves tackling all of the material and social interests associated with our current economy, many of whom are traditional supporters of social democratic parties.

The problem, of course, is that climate change is a most serious issue that warrants priority status. On this occasion, no one can say we haven't been warned of what the economic, social and political consequences of inaction or inadequate action will be. Science has spoken and we would be foolish to ignore its pleas.

Indeed, social democrats have a special obligation to listen and take up the cause of a low-carbon economy. As the world is affected by climate change it will become a harsher, less secure and more combative place in which the liberalising aspirations of social democracy will find the ground hard to till.

However, for a not-insignificant portion of the electorate in the democratic world, social democracy is seen to lack the leadership, energy and commitment to initiate and complete the change process required to deal with climate change. So it is that we have seen the emergence of green parties competing for votes previously the preserve of social democracy.

Nor is it just a case of environmental and climate-change politics. The Greens have a far-reaching agenda for change in the economy (more intervention and more regulation of the sort once the hallmark of social democracy) and in the society (more freedom for the individual and less legal restraint on differences within society). They fight for a continuation of the human-rights agenda that emerged in the 1960s and they question the war on terror, the war on drugs and the philosophy of zero tolerance.

It is as if social democracy has tried to be all things to all people — a little bit of this and a little bit of that, but not too much overall! This shouldn't just be seen as a negative, as in many ways it represents the maturing of the left in a democratic and pluralist society. Nor can there be a turning back to the social democracy of the post-war era. Economic rationality and the market cannot be ignored. The insecurities of people in the face of the international uncertainties of our times cannot be underestimated. Nor can their feeling that something is wrong in the way society and the Welfare State is working. Climate change can't be treated as an intellectual fad and its potential implications ignored.

## Social Justice and the Politics of Climate Change

However, none of this should mean that the traditional social-democratic focus on social justice is no longer relevant. In fact, it is quite the reverse. If climate change is to be managed effectively it needs to be justly managed. Fairness is not just an aspiration for society generally but a real force for security in a world of change. We saw this in Australia in the 1980s and 1990s, when microeconomic reform was coupled with a commitment to the social wage. Indeed, social democrats need to re-emphasise their support for initiatives which guarantee equal opportunities, even when expanding freedom of choice and market competition. As a slogan, I would suggest "liberty, equality and community" — the latter as opposed to the too nationalistic and collectivist alternatives "fraternity and solidarity".

However, focusing simply on the move to a low-carbon economy and a just society, even if coupled with more freedom of choice, still leaves unanswered many questions about politics and political positioning. The balance of power in the world is changing as countries like China and India exercise their new-found muscle. The instabilities of the Middle East and the renewed confidence of Islam has become an issue for us because of foreign policy considerations and new patterns of immigration. Nationalism has re-emerged as a force driving political change. The inherent internationalism of a commitment to a low-carbon economy doesn't fit easily into the politics of North America and Europe, let alone in a resource-rich nation such as ours. Short-term self interest and climate scepticism make a formidable team, especially when linked to a politics of national and cultural unity.

These weren't the issues when social democracy was born and came into prominence. Then it was a case of civilised capitalism versus authoritarian socialism. By linking its policy agenda to the material and social interests of the majority, social democrats provided a large portion of the social cement necessary to keep capitalism alive and ticking.

In the latter years of the twentieth century, social democrats made an appeal on behalf of the economic interests of the nation and the desire of the newly suburbanised citizens for environmental amenity and social order. Some listened but some didn't. A portion of their traditional base saw the greens to the left as a better bet for the environment, and another portion the neoconservatives to the right as a better bet for security and law and order.

Today it's even harder — an appeal on behalf of our children and grandchildren, an appeal for a just world and an appeal on behalf of civilised life on the planet itself. It is clear for all to see but not so clear for all to respond.

## The Political Alternatives

It's my judgement that for all their insight, energy and enthusiasm, the Greens are not in a position to successfully complete such a reform project. Their economics is too reactionary and their international perspective too utopian. David Miliband put it so well when he said "climate change must enter mainstream political parties rather than remain in a separate green culture".[1]

Neoconservatives, however, are unlikely to be at the forefront of climate-change politics. They could be, and indeed should be if we are to create a political consensus on the matter. However, their distrust of the state, the temptations of short-term political interest and a more-than-healthy gaggle of climate sceptics in their ranks make it hard to imagine them as leaders in this space.

What climate-change politics needs is not just a mix of policies for a low-carbon future, but also a strategy to achieve it. It needs social and political cement, just as capitalism did in the twentieth century. This means social justice in the distribution of the burdens and benefits involved in the realisation of a low-carbon economy. That means international co-operation in policy and implementation. That means an interest in and support for international institutions at the regional and global level. That means social democracy.

It must also mean interest in and leadership around the many issues that trouble societies like ours today — citizenship and engagement, rights and responsibilities, life in the cities and suburbs, social dysfunction and disadvantage, multiculturalism, the proper regulation of finance, and health and well-being. Social democrats should be the agents for effective public policy and participation in the interests of social inclusion, harm minimisation and respect for the individual. Where radical responses are required they should be taken up on issues like gay marriage, drug policy, euthanasia, and congestion charges in the cities. Thinking that being conservative on all issues is good politics is misguided.

This may be too much for a political movement that exhausted much of its leadership, energy and political capital in the globalising years following the collapse of communism. It's a movement whose power and status have been dented, but whose role and influence are going to be crucial if we are to meet the challenge of our times, most notably climate change but also the global instability fuelled by fundamentalism, financial failure and economic re-alignment.

**Notes**
1   See "Red-Green Renewal" http://www.fabian-society.org.uk/events/ speeches/red-green-renewal-the-future-new-labour

# Whatever Happened to the Left?

Speech delivered at
New South Wales Fabian Society,

Sydney, 17 September 2008

How often do we hear political commentators today lecture the Labor Party on the failings of the left? "Whatever you do", they say, "don't listen to the advice coming from the intellectual left". And how often do we hear politicians talk of the need to take politics beyond left and right and then proceed to define a political position that is essentially neo-conservative? It would appear that it is much easier to move beyond the left than it is to move beyond the right. Why is this so?

It all began, of course, with the collapse of communism and the triumph of globalisation in the last decades of the twentieth-century. Not only did we see the incorporation of previously socialist countries into the market economy but a significant change in the public sector in the democratic capitalist world itself. It was the era of corporatisation and privatisation, the purchaser–provider split, the level playing field, user pays and individual choice. It was a revolution in political economy as significant as that which had seen the creation of the welfare and opportunity states in the post-1945 world.

What had defined the left for a good part of the twentieth-century, the public ownership and control of the means of production, distribution and exchange, became a discredited policy option, not without continuing value in particular circumstances, but certainly without value as a comprehensive governing principle for a political party seeking relevance in a world of constant change.

That this happened should have surprised no one. The idea that a government plan could replace the market was always flawed. This was understood by John Stuart Mill as far back as the nineteenth-century, when he proposed co-operatives and an appropriate mix of social and economic reform as the best antidote for commercial capitalism.

This takes us into the territory of what we might call a left-liberal view of the world. Here we see a strong commitment to political and civil liberty coupled with an understanding that social and economic equality are also crucial ingredients of the good society.

For the left liberal, equality matters. It may be political equality and ability to influence and control government. It may be social equality and the respect it means for all, no matter their race, gender, sexuality or background. It may be equal opportunity and fairness in the distribution of the burdens and benefits of life. Certainly it means access to those services and that support needed to guarantee the development and realisation of an individual's talents and capacities.

In contemporary political and social philosophy there has been no better exponent of this viewpoint that the late John Rawls. In his classic *A Theory of Justice* (1971) he identified two key principles — the liberty principle and the difference principle. Each of us, he said, has an equal right to the most extensive liberty compatible with similar liberty for others. Social and economic inequalities were justified so long as they were attached to positions open to all and so long as they were to the greatest benefit of the least-advantaged members of society. By arguing this way, Rawls puts the onus on those who support inequality to justify their position. His benchmark is the community of equals about which we hear so much in the major religious texts.

It is this commitment to equality that marks out the left. However, it is not just a case of faith, belief or values. There are also definable institutions and policy prescriptions that flow from such a commitment. They are not watertight; indeed, some may not even be necessary conditions for equality in all circumstances, but they stand out when the experience of history and government is taken into account.

Firstly, that the collective aspects of human society are indispensable. To put it in simple terms — that which we share and enjoy collectively is a crucial element in determining our quality of life. It is a recognition that the individual needs strong social support and the marketplace proper rules and regulation. Social and economic equality do not emerge spontaneously and need to be promoted and protected by the collective arm of society, most notably governments be they central, regional or local. In particular, guaranteed access to services like health and education, as well as the rule of law and effective systems of economic regulation will be vital.

Secondly, that the question of redistribution cannot be avoided. Only on the narrowest of interpretations of equality is it possible to conclude that growth can replace redistribution as a mechanism for fairness. What is involved will vary from case to case — it may be a redistribution of political power to a previously disenfranchised group, it may be anti-discrimination laws that require employers to justify their hiring and firing decisions, or it may be the priorities chosen when taxes and expenditure are determined and budgets finalised. Inevitably, the pursuit of equality will mean the tackling of vested interests and the ruffling of some feathers.

Beyond this, however, there remains a good deal of disagreement about the sorts of institutions, programs and policies that will best promote equality. From within the Left, questions about the precise role of the state, the precise balance between rights and responsibilities, organisation principles for service delivery, the role of the private and community sectors, the importance or otherwise of the principles of decentralisation and subsidiarity, the extent and depth of political participation and the status of cultural pluralism are as much the subject of debate as they are more generally across the political spectrum.

What defines the Left is the commitment to equality and the need to redistribute political, social and economic power to achieve it, as well as a belief in the power and importance of our collective obligations and the institutions required to support them.

This leads me back to the original question: Whatever happened to the Left? In the wave of reform which followed the collapse of communism, the very idea of redistribution was all but dropped from the vocabulary and the belief that individuals were and should be their own masters reduced the space deemed acceptable for collective action. It was assumed that growth could provide adequate opportunities for all and a revenue source to help for those who by illness or misfortune were incapable of participating in the market.

However, it wasn't as if equality itself was completely lost to the political debate. In the first place, many of the newer movements around gender, sexuality, race and ethnicity provided significant ammunition for left liberals. This is still the case today.

In the second place, a link with the Left was preserved with the development of an agenda of social inclusion. Indeed, the very aim of tackling social exclusion raises important implications for governments and communities. Once again, however, the potentiality of the politics of social inclusion has been limited by assumptions (or should I say prejudices?) about the extent of acceptable redistribution and the role of individual choices and responsibilities in the journey of life.

There was a strong feeling that history had come to an end. Democracy was triumphant as a political system and market capitalism, modified by appropriate actions by government and community, was dominant as an economic system. With respect to society, there was still unfinished business to be taken care of by new social movements around race, gender, sexuality, and ethnicity. Politics was not completely but mostly about management, with the needs and requirements of the market the benchmark for decision-making. What had been a "light on the hill" became a "flickering candle in the valley", inadequate perhaps for those who had been inspired by the ethics of socialism but certainly a basis upon which centre-left parties could be and have been elected and re-elected.

By this time, a completely new issue had emerged — the environment. The quality of the natural and built environments became an important element in the contemporary public policy agenda and sensible parties to the left of centre realised that their support for collective action was a powerful base upon which to mount a case for the votes of the post-materialist generation. In more recent times, the argument was broadened to become a critique of the very ways and means of our greenhouse-gas producing economies. Ecology joined economics as a primary discipline in the political and policy debates and an alternative green vision emerged for the economy and society.

What has all this meant for the nature of politics in Australia?

Certainly it has meant that a good deal of the energy and enthusiasm that supported left-of-centre parties in the past has moved to the Greens, with their vision of an alternative economy and society. In many ways, what used to be the Left has become the Green Left. This is pretty obvious for all to see. Not so obvious, perhaps, but just as important, has been the political space opened up for populism. The populist picture of an "us" versus "them" has been utilised to foster division between a "middle-class elite" and "the people". Under fire in the populist world view are judges, bureaucrats, politicians and all those who are seen to pander to "minority interests". Populism is a politics of the majority. It's particularly potent, of course, when linked to the traditions of Australian nationalism.

These things said, it cannot be concluded that parties to the left of centre have exhausted their capacity to win and hold power. Quite the contrary. We see many Labor governments based on a mixture of market economics, improved public health and education, a smattering of populism, support for a healthier environment and an extensive rights-based agenda for those previously excluded by culture and tradition. It needs to be said that in the area of economic and social policy the balance was shifted away from collective action towards individuals and markets. Not surprisingly, many inequalities were intensified.

Not only did this form of politics kill off socialism but also the left-liberal vision of an alternative to commercial capitalism. The number of policy instruments deemed appropriate to a modern government was narrowed, and in Australia, political and economic strategies like the Accord lost relevance as the power and influence of trade unions declined and the idea of the social wage was increasingly privatised.

In many ways, however, this is a world that has passed. Critics of the Left are sounding shrill and irrelevant. Indeed, what they recommend is unsustainable in a world of complex social problems, global warming, environmental stress and a re-alignment of economic power. We will need not only a strong state and good government but also significant community engagement to see us through. Indeed, I would argue that the current situation provides circumstances for a renewal of what we might call a left narrative and politics. The continuing drive to improve productivity in a world of increasing competition, coupled with the necessity of moving to a low-carbon economy, is bound to require substantial public initiative and investment and have significant short-term distributional impacts which cannot be avoided. And we are going to need a new and more demanding set of rules for market exchange. The good management of this process will be crucial. One might ask: "Would it not be easier to manage in the context of a society which actively supports and promotes equality?" Certainly this has been the experience of the Scandinavian countries with their radical mix of market economics and social support. They have shown that equality is not only a matter of belief but also an effective way of governing in a world of change.

Let me be even more specific. We are all aware of the Australian government's commitment to "close the gap" in health, education and employment outcomes between Indigenous and non-Indigenous Australians. Why not adopt this principle more generally and pursue an objective of tackling the many inequalities that still disfigure our society, whatever their source? Equality would make an excellent organising principle for governments, working individually or together, and for partnerships between the government, community and private sectors. It's good in itself and as a strategy for the times. It can be situated within a broader policy agenda that is concerned with issues like climate change, productivity and national security. Indeed, if managed well, it could provide strong support for these other important objectives. It would give a sense of long-term moral purpose to government but it is not an "all-or-nothing affair". It can be approached in an evolutionary manner and, most importantly for Labor, it gives us that much needed "light on the hill" that Ben Chifley spoke about in 1949.

# 5.

# Australian Democracy

# Where is Government Going?

Speech delivered at
Key Directions Public Lecture,
University of Sydney

Sydney, 6 June 2007

In tonight's lecture I want to reflect on government and where it is heading in our society today. I do so because we have seen a plethora of commentary on what governments should be doing — not surprising in an election year — but less on how government is functioning as a key institution in our nation.

I will be arguing that the nature of the times we are living in, and the external and internal pressures being generated, means that we will need to be thinking about the way we are being governed. Government is not just a means to an end or a vehicle for a set of policies, it is an institution central to our democratic society.

By government I don't mean the whole system of governing, but rather the executive that is at the centre of that system. Included, then, are the leaders of government (Prime Minister, Premiers and Chief Ministers), the cabinets they lead, and the public sector that supports them.

About the institution of government two sets of questions can be asked.

Firstly, how is the government itself being managed? What are the relationships within: between leaders and Ministers, and between the political and administrative areas of government? Do these relationships, and the accountabilities that underpin them, help or hinder good government?

Secondly, how is the government relating to the other parts of the political system and to the broader community? In particular, are these relationships being managed in a way that leads to good and sustainable outcomes for the citizens?

## What Has Been Happening in Government?

In focusing on government in this way I am conscious of the fact that there are differences in approach across the nation — between the different leaders, between the parties and between the federal, state and territory jurisdictions. This being said, there are some common themes that can be identified from within this complex pattern which will be the subject of my lecture tonight. They are as follows:

1.  The clearly established power of the Prime Minister, Premiers and Chief Ministers within government
2.  The clearly established power of the political over the administrative arms of government
3.  The growing power of the commonwealth over the states and territories
4.  The development of New Public Management principles and associated mechanisms of accountability in the practice of government

Let me say something about each of these.

It is clear that our political system has become presidential in both form and content. It is to the leaders that the public turns when evaluating parties. It is to the leaders that the media turns for daily comment and clarification. It is to the leaders that the Ministers are accountable and it is to the leader's office that power and resources accumulate. All political parties need a centre from which generates the drive to gain, hold and use power. Leaders are that centre in a world of shifting loyalties and increased volatility.

Within government itself the power and authority of the political arm over the administrative arm has been well-and-truly established. It all started as political necessity back in the 1970s with the reforming Whitlam government, and has continued ever since — at all levels and within all governments.

Ministerial responsibility has been joined with administrative responsibility. The old Public Services Boards have gone and departmental heads are appointed by and accountable to the Ministers, most notably the Prime Minister, Premier or Chief Minister. Ministerial Offices have grown in stature to become important political institutions in their own right.

The financial position of the commonwealth has always made Australian federalism more centralised than its overseas counterparts. However, in recent years we have seen a concerted push to use that power more extensively and to successfully expand the boundaries of the Constitution in respect of the corporations power. It is true that the GST revenue has been given to the states and territories but at the expense of fiscal flexibility. It is, after all, a commonwealth tax which replaced a range of other taxes.

Increased commonwealth interest in areas traditionally the responsibility of the states and more intra-governmental co-operation around objectives deemed nationally important has taken Australian federalism into a new era of complexity and conflict. More often than not, the commonwealth emerges the victor when what are said to be "sectional" interests get in the way of what is deemed the "national" interest.

Connected with these shifts in the balance of power has been significant change in the way we are governed. Many previously publicly owned corporations have been privatised and corporatised, and new regulatory regimes established to ensure competitive neutrality. Market principles have been applied to government and contracting out adopted for a range of services.

Part of this process has also been the use of a much wider range of policy instruments to achieve government objectives, ranging from partnerships with the private sector and community to mutual obligation in welfare programs.

## What Does It Mean?

I would say that it is the overwhelming view of those who comment on these matters, but it is certainly a widely held view that this concentration and centralisation of power and what has come with it is a rational and therefore a necessary response to issues like globalisation, terrorism, global warming and the way politics is conducted today.

It is also seen by some as a continuation of the process of nationalising Australian politics and culture. In this world view there is an inner logic to the move towards centralised uniformity. It is seen to represent Australian values (as opposed to parochialism) and economic efficiency (as opposed to populism). There are few better illustrations of this point of view than John Howard's speech to the Menzies Research Centre in April 2005.[1]

My own reading of a range of these developments and what they mean is different. You might say that is not surprising, coming from someone born and bred in regional Western Australia and who served the Western Australian Parliament for twenty years, five as Premier. To the charge that I am prejudiced in favour of federalism and an active role for government, I plead guilty. However, to the charge that this represents out-of-date thinking, I would plead differently. Indeed, I would assert very strongly that the contemporary debate about these matters and about government in general is severely deficient.

However, it is not enough to simply contest the arguments of those who claim the contemporary trends are necessary and inevitable. To be effective, criticism needs to be constructive, and that means coming to grips with the range of contextual issues that lie behind developments in government today. It also means having a good understanding of what works and what doesn't work.

Let me begin that exercise by asking a straightforward question: What do we know about good government? What makes for good government? To answer these questions we need to consult with political philosophers and social scientists as well as the business and political elite. All too often it is only to the latter that we turn. This has unnecessarily limited the debate and the options we put on the table for consideration.

After all, those on the inside looking out will be primarily concerned with power and how to use it. Those on the outside looking in have more space to look at how the power is being used and how it is impacting on the community. As is the case in all things, we need a balanced consideration of these matters.

## Six Rules of Good Government

My readings about and experience of government leads me to conclude that there are six rules for good government.

Firstly, good governments have the strength and purpose required to defend the public interest. Politicians and public officials create and administer a range of laws and regulations that are being tested and challenged on a daily basis by a range of private and group interests. The public interest may be a slippery concept that is difficult to define. However, its absence is easy to see when government becomes the plaything of particular interests or when it fails to protect its citizens when their rights and dignity are threatened.

Secondly, good governments take a strategic, long-term approach to their work. Change is sometimes unpredictable, but not always. There are methodologies for anticipating and planning for change, and governments that adopt them are better placed to serve their citizens. Geoff Mulgan, who worked in Downing Street in a number of senior roles from 1997 to 2004, put it this way:

*... a combination of sound analysis, rigour on priorities and realism about capacities to deliver does pay dividends. This is evident internationally, but it is also clear from recent British history.*[2]

Thirdly, good governments understand that they are part of a much larger whole. This is part of — but more than — a recognition of the importance of democratic accountability. Government works best when there are proper checks and balances, a vigorous civil society, an energetic market economy and an active citizenry. As Robert Putnam observed in his study of Italian regional government:

*The correlation between civic engagement and effective government is virtually perfect.*[3]

Putnam demonstrated that rich networks of community associations, organised horizontally, help create not only better governments, but also richer economies and more social and intellectual progress generally.

It is, of course, not always easy for governments to see that their effectiveness is partly determined by external as well as internal factors. Power has an unfortunate habit of drifting from a means to an end to an end in itself!

Fourthly, good governments are not just strong and purposeful, they also have breadth of vision. In today's language we would say they are committed to the triple bottom line of economic, social and environmental objectives. It also means that they are aware of the wide range of policy options available to realise these objectives. Government is not just about rule-making, budgets and service delivery. It can also be about information provision, partnerships, facilitation, community leadership and negotiation.

Fifthly, good governments engage the people beyond the requirements laid down by regular elections. Proper methods of consultation can be used as part of strategic planning and in the course of day-to-day government. They assist in providing for more relevance in service delivery, helping deliver projects more efficiently and in giving the community a greater stake in the political process generally. It is all part of a process of bringing elected officials "into a far richer dialogue with the people they serve, by giving those people real power to shape the state's actions".[4]

Sixthly, good governments will care for their public sectors. Government is about philosophy, policy *and* implementation. Good governments need a public sector that has the right people, the right numbers and the right capacities to carry through on the types of qualities listed above — acting in the public interest, thinking strategically, being aware of all the options available and properly consulting the community. As Henry Mintzberg put it so well — there is no gap between strategy and implementation, just strategies that don't account for implementation.[5]

## How Good is Australian Government?

Using these rules of good government, we need to ask today whether there is a mismatch between the style and practice of government we have inherited and the needs of the new century. We also need to ask whether there are any important issues that were not dealt with at all, or which were not addressed adequately, by the system which was developed in the last decades of the twentieth century.

There is no doubt that the centralisation of power within executive government facilitated significant change. Indeed, the destruction of what has been called the old Australian Settlement based on protection, regulation and arbitration required leadership and collaboration efforts across the system. A range of vested interests in both the private and public sectors meant that a concerted effort was required — and it was given.

In as much as strategic government was involved, it was focused on this neo-liberal transformation of public policy and practice, seen as necessary to ensure the productivity and competitiveness of the economy in the new era of globalisation. Just as the relationship between state and economy was altered, so too was the structure and organisation of the public sector with managerialism, corporatisation, competitive neutrality, contracting out and performance management being the order of the day.

Not only did the neo-liberal agenda dominate the debate about the public sector, it also dominated the inter-governmental agenda which took shape as national competition policy. No matter what their party backgrounds, there was agreement amongst the various governments that this was the way forward for the nation. It was this ideological agreement at the top which facilitated the transition.

The positive aspects of the legacy from this era are bound to withstand the tests of time and change. For example, leaders with the ability to respond rapidly to changed circumstances and a public sector geared up to implementing a range of possibilities required of it are indispensable elements in any regime of good government.

So too, I would predict, will the newly emboldened state governments continue to be important. The neo-liberal revolution gave a new stature to Premiers and Chief Ministers and created an environment that favoured policy innovation in general. Indeed, it should be remembered that the genius of the national competition policy was that it gave financial incentives to the states to undertake reform but it preserved their autonomy. Despite a range of compromises and intrusions on their power, they are still providers of core services like policing, health, education, transport, community services and planning.

The Commonwealth push to achieve uniformity through centralisation will be resisted and should be given the all-important need for creativity and innovation in a forever-changing world. The formation of the Council for the Australian Federation is a sign of this fight-back, with its first major publication being a vigorous defence of the role of the states in our system of government.[6]

There is a logic to the development of a presidential pattern of leadership and real political control over the bureaucracy, and there is a logic to more collaboration between the different levels of government around agreed priorities. However, unless you subscribe to a nationalist sentiment that favours Commonwealth power and uniformity of laws, regulations and services, there is less logic to the centralisation of power. Not only are there important differences in circumstances across the nation, but policy innovation is important and multiple centres of power are demonstrated means of achieving it.

Indeed, the encouragement of innovation in service delivery will require a degree of devolution within bureaucracies as well as a defence of autonomy within the federation itself. Place management, local area agreements and community partnerships are recognised as important vehicles for reform, particularly when dealing with difficult issues like entrenched poverty, family abuse, and long-term unemployment. If public servants are not given an adequate degree of space it will be difficult to ensure such developments are effective. This obviously poses a challenge for their political masters and the system of administrative accountability that have been developed.

Whilst the new public management revolution had a range of positive benefits and set up a framework that allows for more agency responsiveness, there is little doubt that its focus was largely on society-wide allocative efficiency and efficiency in the delivery of government programs. Although effectiveness in delivery was part of the equation and some innovative ways of measuring it were developed, the main thrust of change was to make government more efficient.[7]

A more broadly based approach based on social, economic and environmental indicators of success is now recognised as more appropriate. The degree of freedom and power possessed by political leaders today needs to be put to work on behalf of this more broadly based approach to governing. This is bound to create a busier form of government as the public sector is activated and policies and programs are developed to pursue the desired targets. It means judging government on the effectiveness of the strategies it has developed to bring about change, rather than just in terms of operational efficiency.

Nor does it necessarily mean more government. It means a different way of doing government. Indeed, we can observe today a clear shift in what we expect of government. Does government simply seek to deal with problems or should it also seek to solve the problems? It's the difference between a view of service delivery geared to fighting crime, treating illness, delivering a curriculum, providing income support and facilitating development to one of preventing crime and illness, producing a range of outcomes from education, lifting the capacities of those on welfare and influencing the type of development. What this means, of course, is considering extra programs and services along with traditional services associated with policing, hospitals, schools welfare provision and planning departments.

Many of these innovations in government have been associated with state governments. Indeed, many of the states have engaged in a strategic planning process for their jurisdiction. In the case of the *Tasmania Together* program initiated by the late Jim Bacon, the community was fully involved in the setting of objectives, benchmarks and targets. Community engagement was also a feature of New South Wales' recently published *State Plan*.

However, perhaps the most interesting of these innovations in democratic engagement came in Western Australia by way of the 2003 *Dialogue with the City*. Involving 1,100 participants (one third randomly selected, one third invited and one third self-nominated from newspaper advertisements). It was the largest deliberative forum in the southern hemisphere and sits alongside other initiatives like citizens' juries, consensus conferences, consumer forums and other consultative techniques used in Western Australia.

*Dialogue with the City* utilised modern technology and scenario planning techniques to develop a plan for the future of Perth. It was clarified at the outset of the program that the findings of the forum would be integral to the state government's decision making and that participants would be involved in monitoring the implementation. By guaranteeing this influence, these forms of consultation take on a greater meaning for those participating.[8]

This still leaves us with the important issue of how accountability regimes are working across the nation. There is no doubt that despite declining influence of the doctrine of ministerial responsibility, the era of new public management saw a range of accountability mechanisms put in place around the theme of performance management. This was a feature at all levels of government and has significantly multiplied the reporting requirements for the agencies and personnel of government.

Whilst all of this is important, the real test of accountability comes from a genuine system of checks and balances and independently constituted centres of power. That's why proportional representation in our Upper Houses — first established for the Senate but incorporated in political reform agendas in the 1970s and 1980s — has had a significant impact on the accountability of government. The last federal election was the exception to the rule, and I would expect that more often than not governments would not enjoy a majority in their Upper Houses.

However, there have been two other changes — both at the state level — that have the potential to impact more widely if they gained universal acceptance.

The first of these is the establishment of Corruption Commissions in New South Wales, Queensland and Western Australia. It is clear that the level of transparency created by such powerful commissions of inquiry is significant.

The second is the establishment of a Charter of Rights in the A.C.T. and Victoria. Although such charters are not the constitutional equivalent of a Bill of Rights, they provide an important check in an era of extensive government initiative.

## The Way Forward

What we see throughout Australia is change that takes government beyond the principles of new public management and executive dominance. However, the process is hesitant and patchy. We see elements of strategic government, sustainability, democratic engagement and checks and balances, but short-termism, day-to-day events management and populist posturing still have their attractions, most notably in terms of proven strategies for political power. However, this can only work as long as there is a settled pattern for government as a whole. Such a pattern seemed to be emerging with the end of the Cold War and the onward march of globalisation. Some even spoke of "the end of history".

No sooner did this seem to be the case than the world was shaken by the terror attacks in America and elsewhere, including Indonesia, and the realisation that global warming was not simply a debating point but a pressing reality. This takes us into that political territory where systems of thinking and practice have to be questioned and changed. It certainly makes the case for strategic planning and co-ordination across government, but just as importantly, it forces us to consider the costs that may result if in the war on terror and the war on global warming we ignore the political, institutional and cultural foundations for policy responsiveness, innovation and human rights.

We are living in an extraordinary time, with external pressures requiring collective and whole-of-government action and internal pressures requiring greater freedom, more democracy, and the individualisation of service delivery. To bring these together we need to think of government in terms of a partnership

- between the government and the community
- between the cabinet and the public sector
- between the levels of government.

To work properly, such partnerships need to involve mutual respect and shared responsibilities as well as dialogue that is open and inclusive about both ends and means. We need, as one of the candidates in *Primary Colours* said, to calm things down a little and see if we can start having a conversation about the sort of place we want ... to be in the next century.[9]

## Notes

1   "Reflection on Australian Federalism", Menzies Research Centre, April 2005.
2   "Lessons of Power", *Prospect,* May 2005.
3   "What makes Democracy Work?", *IPA Review,* vol. 47, no. 1 (1994).
4   Simon Parker and Duncan O'Leary, *Re-imagining Government: Putting People at the Heart of New Zealand's Public Sector* (Demos, 2006).
5   According to Mintzberg, strategy creation and implementation are interdependent. Good managers are like potters sitting at a wheel, moulding the clay and letting the shape of the object evolve in their own hands. See Morgan Witzel, "Guru Guide: Henry Mintzberg — the great iconoclast", *Financial Times,* 5 August 2003.
6   Ann Twomey and Glenn Withers, *Federalist Paper 1 – Australia's Federal Future* (April 2007),
7   See Janet Hartz-Karp "A Case Study in Deliberative Democracy: dialogue with the city". www.activedemocracy.net/articles/jhk-dialogue-city.pdf.
8   See Geoff Gallop, "Strategic Planning: Is it the new model?" *Public Administration Today,* January–March 2007.
9   *Primary Colours: A Novel of Politics* (1996).

# The Real World of Politics

## Some reflections on politics today

When academics think about politics they tend to focus on values, institutions and relationships, for example, between the three arms of government — the legislature, the executive and the judiciary. Such an approach produces an enormous amount of useful knowledge but not enough to cover the complexity that is modern political life. Not surprisingly then, voters, parties and pressure groups are added in an attempt to put some flesh on the bones. Even then, however, the analysis tends to remain on the surface of things. What we need is an approach that involves ethos as well as ideology, and people as well as institutions. Indeed, a comprehensive description of politics will focus on the different types of people who are involved and what they think and do. It's partly a question of position and role, but also one of the attitudes and values that they bring to their work.

In looking at it this way I can identify seven major groupings. At the centre of politics we see the *politicians* and their *helpers* and *officials*. They have power but need ideas and numbers to sustain their work. These are provided by the *advocates* who generate ideas and the *voters and activists* who generate pressure on the system. Add to this list the custodians of transparency, be they defenders of principle — the *institutionalists* — or seekers of information — the *interpreters* — and we have our system personified.

## The Politicians

You can't have democracy without politics and you can't have politics without politicians. They live and breathe power and how to get and keep it.

1. *The Leaders* are at the centre of politics, the focus of attention for the general public, the major interest groups and the media. Within the parties and the Parliament they are the ideological and political agenda–setters and managers. They mean business or they die. They need ambition just as a motor vehicle needs petrol, but even more so they need good political judgement.

2. *The Ministers* are at the top of the system but constrained by their collective loyalties and responsibilities, as are their shadows. Once upon a time, Ministers were fully responsible for what happens in government but now they share that fate with public servants. The party leaders are the masters of their fate, but many others, most notably the media, are ready, willing and able to give advice on performance.

3. *The Party Hacks* provide the numbers in the Parliament. Party loyalty in all matters is their guiding principle and although intellectual "flexibility" is a must, they get very angry if their loyalty isn't recognised and/or rewarded in some way or another.

4. *The Headkickers* are the faction leaders who organise numbers and impose discipline in the parties, often on behalf of outside interests. They are willing to do whatever it takes to achieve their ends, sometimes at the expense of good government and party credibility.

They can act rationally in the interests of the "greater good", but it is dangerous to assume that this will always be the case.

## The Helpers

Politics at the top also needs its helpers (often called advisers) and I'm not referring here just to the strategists and policy wonks, but also to those who operate at the sharp end of the political process. Machiavelli's "The Prince" is their bible.

5. *The Fixers* seek order out of the chaos which is politics and government. They bring antagonists together, overcome roadblocks to implementation and make sure the messages at the top are understood at the bottom. In an ideal world they wouldn't be needed, but in the real world they are a necessity. They like comparing notes with the headkickers.

6. *The Spin Doctors* develop the stories about what the politicians and others are doing (and why they are doing it) and then proceed to seek influence over the views of those whose business it is to describe and interpret events. They can be creative with words and love writing or reviewing speeches. Today we find them in all the major institutions of politics, inside and outside of government. The science of communication and the art of influence are their majors.

7. *The Pollsters* survey public opinion on just about everything that is pertinent to power and politics, and politicians can be addicted to their findings. They help in the determination of priorities and the formulation of messages, but are often used to make policy itself — the ultimate in populist democracy.

## The Officials

All governments need their officials for ideas, support and delivery. They add the "how" question to "why" and "what" questions of government. They are the philosopher kings of implementation.

8. *The Mandarins* are the heads of government departments and agencies who are the conduits between the political and administrative parts of government. They give advice and manage organisations. They can be supportive or awkward, even devious if necessary. They know they're not supposed to admire Sir Humphrey but they do. As noted earlier, they share responsibility with their political masters for success and failure.

9. *The Administrators* run systems of human, financial and information management. Politicians are often bewitched by the methodologies (the latest management fad) and technologies (the latest ICT application) they introduce and manage. Rarely seen but not to be underestimated, they are the engine room on the ship of state. When things go wrong they are called to account, but don't handle political conflict very well.

10. *The Service Deliverers* are the face of the government in the community — in schools and colleges, hospitals and health centres, and offices and outreach services. For them the general public are clients or customers, just as they are citizens for politicians and subjects for enforcers. Today, however, they are being asked to individualise and localise the services they deliver and this is never easy.

11. *The Enforcers* exist to support peace and order according to law. Someone has to enforce community standards and call to account those who transgress, be they speeding drivers, dodgy politicians, irresponsible employers, negligent builders, greedy developers, and thieves and vagabonds generally. Enforcers need courage in the face of danger and integrity in the face of temptation. Like football umpires they aren't liked, but we need them.

## The Advocates

The advocates generate ideas and seek influence. We need to distinguish between the different levels at which they work.

12. *The Ideologists* are the philosophers of modern politics who provide us with the general theories about human nature, human society and human history. Theirs are the big ideas of the human imagination like liberalism and socialism, and their abiding interest is the human condition itself.

13. *The Strategists* are the political gurus who put these big ideas into context and develop narratives for those seeking power. They are concerned with relevance as well as ideology. Thus it is that some of the big ideas become "factionalised". In our time, we have seen influential examples like "the old left" versus "the third way" or "neo-liberalism" versus "left liberalism".

14. *The Policy Wonks* are the public policy and public administration experts who design systems, programs and policies for use by governments. We find them in the private sector, the public service and ministerial offices. Their very existence is a reflection of the changing nature of political debate in democracies like ours — away from comprehensive ideology and towards context and evidence-based policy.

## The Voters and Activists

Politics is, of course, much more than ideas and government. It is, as Bernard Crick reminded us, freedom in action. This takes me to those who challenge and create and who push and pull, not only in the cities, towns and regions, but also in the corridors of power.

15. *The People* are the ultimate point of democratic reference. Politics runs on the energy generated by citizen initiatives — from letter writing to petitions, from protests to boycotts, and from demonstrations

to sit-ins. Today, they can also play an indirect role through participation in opinion surveys and focus groups. Ultimately, however, it is the power of their vote in an election that gives them real influence. The people aren't, and in all likelihood will never be, a spent force. Radicals describe them as "the masses", conservatives as "the mob" and spin doctors as the "punters".

16. *The Organisers* are the machine men of politics who organise the people on the basis of issues and ideas. They understand the power of numbers and organisation, and spend a good deal of their time in the pursuit of both. For them, ideas are as much a means to power as they are the ends of political activity. They may be boring but they are effective.

17. *The Lobbyists* advocate and act for specific interests and movements. Industries, unions, NGOs, churches and communities are all involved. Such lobbying may be sophisticated and upfront, or crude and behind the scenes. They can use spin as well as argument and threats as well as advocacy. Sometimes they rely on research, but inside knowledge can be especially useful. The good ones never take anything for granted.

18. *The Legal Eagles* are the lawyers who provide ammunition for both defence and attack. They see the law as a weapon in the struggle for power and remind us that politics and the law can't be separated. They live and breathe the politics of "due process". Politicians either love them (defence lawyers) or are suspicious of them (human rights lawyers).

## The Institutionalists

The institutionalists are the true believers and custodians of constitutional democracy. They like to see that things are done properly. They keep alive notions like honour, and believe in principles before power. Amongst their ranks we find the following:

19. *The Vice-Roys* are our Governors and Governors-General who operate at the apex of the system as the representatives of the Queen. They give authority to government and take an interest in and support civil society. We never see most of what they do, and their reserve powers remain contentious, even more so after the events of 1975, when Sir John Kerr dismissed the Whitlam government.

20. *The Judges* interpret the constitution and the laws. They need and support the separation of powers. What they think and how they go about their tasks really matters. Politicians (and others) who ignore them do so at their peril.

21. *The Parliamentarians*, aided and abetted by the officers of Parliament, are vigilant in defence of parliamentary privilege, debate and inquiry. They find their role much easier if they are independents or if they are from minor parties. Indeed, they yearn for a return to nineteenth-century practice. Scrutiny of the executive arm of government is seen as a duty. However, most MPs are not like this. For the majority, process is not unimportant but it is not the main game. They seek and support power. They are politicians.

22. *The Supervisors* are there to monitor performance. Democratic accountability is characterised today not just by elections but by a range of monitoring agents who supervise on behalf of the public interest — Auditors, the Ombudsman, Corruption Commissioners and Public Service Commissioners. On occasion they are joined by Royal Commissioners (and by Parliamentarians for that matter). Their powers are extensive and their findings can be political dynamite. There are even a range of NGOs in on the act today, seeking information in order

to judge performance on the key questions related to good government.

## The Interpreters

To complete the picture we need to examine those who seek to make sense of it all. In their approach we more often than not see advocacy as well as description. However, many of them deny this in order to make a claim for "objectivity".

23. *The Media Barons* have always sought power and influence through the media outlets they own. They need and have their own legal eagles, fixers and spin doctors. Some seek to frame the debate, others to pick winners and many attempt to impose their views on what is acceptable and what isn't. Their commercial interests are especially important and politicians struggle to find a regulatory framework that satisfies all.

24. *The Journos* describe events for us all and love to add colour and light. They have clear views on what is news and what isn't. When it comes to politicians, most journos are suspicious and some are hostile. They believe in protecting their own sources but exposing others. Some seek to describe and others to influence outcomes on the basis of their own attitudes, ideas and even prejudices. Politicians and journalists need each other, but the relationship is always rocky, with journos rarely able to resist a good headline.

25. *The Cultural Critics* are progressive or reactionary, and restless in the face of commercial and political reality. They don't like compromise ("hypocrisy") and pragmatism ("opportunism"). They are well-and-truly on the outside looking in, and tend to be of a religious or ideological disposition. Cartoonists are often amongst their number. For the critics, the pen is mightier than the sword. They occasionally form alliances with politicians but inevitably fall out with them. After all,

politics is the "art of the possible". However, whilst there is an air of unreality about their criticism, they do raise important issues for us all

26. *The Academics* are our scholars and researchers who are given freedom to investigate and analyse all aspects of the system. From their research, many a grand theory about how to understand politics has emerged. Science is their weapon. However, recognising the implausibility of the complete separation of fact from value has led some academics to become ideologists, strategists or policy wonks.

## Conclusion

In terms of objectives, it works something like this: the politicians, their helpers and officials want the power to do things, the institutionalists want ensure it is done lawfully and ethically, the voters and activists want the freedom to participate and pressure, the advocates want to be listened to and the interpreters want information about it all.

When you look at the system this way, you can see that complicated mix of principles and politics that is necessary for democracy to work. It's neither applied ideology nor value-neutral manoeuvring. It's about power and principle, and involves the vicious as well as the virtuous. All too often the good people fail because they refuse to dirty their hands in the rough-and-tumble of political life. However, they too need their supporters, organisers and strategists.

# 6.

# Leadership for the Future

# Re-thinking Australian Politics: Engaging the Disenchanted

Speech delivered at
The 2010 Annual Hawke Lecture

Adelaide, 13 October 2010

I feel very honoured to be able to deliver the Annual Hawke Lecture and to follow such a distinguished list of lecturers. Bob Hawke acted as an inspiration to many Australians of my generation. I remember writing a lengthy essay on resale price maintenance whilst studying economics at the University of Western Australia. This had followed Bob's campaigning on the issue as ACTU Advocate and President. I was particularly interested in his view that trade unions ought to expand their horizons to take on issues like the collusive practices of big business and their impact on Australian consumers. Already we can see developing here what was to become the Labor case for a more competitive and therefore more productive Australia. In fact, by engaging and involving the trade union movement in economic reform, Bob Hawke restored Labor's status as an international leader in social democratic thinking and practice, a position it had held — along with New Zealand — in the early years of the twentieth century.

Speaking tonight also allows me to remind us all of the energy and commitment that were displayed during the years of the Hawke government. Serious economic and tax reform, wide-ranging social reform and some major decisions to protect the environment, most notably stopping the construction of the Franklin Dam, were the order of the day. Hawke and his Ministers managed government well and had an eye to politics but weren't afraid to take risks in the interests of a better and more compassionate Australia. When it was necessary they took a lead and fought for their proposed reforms. Indeed, it is to these themes of leadership, engagement and reform that I intend to return later in this lecture.

## Politics, the political system and political reform

My focus tonight is on politics and the political system. I don't hold the view that Australian political debate should just be about economics. The economic debate is crucially important and I strongly support a continuing program of micro- and macroeconomic reform to ensure our economy is internationally competitive and efficient. We can ill afford to be complacent about productivity, and the legal, human and physical infrastructure needed to support its improvement.

The truth is, of course, that there are a range of issues that need to be addressed if we are to secure the future — the economics of productivity being one. Others include our foreign and trade policies, our approach to education, health and welfare, our policies for climate change and environmental renewal, and our agenda for population, immigration and religious and cultural diversity. Some are pressing issues and some are evolutionary by their nature, needing long-term and persistent attention.

What, then, of the way we are governed and the challenge of political reform? Some say we should leave such questions to one side while we get on with the "real" issues mentioned above. To argue that our nation is incapable of debating and acting on political reform at the same time as it moves forward with economic and other reforms is to underestimate the capacities and misrepresent the interests of the electorate. What happens in politics is understood to be important and seen to be in need of repair. Politics is not an issue which can or should be avoided.

Political reform can mean many things, ranging from changes to the Constitution, to changes in parliamentary practice and behaviour, to changes in the electoral system. We may seek changes to the formal arrangements under which we are governed or changes to the culture under which we are governed. Whatever the proposals for change, they will need to be assessed, not just for their guarantees of extra responsiveness and accountability, but also for their capacity to promote good and effective government.

The attitude that electors take to the system and the politicians that run it is important. They may be disillusioned and apathetic. They may be supportive and energetic in their citizenship. If they feel confident about and trust the system making important and necessary changes is going to be easier, even if still difficult. What is needed is an atmosphere of trust that makes it possible for governments to tackle issues that they may otherwise seek to avoid.

Thus the title of my lecture tonight: "Re-thinking Australian politics: engaging the disenchanted".

The questions I seek to answer are as follows. What do we mean by disenchantment with Australian politics? How extensive is the phenomenon? Who are the disenchanted? What form is their disenchantment taking and is it the same thing as disengagement? Do disenchantment and/or disengagement matter and, if yes, what solutions have been proposed? Will these solutions address the issue as intended or are they based on a merely impressionistic and largely faulty view of what is really happening? And finally, given my answers to these questions, what is the way forward for Australian politics?

To assist me in this endeavour I commissioned Ipsos Marketing to engage in some research. They used a sample demographic profile to ask 1,040 electors the following questions: How important is it to you personally which party is in government? What do you think is the best thing about Australian politics? What do you think is the worst thing about Australian politics? If you had a magic wand, what one thing would you change about Australian politics? Thinking about politics over the last decade, which federal politician do you most admire? I have attached the overall findings as an appendix to my lecture.

The survey found that 73 per cent of respondents still thought that it was very or somewhat important to them which party was in government. However, the younger the respondent the less likely they were to report that the party in government was "very important". Whilst 27 per cent said there was nothing good about Australian politics, only 4.2 per cent reported that everything was bad! As Ipsos reported to me; "cynicism has not yet triumphed!" However, there is disenchantment with the parties, the politicians and the culture they support, particularly in terms of in-house fighting, negativity, honesty and accountability. The theme of freedom featured prominently as a positive — freedom of choice, freedom of speech and the freedom to vote. This being said, more reported compulsory voting to be the best thing about Australian politics (3.9 per cent) than reported it the worst thing (2.9 per cent). Of politicians most admired, John Howard and Kevin Rudd scored the best with 31.4 per cent and 24.3 per cent, respectively. Most desired by way of change was more honesty and integrity in politics. Electors like their politicians to stand up for what they believe in even, if they disagree.

I include this research not to indicate that my argument is based upon it but just as background to the discussion of disenchantment and disengagement. Such findings don't tell us everything, still require interpretation and, as you will see in my lecture, I believe the key issue to be the way political leaders frame the debate that follows from digesting such findings.

## The 2010 Election

It has been a remarkable year for Australian politics — a Prime Minister deposed by his own party and an election that produced a hung Parliament and a minority government. For the first time, the Greens have captured a seat in a general election for the House of Representatives and there are now four Independents in that chamber as well. The resurgent Nationals in Western Australia gained a seat at the expense of the Liberals, proving once again the power of the "City versus Country" narrative in Australian politics.

The changed circumstances have seen renewed debate about the role of Parliament, the place of the Speaker and the conduct of politics generally. Indeed, the concept of a "paradigm shift" has re-emerged in our political vocabulary. The new paradigm, so the argument goes, involves a spirit of compromise across boundaries rather than claims of a mandate to rule. Strength in politics is being defined less in terms of the will to power and more in terms of the capacity to listen, negotiate and influence.

That this would be the result of the election comes as no surprise. Never before have we seen an election that was as much about itself as it was about the issues facing the nation. The commentary was highly critical of both the major parties and their attempt at risk-free campaigning. Ideas were out and images were in. It seemed everyone was dissatisfied — the true believers on both sides, as well as the media and the electorate. This was manna from heaven for the Greens and the Independents, and they were only too happy to occupy the territory left uncontested by the big boys.

Add to this the intervention by Mark Latham and his case for an informal vote. This was consistent with the view he had been putting: that we ought to drop out of mainstream politics and focus on building social capital in the community. It would appear that his cynicism was shared by many others, and the trend to an increase in the informal vote continued. In some Labor seats, it actually exceeded 10 percent.

## Conservative and Radical Interpretations

What, then, do we make of this new situation? There is both a conservative and a radical way to interpret these events.

A conservative interpretation would go as follows: Australia is a well-governed country with a sound Constitution and political institutions that have stood the test of time. Outcomes from this system have been good even though there are new challenges, such as climate change, and older challenges, such as Indigenous disadvantage, requiring more attention.

More importantly, it is a system that allows for change, but change of an evolutionary nature initiated by voters dissatisfied with the two major parties. We can see these evolutionary changes happening today in relation to both process (parliamentary and political finance reform) and outcomes (climate change and the city–country divide). Adjustments are being made to reflect the new reality — more resources for regional Australia and a new attempt at pricing carbon.

According to this view, politics will change, but only at the margins where the Greens and the Independents are chipping away at the centrist consensus. Strategic and political power will still lie with the major parties and they can be expected to return to their dominant positions once the new policy equilibrium is established.

Behind such thinking is the assumption that political restlessness within the electorate doesn't equate with radical fervour. Indeed, the so-called "hollow men" of party politics are confident that what they face is a management problem rather than a political and cultural challenge.

This takes me to the alternative, radical interpretation of current politics. Here it is held that there are indeed deeper forces at work. They point to the decline in the status and influence of the ordinary members of the major parties. Party conferences are stage-managed affairs and party organisations simply exist to fight elections rather than develop policy for the future. The once powerful forces of class, party and ideology still exist but no longer drive the system as they once did. Politics has become a science, the science of political management where public opinion and public policy interact.

No matter how hard the major parties try, radicals believe such organisations are incapable of regaining their strangle-hold on the nation's imagination. Their mission has been played out, they are hollow and exhausted and they are incapable of meeting the challenges of the times. They know no world other than focus groups, political slogans and political marketing. They find cause in a limited range of policies and plenty of empty and often contrived adversarialism played out in Question Time and through the media.

Although the radicals see the major parties as the problem rather than the solution, some continue to work within for change on issues like party democracy, party finance and policy development. For example, there has been talk of establishing the American system of Primaries to broaden the basis for pre-selection. It is quite remarkable, however, that there are so few party activists pursuing a reform agenda within the major parties. In and of itself this tells us something about change in our political culture.

For an increasing number today, new forms of political participation and/or allegiance are seen to be necessary if change is to be achieved. Their slogan is vote Green or Independent to bring new voices into the Parliament. Back this up with support for GetUp or Australian Conservation Foundation-style campaigns around individual issues like climate change and mental health reform and a whole new dynamic is created in the political system. In relation to this, one can only say that it has already proved to be feasible and effective. Not only does it perform the crucial role of mobilising and energising electors — something the major parties have downplayed at great expense to their support base — but it has notched up enough wins to encourage those for whom outcomes are as or more important than processes.

## Disenchantment and Disengagement

Re-adjustment or reform? What is the answer? In order to tackle this question properly we need to analyse the phenomenon of political disillusionment and distinguish it from disengagement.[1] We need also to recognise that politics ought not to be about just responding to change, it should also seek to shape the world in which we live. This takes us to the question of leadership and one of the ironies of modern politics. At the very point at which our major political leaders have emerged with more status and influence than the parties that have created them, they have narrowed their vision to the science of political management. This is a story to which I will return later.

What, then, is political disenchantment? Digging beneath the surface of this phenomenon reveals two sets of attitudes, one about politicians and the other about the system. What we see is declining trust in politicians, cynicism about their motives, concern about their behaviour and disillusionment about the capacity of the system to deliver good results. However, none of this necessarily means disengagement from the political process by opting out, not voting or voting informal. Cynicism and disenchantment don't automatically link with apathy or despair. Indeed, it may be linked to greater and different levels of activity in the interests of change.

But back to disengagement. It is the opposite of what we might call active citizenship. It may be that electors drop out of involvement with a party, take little interest in what is happening in politics and stop voting or vote informal.

I include voting informal but acknowledge that for some it may be a form of political protest to shame the political class into action. What it means, however, is a diminution in the representational value of our political system and a weakening of the all-important link between civil society and government, so strongly supported by our institution of compulsory voting.

Such political alienation is a cause for concern that warrants attention even if one is not inclined to agree with those who say our very democracy is on a course of self-destruction. I, for one, don't believe we are on the edge of the precipice. I recognise the problems but can see a way forward. Part of the reason for my confidence in the future is that a good deal of the disenchantment we have seen has not yet translated into disengagement. For all its weaknesses, Australian democracy is robust with those seeking change, full of energy and action. Such pressure from without should force a rethink of Australian politics.

My confidence, however, is qualified. What we need to analyse is what is being proposed by way of change, and whether or not it will achieve what is being sought. So, too, do we need to ask: Even if the proposed reforms could achieve their intentions, are there other negative consequences that should be part of the calculations?. In other words, we need not just to analyse the viability but also the desirability of the proposed changes. In saying this I reveal my own bias in support of the major parties. This should come as no surprise. After all, I worked as a Labor parliamentarian for twenty years, a local councillor for three and a party activist for a decade prior to that, including a brief stint as a union organiser for the Miscellaneous Workers Union. I have loyalties and I have an ongoing belief that the Labor versus Liberal division has meaning and is still important in giving context to our day-to-day arguments about policy directions for the future.

What we need to understand is that the mixture of disenchanted and/or disengaged is not consistent or uniform. There is, in fact, a fundamental divide here which is as important as the divide between the conservatives and the radicals. Disenchantment has its own divisions and internal tensions. There is what I would call a "left-green" as opposed to a "right-populist" disenchantment.

## Left Green and Right Populist
The left-green movement seeks fundamental change in the political system, including proportional representation for the

House of Representatives. They are republicans and supporters of human-rights legislation and a re-prioritised public policy agenda that replaces economic rationalism with the principles and practices of sustainability. The unfettered capitalism associated with globalisation is the target of much of their campaigning.

Globalisation is also a target for the right populists. They are less a political movement these days, particularly since the collapse of One Nation, but more a political tendency active in civil society and in the world of politics. They want strong government based on the will of the majority in areas like law and order, immigration and economic development. For such electors, the republic and human-rights legislation are the province of the chattering classes. They see government as having been captured by middle-class liberals at the expense of working people like themselves, particularly those who live and work outside the major cities.

Some within the right-populist tendency are engaged in the Australian version of the culture wars. For them, politics is about values independent of the consequences of applying them — a Judeo-Christian Australia, the right to life, the sanctity of the family and a drug free community. We have seen faith-based politicians elected to parliament and strong campaigning around issues like abortion, stem-cell research, euthanasia and same-sex marriage. They wish to turn the tide of late twentieth-century left liberalism.

Inasmuch as we can see a political reform program associated with right populism, its focus is majority rule and accountability. They want the silent majority to be given a voice and have, on occasion, flirted with the Swiss model of direct democracy and its institutions of citizen-initiated referenda and a popular veto power. A less sophisticated but equally powerful version of direct democracy is government by opinion poll! Different method but same result — rule by majority opinion at any point in time.

Right populists may be disenchanted with the political culture and system, but they are certainly not disengaged. We see their influence in both the major parties, even if more obviously within the Liberals since the ascendancy of John Howard. What they have challenged is the bipartisan agenda of progressive social reform associated with Whitlam, Fraser and Hawke.

These two forces — left green and right populist — have energy and commitment and are growing in self-confidence and power. They have been outflanking the mainstream political parties and squeezing their support. Politics in Australia is changing. The only question left is how far will the process take us? More important is the question: how far *should* the process take us?

This takes me back to the conservative versus radical interpretation of the current situation. What the evidence tells us is that there is certainly a growing level of disenchantment which is associated with a degree of disengagement. However, it is my view that we need to penetrate deeper beneath the surface if we are to fully understand this disenchantment. It is a complex process with a range of cross-cutting elements. I have already mentioned the left-green and right-populist forms of disenchantment. Inasmuch as there is a program of political reform associated with these tendencies, it is not necessarily the same as what is in the minds of those voting for them. There are protest voters as well as conviction voters and, as we noted, some choose to vote informal or opt out altogether.

## Leadership Shaping and Responding

This leads me to a fundamental point I wish to make — politics needs to be about leadership as well as responsiveness. Electors want their leaders to stand for something and to craft a narrative and policy agenda for the future. Part of the disenchantment we see relates to a belief that the political class has been too short-term and risk-averse in its thinking and practice. Even the language of politics is seen to have become too managerial and insufficiently ideological. We should consider such criticisms when designing a political reform program. Take direct democracy, for example. It would certainly give power to the people. It would mean majority rule, but at what price? To go beyond the valid requirement that our Constitution only be changed with the support of a majority of electors overall and a majority of states and incorporate a popular veto for all matters would make legislative change difficult if not impossible. One of the good things about our current system is that it provides room for change that may be disapproved of today but accepted tomorrow. This is how a good deal of economic and social reform has been achieved in the past. Such a leadership function can be best exercised in a representative rather than a direct democracy.

What of the left-green agenda or proportional representation? This has been the system in Tasmania since 1909 and has become accepted throughout Europe. After the intense debate about the unfairness of New Zealand's first-past-the-post system, they, too, changed to proportional representation.

There are, of course, many different versions of proportional representation and it is not my concern tonight to analyse them. Rather, I would like to address the logic of proportional representation and how it relates to the theme of disenchantment.

Proportional representation will certainly give the minor parties a greater say and will guarantee that there is a balance in the relationship between votes and seats. Coalition government (or minority government) will become the order of the day. Politics will be more complex and outcomes less predictable.

In relation to this let me say a number of things.

Firstly, I note that we already have proportional representation for our Senate. Smaller parties and Independents have won seats there and come to play a not-insignificant role in legislation and public policy. Proportional representation is well entrenched and well understood in the electorate. This is reflected in different voting patterns for the two Houses of Parliament.

Secondly, it would mean that the capacity for a party to form government in its own right would in all probability be lost to the system. It is true that the major parties are under pressure and have been found wanting, but do we want a system that would forever prevent them from achieving a majority presence in the House of Representatives? Systematic change is already difficult to achieve in Australia today; why would we want to make it even harder?

Those who advocate change will need a carefully crafted agenda that is relevant, feasible and acceptable. It needs to take into account the views of the disenchanted on the way things are done and what is prioritised. Such views cannot be swept under the carpet and ignored. Sitting still and waiting for the world to return to where it once was is not an option. However, it will need to transcend the political reform politics associated with the left-green movement and the right-populist tendency. It needs to lead and that means engaging with electors and mobilising support for change. To be engaged, electors will need to hear a message they can understand and support and which is based on conviction as much as it is based on attitudes within the electorate. Necessarily it will challenge as much as it responds. Indeed, there can be no such thing as a genuine re-engagement that is free of risk or devoid of conflict.

How then can we create such interest and harness such energy? Our political class needs to send out a message that they wish to engage the electorate around sound principles of democratic reform. Our citizens need a light on the hill as well as an extra penny in their pocket. Given the right-populist tendency to seek rule by the majority and the left-green tendency to seek rule by the percentages this is not going to be easy. Both have helped create the necessary pressure for change but defend or promote political institutions that fall short of what the nation needs.

## A New Radical Centre

When it comes to political reform we need a new radical centre built around the consolidation of parliamentary reform in the short-term, a Charter of Rights and Responsibilities beyond that, and a meaningful republic in the longer-term. This needs to be linked to a new concept of political leadership that seeks to better engage the public on a range of issues including political reform. Indeed, a move to a republic will need to involve the public every step of the way if it is to be successful.

In recent decades, both here and abroad, we have seen very successful exercises in political engagement that have taken us beyond the politics of public opinion and parliamentary power. Parliament can — and should — play a more active role in the development of national policy. Hopefully the Climate Change Committee created by Prime Minister Gillard will prove to be a good example of what can be achieved through focused and non-adversarial consideration. However, it should not be seen as being in competition with alternative mechanisms of deliberation such as my own government's *Dialogue with the City* which developed planning policy for metropolitan Perth.

One third of the participants in the *Dialogue* were randomly selected from across the city to join representatives from government, business, academia, interest groups and community associations. The government made it clear that it would follow up on the recommendations made and we did with *Network City: Community Planning Strategy*. So, too, did we involve representatives from the *Dialogue* in the Implementation Team set up within government. For such initiatives to add real value to our representative system they need not only to guarantee influence for the participants but they also need to be genuinely representative of the population and facilitated to ensure there is open and informed deliberation.

The commonwealth government's ill-fated "Peoples' Assembly" proposed during the election campaign would have been a good idea for the 1990s when it became obvious that climate change was real and threatening. Imagine, too, if it had used some form of deliberative process to assist in the matter of tax reform, particularly for the resources sector.

There are many issues for which such processes would not be appropriate, most notably areas of strong political commitment and mandate. However, it should not be ruled out as an option on the grounds that Parliament is the font of all wisdom. Just as citizens are now involving themselves in politics in a range of different ways and not just through party membership, so, too, should government develop policy in a range of ways that are more participative and deliberative.

Power is a wonderful thing, but if not shared it may become a liability. What we need is power with authority. So, too, does power need to be regulated, particularly executive power. We need a Charter of Rights and Responsibilities as recommended by the Brennan Committee and as instituted in the A.C.T. and Victoria to place individual rights and liberties at the forefront of our decision-making and public administration. Such proposals have well understood that rights have to be defined and their boundaries marked out. What are the limits of free speech? How do we best institutionalise the right to vote? So, too, has it been recognised that rights may come into conflict with each other or with wider public interest considerations such as national security.

The aim of a Charter is to open up a proper dialogue between the Legislature, the Executive and the Judiciary. It does this without undermining the pre-eminence of the Parliament and with full recognition of the need to balance rights against each other and against competing public interests. By requiring the Parliament to carefully consider the rights implications of its work and the public sector to act in ways that are compatible with human rights would add a new dynamic to our political processes. It sends a powerful message to our legislators and to our administrators about the accountability of government to the people. Indeed, the British experience with such a system tells us that public authorities have been encouraged to search for solutions to situations that had previously been viewed as unavoidable and unalterable. In other words, it helps avoid that tunnel vision that all too often operates within executive government.

Finally, there is the question of the republic. It is unfinished business in Australian politics, and debate about it necessarily takes us to debate about our Constitution and political system. We need to take the opportunity it provides to take a serious look at our Constitution. A popular vote on the question of the republic would sensibly come first. Should it be a popular vote in favour of a move to a republic we would then do well to refer the matter to a properly constituted Constitutional Convention. Such a convention could examine what type of Constitution we wish to have and what the powers and responsibilities of a President would be.

Attempt to cut off debate beyond a politician-dominated minimalist model would almost certainly fan the flames of disenchantment and populism. This time around, more detailed consideration could be given to models of direct election and presidential power. Indeed, a strong case can be made that a move in the direction of an Executive Presidency separate from the Legislature would be good for Australian politics. Not only does it accord with the evolution of our system in the direction of presidential politics but it creates the possibility for Cabinet Ministers to be selected from outside Parliament. Many Australians who would exercise ministerial office with distinction and effectiveness are simply not willing to stand for Parliament. In the case of some of the smaller states and territories, the pool of talent from which to select is limited. Indeed, an American-style system of government would work well for the states and territories given the service delivery functions they perform. Having Ministers less trapped by the imperatives of electoral and parliamentary politics should allow for better management and more innovation.

Due to our Westminster inheritance, all our Ministers are Members of Parliament. Some rise to the occasion, others don't as the pressures of maintaining a political base in the Parliament and within the electorate overwhelm their best intentions. We know that the way we govern can be improved but seem addicted to the view that Westminster is the only way. This reflects itself not just in the composition of our cabinets, but also in our reliance on conventions to run the system. At a minimum level we ought to be clarifying and properly codifying the powers of the Head-of-State, the role of the two Houses of Parliament and the relationship between the Executive and the Legislature so that the conflict and uncertainty that surrounded the crisis of 1975 is not repeated.

In other words, the republic debate allows us to put on the agenda new ways of thinking, not just about government but also about the functioning of Parliament. By separating the Government from the Parliament, voters could be given a wider range of choices. Who do I want to be President or Governor? Who do I want to be my Member of Parliament? Already electors have shown that such questions are relevant to them by their different voting patterns for the Senate and the House of Representatives.

## A Vision for the Future and a Strategy for Achieving It

It is important, however, that I put these proposals into a political context. I'm not arguing that the Australian government drop everything else it is doing and make political reform the sole focus for its legislative and policy development. Politics should be just as much about vision as it is about the nightly news. What we need is a serious strategy for political reform that distinguishes between short-, medium- and longer-term initiatives.

In the short term, it is important that the current case for a more constructive and policy-making Parliament be consolidated with real support and commitment. Couple this with the utilisation of new forms of public engagement where it is appropriate and a strong message is sent to the community about support for change. It will signal a turning of the tide.

The current government has thus far rejected the full program of human-rights reform recommended by the Brennan

Committee. This indicates the role right-populist thinking plays within the ALP either as a phenomenon to be feared or as an approach to politics that should be endorsed. However, like the republic, it won't go away as an issue. Resistance of its embrace on the grounds of popular opinion and the greater importance of the needs of executive government diminishes us as a political community. However, it is an issue that requires more advocacy and campaigning around the role such a Charter can play, particularly in respect of services provided by public bodies. As the British Institute of Human Rights put it when reviewing the day-to-day functioning of the UK's Human Rights Act:

> *Too often the Human Rights Act is associated with technical legal arguments or perceived to be limited to high profile — sometimes spurious — claims by celebrities and criminals. These case studies reveal a very different picture. They show how groups and people themselves are using not only human-rights law, but also the language and ideas of human rights to challenge poor treatment and negotiate improvements to services provided by public bodies.*[2]

Even though I can imagine the difficulties of campaigning on the question of a Charter, I see it as an important political reform because it talks to us as free citizens with wider responsibilities, just as the new forms of political engagement do. It institutionalises the values we purport to hold and makes it clear that the exercise of power is a most important business that needs ethics and sensible regulation. By requiring governments and law-makers to think carefully about what they are doing it has the potential to create greater confidence in the quality of the outcomes. Once again we have entered that territory we call "trust in government".

The move to the republic should involve a longer process of consideration. Firstly, we need a vote on whether to cut the ties with the English Monarch and secondly, the creation of a Constitutional Convention to consider the future government of the nation. Properly engaging the people on the question is not only good in itself, but also increases the chances for a consensus to emerge on the twin questions of democratic accountability and effective government.

## Re-engagement Through Leadership

By way of conclusion let me return to where I started.

There is a level of disenchantment about, and a degree of disengagement from, Australian politics. It is neither uniform in its expression nor internally consistent in its arguments. There are overlapping currents and a range of complaints about the way our political class is discharging its responsibilities — the rigidity of their adversarialism, the narrowness of their agendas, their defensiveness when it comes to community engagement and their attraction to the "quick fix". However, proportional representation or populism doesn't represent a solution. The disenchanted don't just want a better Parliament, they also want better and more principled government. This is why I believe a Charter of Rights and Responsibilities is necessary alongside new and innovative forms of public engagement. I have sought to find that political reform formula that achieves the right mix between principle (rights and responsibilities) and responsiveness (public engagement).

So, too, do I think it is the case that our current method for producing cabinets is putting too great an emphasis on politics and not enough on creative administration. Good government built upon long-term strategic planning and administration has become a necessity if we are to secure our future. That's why the move to consider a republic should open up the debate to wider considerations than those we have inherited from Westminster. Indeed, it is worth noting that two of the better reforms in Great Britain in recent years — the Human Rights Act and Devolution — challenged traditional Westminster thinking rather than endorsed it!

Re-engagement shouldn't just be about giving electors what they want as indicated by opinion polls. It requires leadership

around the very principles under which we say we are governed —
human rights and democratic accountability. Putting them
together in a way that produces good and effective government
requires a commitment to reform and a commonsense attitude
to what is required from our political system. Yes, the numbers
matter as to the proportions but politics ought to be about
more — our long-term productivity and environmental
sustainability, the rights of the minorities and the marginalised
and the public interest generally. However, should the major
parties not take up the challenge of political engagement and
involve the population in a deliberative dialogue about these
issues there is the risk that we drift into a system that makes
change too difficult and which may even take us back to a more
insular, defensive and protectionist Australia. Re-engagement
is not just about re-adjustment, it must also be about leadership
and reform. On this conclusion it will either stand or fall!

**Notes**

1    See Gollop, Leigh. "Distrustful, disenchanted, disengaged citizens: Are
     Australians an exception?" Paper presented at Australasian Political Societies
     Association Conference, University of Adelaide, 29 September – 1 October
     2004.

2    *The Human Rights Act – changing lives*, (BIHR, 2008), p. 5.

# Leadership and Politics Today

## Speech delivered at
### an address to the Banksia Club, Murdoch University

### Perth, 16 August 2007

The headline for Phillip Adams' column in the *Australian* last week said it all: "It's primarily a race for the lodge: the focus on Howard v Rudd is in keeping with Australia's de facto presidential system."[1]

Adams hits the nail on the head: politics today is primarily about the leaders. Indeed, it's not just about them, the whole process is built around them. To quote Adams again:

> *Australia has had a de facto presidential system since the end of the Menzies era, accelerated and intensified by the influence of television.*[2]

In today's lecture I will examine the background to this development and how it has progressed to create a system within a system. I will conclude with an examination of how leaders might rearrange their political and policy priorities to better deal with the long-term challenges our community faces today. I will begin, however, with some reflections on Adams' account of the politics of leadership and how it fits with accounts based on class, party and ideology.

## What Happened to Class, Party and Ideology?

Increasingly, political science has come to recognise the truth of this description of modern politics. Go back thirty years and much more emphasis would be given to class, party and ideology. However, with the increased volatility of voting, reduced identification with the major parties and less disagreement on political economy, the focus has shifted to the "leadership factor".

There are different ways that this development can be interpreted. It may be said that leaders have emerged to fill the vacuum created by the declining resonance of class, party and ideology. On the other hand, it could be argued that leaders, and the political machinery that surrounds them, have captured the commanding heights in a type of cultural coup d'état.

Whichever way you look at it the conclusion is the same: we have a political system built around leaders. They will either be in power or the major contenders for power. Their character, style and policy will be the focus of political commentary and they will be expected to be across all the major issues of the day.

If in power, the process of government will be organised around the leader's political office and the central agency under his or her control. If in opposition, the same rule applies even though the resources available are more limited.

Leaders have power and resources to develop policy and define strategies. Most important of all, however, is the expectation of their supporters that they will lead. In the balance between the opportunities and constraints that go with leadership, there is no doubt in my mind that opportunity is the clear winner. Indeed, many elected to positions of power underestimate the freedom they have to shape and define policies and processes. It is often this caution in a world of complexity and risk that undermines rather than consolidates power.

All governments (and oppositions, for that matter) need a centre from which is generated the will to gain, hold and use power. Leaders are that centre in a world of shifting loyalties and increased volatility.

Even the Labor Party, with its tradition of party and platform accountability, has given way on this fundamental point of leadership power. Just look at the changes that were made to the ALP's approach to the public sector and the market economy under Bob Hawke and Paul Keating. Labor was taken into new territory for which there was no precedent and from which there has been no return.

A more recent example is John Howard's embrace of centralism in the name of nationalism. Howard has not only questioned the reality of state loyalties but also the ongoing relevance of the federal idea. He went so far as to say last month that the Australian people are "not fussed about theories of federalism". According to Howard, the "two great sentiments regarding governance today are nationalism and localism".[3]

Of course, there are constraints and boundaries which it would be foolish to cross, but they can be overcome by a leader skilled in the arts of politics and management — and for which there are plenty of text books and plenty of advisers. Leaders also hold the trump card in the face of internal dissent. "Oppose me", they say to their followers, "and you threaten the only basis upon which you can gain and hold power — the strength of my leadership."

Nor is it the case that class, party and ideology are dead. Loyalties built around class still exist but are overladen with so many complicating factors — nationalism for one — that they lack the unified political expression they once possessed.

Political parties and their members are important, but now function more as workhorses for the leaders rather than radical constraints on their power. They are first and foremost campaigning organisations focused on fundraising, networking and polling.

What about ideology? There is still a divide between Left and Right as can be seen in the debate over labour law in Australia today. However, even here it is muted to some extent with the Liberals searching for a "fairness" test and Labor stressing the importance of "flexibility".

The traditional ideologies may be less relevant, but political ideas are alive and well. How often do we hear our leaders talking about rights and responsibilities, family and community, identity and citizenship, and freedom and security. Some even talk of democracy and sustainability. All of this adds up to an ongoing debate about values and how they relate to public policy and political practice. Of all the political commentators who seek to inform us on a daily basis, Paul Kelly is the one who understands this most.[4]

## The Leadership System

What we see in all of this is less traditional accountability *within* the major parties but more responsiveness to the wider public — and the range of institutions that help to define it, most notably the media. The leadership agenda can be defined as projection without and management within. Another way of describing the same phenomenon would be to say that leaders are required by political reality to look beyond the boundaries of their own party traditions in order to find that elusive but nevertheless all-important centre ground. It is important (and interesting) to note that part of that centre ground is the very process of seeking it — and managing the party along the way.

What I have described is a type of political system within a political system. Associated with it are a set of ideas and campaigning techniques as well as a set of political institutions around the leader's political office. No matter who is in power, the "look" of their operation will be the same. In fact, it would be true to say that the way they operate, particularly on a day-to-day basis, is remarkably similar.

So far, my only references to the ends of contemporary political leadership have revolved around two words: "power" and "the centre ground". This tells us a good deal about the boundaries within which politics occurs: investment and growth, a fair society and concern for the environment. Market solutions are favoured in most areas, but not without proper regulation in the public interest. Personal, community and national security are always important as is leadership strength and integrity.

This is not to say that there are no variations on a theme within the "centre". These variations provide the raw material for adversarial politics. Add a touch of leadership vanity and an aggressive and conflict-seeking media to the equation and you have a fully fledged system of "us" versus "them".

On the question of power, there will never be a shortage of political operatives willing and able to offer advice to their party leaders about how to capture and retain power. They are an essential part of the political process, never to be ignored, even if not always to be believed. The world they inhabit is inevitably short-term, a mixture of day-to-day events management, and planning for the next election. Inasmuch as there is science, it is the science of public opinion, backed up by the opinion poll and the focus group.

This world of contemporary political leadership, centrist ideas and professional campaigning techniques is the defining feature of contemporary politics. The way leaders project themselves into the community and manage their own constituencies will be crucial in determining whether they succeed or fail in the court of public opinion. Whilst the "centre ground" is a useful description of the boundaries of politics, it still needs political definition by way of combinations of position and policy on a wide range of fronts. Indeed, the capacity of political leaders to incorporate seemingly contradicting positions often proves to be the key to success. A good illustration of this has been the co-existence of "populism" and "economic rationalism" in many an election platform. In the world of politics, philosophical clarity may come at the cost of irrelevance. As they say, politics is an "art", not a "science"!

## Leading and Managing Change
This takes me to the point I want to make today. Power is never exercised in a vacuum. Leaders need a strong grasp of

how the world is changing and what are the drivers of change. However, it's one thing to manage a system, quite another to steer it in a new direction. Political leaders have been good at steering their own parties towards the centre ground. It has meant challenge and change for many. So, too, we have seen enormous changes in the structures, processes, and conception of government over the last thirty years. They were driven through the system by a series of reform-oriented leaders in the 1980s and 1990s. The changes were even given a name — "New Public Management" — as part of what has been described as "globalisation" and the "neo-liberal revolution".

As we entered the twenty-first century, this new system of governance and the political economy associated with it had become entrenched. The primary task of political leadership was to manage the contradictions it contained. The Right complained that the reform was being compromised and the Left complained that the reform was being consolidated. Liberals complained about the influence of populists, and populists complained about influence of liberals. This was, indeed, a type of "third way". To some it even looked like the "end of history" — enough, certainty, to keep people relaxed and enough conflict to keep them excited.

Such a system of power and politics has been very effective, but one needs to ask: has it become too insular? Is it too resistant to long-term thinking and structural change? The fact that such questions are being asked points to a restlessness within the body politic about the sustainability of our current attitudes and priorities. Not only is it clear that the international economic and political environment is more uncertain and unstable, but climate change and generational politics have emerged to place a question mark alongside so much we take for granted.

This takes me back to a point I made earlier — leadership is about opportunity *and* constraint. It is also about power *and* responsibility and about management *and* change. Of all leaders we can ask: are they focused on the next election or the next generation? Are they focused on growth or sustainability? Are they reactive or proactive? Are they managers or are they leaders?

The truth of politics is that if leaders are to be effective they will need to occupy both sides in this set of contrasting approaches to power. From the world of short-termism, adversarial politics, day-to-day political management and a degree of populism no democratic politician can escape, particularly given the attitudes and approach of the contemporary media. However, a re-assessment of priorities is possible. The current world of politics is more like a home than a prison. This means the doors and windows can be opened and the wider world explored in the interests of a more sustainable future. It might be said that the choice we have here is between politics as government or government as politics.

## Sustainability Planning, Strategic Government and Democratic Engagement

If I may be so bold as to say that the ability of a leader to incorporate long-term with short-term politics will be dependent on their embrace of three methodologies: sustainability planning, strategic government and democratic engagement.

This means setting long-term objectives for government along with strategies, programs and policies for their achievement, ensuring that social and environmental factors are given equal consideration to economic factors, and fully involving the public in both the planning and implementation phases of the process. It is a comprehensive package involving both the ends we pursue and the means we choose to achieve them.

The image here is that of a conversation between government and people that breaks through a system that is all to often simply "a manipulative exercise utilising the tools of persuasion that were developed by advertisers of commercial products in co-operation with psychologists and researchers who plumbed the inner workings of our thought processes in order to devise ways to de-emphasise facts and logic and reason".[5]

The system of policy and practice set up by political leaders to manage the tensions inherent within globalisation have hinted at these developments. Indeed, there are some splendid case studies of these methodologies being applied. However, with the possible exception of our friends in Scandinavia and a good smattering of regional governments around the world, the realisation of purpose in and across government as a whole has proved too difficult. "It may be good public policy", says the hard-headed politician, "but is it good politics? Hasn't short-termism, day-to-day events management and populist posturing been a proven winner?"

In a settled world that may very well be an appropriate answer. However, in a world where there is a good deal of unease about the ability of our system to cope with globalisation, global warming and global terror, a narrowly-based rationalism embellished with a dash of populism can quickly become empty or counter-productive and, just as political leaders lose authority when they fail to recognise change, they gain authority when they understand change and offer credible solutions to its challenges.

How often do we see time and circumstance weave their magic in human history? What is necessity today becomes unnecessary tomorrow. What has currency today loses value tomorrow. Our democracy is designed to facilitate and manage this process but it needs leaders to move away from the pack and embrace the new agenda.

## Commitment and Capability

We are back, then, to the question of the balance between opportunity and constraint. Quite often leaders underestimate the freedom they have. Some even become paralysed in the face of the risks that go with change. Taking a strategic approach based on sustainability principles requires discipline and can easily be derailed by events or personality clashes. Nor is there any guarantee that engaging the community more directly will always work. It's a theory whose practice has improved enormously, but it still isn't foolproof.

However, it's not only a question of our approach to politics but also of public policy and priority. We are uneasy because we know our current course is inadequate. We know we need more global co-operation to promote exchange and reconcile differences. We know we need a stronger emphasis on personal and social values in the way we live and work. We know we have to reduce our carbon imprint. We know we have to watch out for our liberties in a world mobilising to tackle terrorism.

We know these things but we are reluctant to change. Will it mean offending our American allies? Will it mean unemployment and lower living standards? Will it increase the threat of terrorism? An effective answer for each of these questions on a day-to-day basis provides the political link between the present and the future and will need to be found if that feeling of uneasiness about which I have spoken is to be translated into a base for change. We should recognise, as Ian Marsh and David Yencken have reminded us, that "the public policy cycle is not only a technical process. It is also one that depends on public opinion".[6]

To achieve change we need leaders not just committed to it but capable of delivering it.Building trust and working to win support for change is crucial. Change needs constituencies as well as commitment. It's certainly not riskless, but neither is it pointless as the cynics might suggest. Geoff Mulgan, the former head of policy and director of the strategy unit at Number Ten Downing Street, has reminded us that

>...*a combination of sound analysis, rigour on priorities and realism about capacities to deliver does pay dividends.*[7]

He notes that countries which perform consistently well around a range of indicators all have systems for challenging complacency and focusing on the long term and the strategic.

He goes on to quote an editorial from the *Times*. It provides an appropriate conclusion to my lecture:

> *What looks insoluble to one generation can be sorted out more completely than would have been thought possible… but governments overestimate their influence in the short term and underestimate it in the long term.*[8]

Notes

1   *The Australian*, 7 August 2007.
2   ibid.
3   *The Australian*, 31 July 2007.
4   See, for example, "Ideas Politician", *The Australian*, 11 October 2006.
5   Al Gore being interviewed by Ryan Lizza in *The New Republic*. http://www.tnr.com/doc.mhtml?i=w070611&s=lizza061307. I have developed these ideas further in "Strategic Planning-is it the new model?", *Public Administration Today*, January–March 2007, pp. 28–33, and "Towards a new era of strategic government" in John Wanna (ed.), *A Passion for Policy: Essays in Public Sector Reform* (ANU E Press, 2007), pp. 75–89.
6   *Into the Future: The Neglect of the Long Term in Australian Politics* (Black Ink., 2004), p. 19.
7   "Lessons of Power", *Prospect Magazine*, Issue 110, May 2005.
8   Quoted in "Lessons of Power".

# 7.

# Putting the Public Sector to Work

# Agile Government

Speech delivered at
the Agile Government Roundtable,
State Services Authority

Melbourne, 11 October 2007

Let me commence my remarks by noting that this discussion is part of a wider discussion about public sector reform in recent years.

As your provocation paper[1] points out, the twentieth-century model of the bureaucracy which prized hierarchy, specialisation, efficiency and standardisation was found wanting in the era of globalisation and rising public expectations. Although they differed over the details and extent of change, politicians of both left and right moved to overthrow this traditional approach to public sector management. What followed was described as New Public Management. What we are debating today is said to go beyond New Public Management.

Consequently, we are left with a bewildering variety of objectives which our public servants are expected to pursue, both individually and collectively.

On the one hand, we ask them to be fully accountable, and yet on the other hand, we ask them to be creative and innovative.

On the one hand, we ask them to be efficient, and on the other, we insist that they be effective and produce real change in the community.

On the one hand, we ask them to be inspirational and purposeful in respect of their agency responsibilities, and on the other, we expect them to join up, co-operate and compromise with others.

And finally, we ask them to perform to particular targets and at the same time to be agile and flexible in the way they operate.

Just to complicate matters even further, it should be noted that all of this occurs in the context of ministerial edginess and media pressure, hardly an environment conducive to clear and rational thought and action.

Let me begin my comments today by asking all of us to aim for clarity in all this confusion. This takes me straight to the question of definition: what do we mean by 'agile' government?

## Some Definitions and Categories

Here, there are two options. Are we going to have a broad definition that encompasses much, if not all, of that we seek from governments today, or are we going to narrow the definition and distinguish it from other features seen as desirable, such as joined-up government and network government?

As I read the provocation paper, "agility" is linked to three themes: firstly, working effectively in a world of constant and sometimes rapid change; secondly, dealing with complex problems in an uncertain environment; and thirdly, handling crises, be they natural or human induced.

To discuss each of these themes I suggest that we make some more distinctions, firstly about the different types of activities performed in the public sector. I would suggest four types of work[2]:

1. Law making, rule making and policy development
2. Service delivery

3. Tax collection and the management of government finance
4. Monitoring and enforcing of laws and regulations

I would suggest that "agility" type considerations apply to each of these arenas but in different ways.

## Rules and Policies

With respect to the first, we would expect agility from both politicians and bureaucrats. Indeed, it is worth noting that most if not all of the significant changes that will be needed if governments are to be effective will have to be initiated by the political arm of government. It may even be the case that these changes will sit uneasily with or even contradict the ideological and policy traditions of the party in government. This makes their management a particularly sensitive issue.

One of the problems I have with much of the literature on public sector reform is that it is written as though the public sector is a unified whole. This is not only not the case with respect to functions, but also with respect to accountabilities. Let me illustrate this by referring to the Victorian study *The Future of the Public Sector in 2025*. In the section on workforce capacity and capability it concludes:

> *The public sector needs the capacity to 'think big', test ideas and make bold decisions. It is no longer the role of public institutions to operate principally as production organisations striving for consistent responses.*[3]

I would not disagree with this statement, *but* I would need to add the crucial point that the "big idea" and "bold decision" would need to sit comfortably with the politicians who would be held to account following their implementation. Even an idea like "let the managers manage" — which has plenty of solid intellectual and practical support — has never been easy to implement in the real world of media scrutiny and ministerial ambition. All too often our consideration of public sector reform leaves out the political dimension.

## Service Delivery

When it comes to service delivery it is important to distinguish between the provision of a range of human services like health, education and community welfare, and the provision of crucial infrastructure like roads, railways, telecommunications, water, gas and electricity.

Here the debate has moved on from the provision of particular services to meet particular needs to the provision of bundles of services to solve particular problems. It is in this arena that we talk of "customers" and "clients", those who use government services and for whom the system should operate. It follows that agile governments will need to incorporate proper forms of consultation and engagement into their practices.

The big challenge, however, lies in the move away from "consequences" to "causes". Let me illustrate this by referring to the traditional set of services deemed necessary for good government:

- Hospitals to care for the sick
- Schools to educate around an agreed curriculum
- Welfare to provide support in times of need.

Today, however, it is a more complex issue with each of the above plus

- Illness prevention and well-being initiatives
- Education in personal capacities as well as particular knowledge
- Capacity-building for jobs and community living generally.

In other words, public expectations are pushing governments to press deeper in the quest for solutions to problems.[4]

## Monitoring and Enforcement

The last two functions — tax collection and law enforcement — take us into the harder edge of government–people relations. It is an arena in which people are treated in terms of their obligations to the community. In this context, we don't expect our government officials to be responsive to their needs and interests but rather we expect them to be firm in ensuring that the law is applied without fear of favour.

Agility in this context certainly means being up to date in technology. The way DNA technology is transforming policing is a case in point. The globalisation of crime (and the development of a terrorist threat) has also necessitated more cross-border co-operation between police, tax officials and other regulatory agencies.

This also takes us into the territory occupied not just by our police but also by our armed forces. They face adversaries who employ irregular, unconventional and asymmetrical means. In a research paper prepared for a US Military College, Lieutenant Colonel Christopher P. Gehler draws out the implications of this environment for the military in straightforward terms: "Adapt or Die". He explains:

> *In the volatile, uncertain, complex, and ambiguous environment we face for the foreseeable future if we were to choose one advantage over our adversaries it would certainly be this: to be superior in the art of learning and adaptation...*
>
> *Rather than focusing on a fixed point in a constantly changing future, the Army should create innovational organisations that are agile within the strategic context.*[5]

Certainly, this reference to a complex and ambiguous environment is one that applies across the board. It means "dealing with the unexpected, operating with incomplete information, and making calculated decisions of risk".[6] This takes us to the question of crises and crises management.

## Crisis Management and Scenario Planning
In their paper "Crises, Scenarios and the Strategic Management Process", David Pollard and Saline Hotho address this very

subject. They reach two conclusions which are pertinent to our discussion today:

1. Organisations should employ a strategic approach to crisis management by embodying crisis-management processes and planning in the strategy process itself, and

2. Using scenario planning when making assessments of likely futures and creating methods for dealing with change outside the control of management.

Scenario planning allows us to re-think strategy by asking "what if" alongside "what is" questions. They note that it is a tool which is forward-looking and capable of overcoming the "boundedness" of much strategic planning. From the point of management and governance the benefits are clear:

> *The underlying context is that, the more the organisation is prepared for crisis situations, the better these can be managed and that decision-making in the crisis situation will then be more deliberative and effective. The last thing managers need is to have to make crucial decisions in a context of extreme pressure and stress.*[7]

The Victorian 2025 Study is a good case study of how scenario planning can be used.

However, once again I feel obliged to bring the politicians back into the equation. This is not only crucial for any strategic-planning process but also for crisis management, as they will need to be comfortable with what may be required and with what priorities will be set. Given that there is often ministerial reshuffling within government and, of course, given that governments can change, some reference to Parliament would be helpful, perhaps through the work of one or all of the Standing Committees. This is never easy but if we are to be serious about agility in government it would be desirable, if only to make the elected representatives aware of the issues and their implications for public sector practice.

Defining agility and then asking questions about what it will mean for the various public sector contexts in which it is to apply is one way to tackle the subject. I trust I have added some value to your considerations by taking this route.

## Some Empirical Evidence

The other way to tackle the subject is through empirical study. What does the actual experience of government tell us about this issue?

One such study was by the consulting firm A.T. Kearney of 52 agencies in eight countries. They focused on tax and revenue, health and welfare, and criminal justice and security agencies. Service delivery was their target function and agility defined narrowly as "making government faster, more flexible and more responsive to the needs of customers".[8]

They concluded that there were six aspects of agility:
1. Organisational flexibility
2. Focused leadership
3. A culture of research and innovation
4. Attention to the management of customer relationships
5. Support for e government
6. Commitment to systems of performance management

In looking at the most successful agencies, the biggest impact came from giving priority to customer service, organisational change capabilities and leadership. In particular, a commitment to and consistent support for change from the top was seen as crucial.

## Leadership and Trust

Talk of the demonstrated importance of leadership takes me to an important distinction in the provocation paper, that between responding to change on the one hand and shaping change on the other. This is where the concept of "agility" marks itself out as different from that of "responsiveness". To quote the provocation paper:

*Agile governments are likely to engage in shaping activity over the long term, while seeking to become responsive to changing needs in the short-term.*[9]

It needs to be said, however, that the shaping agenda is a tougher one as it shifts the policy emphasis to the demand management side of the public policy equation and the responsibility side of the rights and responsibility mix. We are back to the illness prevention outcomes from education and capacity-building agenda outlined earlier in this paper. Without doubt, the challenge of climate change will also take us into the province that deals with shaping activity and behaviour.

This is an agenda that will require a re-orientation of government activity, a re-ordering of government budgets and the development of partnerships with individuals and communities if it is to be successful. Once again, the role of the politician will be crucial, not just in agreeing to such a shift in emphasis but in sanctioning the use of different approaches in pursuit of these ends.

Building trust is crucial, not just in relations between Ministers and public servants but also in providing room for experimentation. The implication of this is clear: involving people in the planning and delivery process is not just "good politics", it is crucial if a long-term perspective is to have any chance of success. The sort of agility we are talking about, then, needs to be more than the capacity to respond rapidly and effectively to the latest media crisis.

## Conclusions

Overall, then, I believe the provocations paper provides us with a solid basis for discussion. I would argue, however, that we ought to distinguish between the different activities of government (rule making, tax collecting, service delivery and enforcement) if we are to make sense of the agility agenda.

Secondly, we need to incorporate the political arm of government more directly into the discussion. Politicians are not only involved in one of the activities (rule-making), they are crucial when it comes to the question of implementation. Indeed, they are bound to have strong views on the direction and pace of change. In many ways it is the relationship between governments and the public sector that is the key factor in the reform process.

Thirdly, and finally, I strongly agree with those who advocate the integration of crisis management into all strategic planning, and the use of scenario planning as a methodology for addressing questions about the future.

## Notes

1   Demos and State Services Authority, *Agile Government: A Provocation Paper* (2007).

2   This is adapted from Patrik Engellau, *Four Steps for Saving Money in the Public Sector* (Federation of Swedish Industries, 1982).

3   State Services Authority, *The Future of the Public Sector in 2025* (2006), p. 26.

4   See Geoff Gallop, "Strategic Planning: Is it the New Model?", *Public Administration Today*, January–March, 2007, pp. 28–33.

5   Christopher Gehler, *Agile Leaders, Agile institutions: educating adaptive and innovative leaders for today and tomorrow* (US Army War College, 2005), pp. 2, 14.

6   ibid., p. 15.

7   David Pollard and Saline Hotho, "Crises, Scenarios and the strategic management process", *Management Decision*, vol. 44, no. 6 (2006).

8   A.T. Kearney study on Agile Government, 3 December 2003. Available from http://www.atkearney.com/maintaf?p=1,5,1,140

9   *Provocation Paper*, p. 17.

# Towards a New Era of Strategic Government

Speech delivered at
Australian and New Zealand School
of Government Lecture,
Australian National University

Canberra, 25 October 2006

I am delighted to be contributing to the Australian and New Zealand School of Government's ANU Lecture Program.

The creation of ANZSOG, and, indeed, the Graduate School of Government at the University of Sydney where I teach, is an indication that public administration is returning to its rightful place as an essential element in the study of government and politics.

Politics is not just about theory and policy, it is also about administration and implementation. Systems have to be administered and policies implemented.

The way this has been, could be and ought to be done is a matter that warrants serious theoretical and practical investigation.

The study of public administration has broadened its horizons as governments have come to expect their heads of department not just to administer but to manage change and create value. This has paved the way for new terminology, in this case "public management".

For those who practise public management, the emergence of Graduate Schools of Government has been timely. They have complemented the wonderful work of our Institutes of Public Administration and the innovative thinking associated with our Schools of Public Policy today. To be involved in the public sector is to be at the cutting edge of some of the most creative thinking associated with political and social inquiry. If you want a demonstration of this, look up the website of the Strategy Unit in the UK Cabinet office.[1]

We are interested in systems *and* outcomes, processes *and* outputs, and strategies *and* operations.

The long-standing debate about ends and means has been given new meaning as we explore the relationships involved more intensively.

That public servants themselves have been given the opportunity to reflect on these matters through their participation in graduate programs augurs well for the future.

Of course, I come to these discussions after twenty years as an elected representative in a State Parliament, three years of which were as a Minister and five years as a Premier.

Public servants were always there, informing and advising, helping and counselling, worrying and warning, planning and arranging, and occasionally (and I emphasise occasionally) scheming and obstructing.

Without them the system simply couldn't work. They are part of an equation that involves both the political and the administrative arms of government. Neither can be properly understood without the other. It's all about relationships, as, indeed, is politics in general: government and people, public and private, commonwealth and state, state and local, executive, legislature and judiciary, cabinet and caucus, etc.

Many factors can influence the way these relationships develop, from straightforward events to longer-term tendencies associated with social, economic, environmental or technological changes. I say "influence" because, in the end, politicians have to interpret and respond to these events and tendencies. The way they do — and how successful they are — is a major factor in determining the type of public management we have.

When we reflect on this we should always remind ourselves of the words of John Maynard Keynes:

> *The ideas of economists and political philosophers, both when they are right and when they are wrong, are more powerful than is commonly understood. Indeed the world is ruled by little else. Practical men, who believe themselves to be quite exempt from any intellectual influence, are usually the slaves of some defunct economist. Madmen in authority, who hear voices in the air, are distilling their frenzy from some academic scribbler of a few years back.*[2]

## New Public Management

Tonight I want to reflect on the changes that have occurred over those twenty years. For a large part of that time there was a governing paradigm which we now call the New Public Management. For a couple of years in Carmen Lawrence's government I was it — Minister Assisting the Treasurer and Minister for Microeconomic Reform. I recall representing the Premier at one of the crucial meetings that established the national competition reform agenda for the 1990s.

This was also the time when I had my first of many debates with my media advisers about how to describe and advocate. I had been on talkback radio and was asked "What do you mean by microeconomic reform?"

True to my early education in economics I replied: "The use of competition to guarantee an efficient allocation of resources throughout society."

When I came out of the studio I knew I was in the bad books. My media adviser put it bluntly: "The punters would not have the remotest idea of what you meant. Economic theory is one thing, clarity and simplicity another."

"Okay", I responded, "how would this go: Making sure the production of goods and services follows consumer demand, and only the best and most efficient in the private and public sectors survive."

"That's worse", he said, "not only is it too long, it doesn't speak to the day-to-day needs of the punters."

Feeling challenged but not beaten I made another attempt: "Reducing waste and increasing productivity in both the public and private sectors."

Sensing a breakthrough was close, my word doctor urged me to go further: "You're getting closer, but I'm still not clear on what it means for the family budget."

"Lower taxes and lower prices!" I exclaimed in a Eureka moment.

"Now you're talking the language of the people", he concluded, smiling in the knowledge that mediaspeak had recorded another win in the real culture wars.

What governments took on board were not just new methodologies but a new way of thinking about the role of the public sector itself.

Let me try to define these changes by referring to some of the terminology that was used.

The public service became the public sector as the emphasis shifted from the advisory to the service delivery functions of government.

Senior public servants became public sector managers whose accountability to the government of the day was clearly demonstrated in Public Sector Management Acts that had replaced the long-standing Public Service Acts.

Ministerial responsibility was effectively re-interpreted within the broader context of public sector management generally. Public servants were given more independence and therefore more responsibility. It was a case of "letting the managers manage."

Services to the government of the day and to the community became outputs whose efficiency and effectiveness could be measured.

Concepts like "benchmarking", "comparability", "contestability", "choice" and "competition" became part of the public sector vocabulary, as did "the level playing field".

Citizens and subjects became customers and clients. Government departments became agencies. A range of statutory authorities became government trading enterprises (or GTEs).

Corporatisation and privatisation became public-sector policy options for GTE's and corporate-style management was introduced for departments. In some jurisdictions, a range of government agencies were transformed into self-governing trusts.

The changes that resulted have been comprehensive and far-reaching in their impact.

Many GTE's have been disaggregated, corporatised and made subject to competition. Many, too, have been privatised by both commonwealth and state governments. New independent regulators have replaced Ministers as arbitrators of price and access to infrastructure. Performance management and external auditing are now fully institutionalised, as is accrual accounting. The strict separation of public and private has been broken down by deregulation, outsourcing and a range of public–private partnerships across a range of activities. Contract management, previously the preserve of the infrastructure arms of government, has become central to the work of many public sector agencies. Jeff Kennett's Victoria was actually described as "The Contract State".[3]

Given that these were policies that undermined established patterns of power and influence, their acceptance and implementation required strength of purpose. Increasingly, governments came to seek advice from outside the traditional channels. Consultants were engaged not just as advisers, but to assist in implementation. The size, status and power of Departments of Prime Minister and cabinet and Premier and

Cabinet increased significantly. Top-down change was deemed necessary if public services were to be liberated from the straitjacket of bureaucracy and citizens from limitations placed on their ability to choose.

By the end of the century, the reach of this new form of politics and public management had spread into what had been the Soviet Empire and was exerting influence in Japan, Korea, India and China. In as much as globalisation had its theory, this was it — a new terminology and a new political economy and public administration for a new era. It descended into pure hubris with the declaration that history had come to an end.[4]

But, of course, history didn't come to an end. As Hegel observed of the relationship between knowledge and events: the Owl of Minerva only takes flight at dusk, after the changes have occurred. We only know of the full implications of a major change at the very point that something new is taking shape.[5]

## Strategic Government

In my view, we are seeing something new emerge in the public domain. It is a form of public management that is a response not just to terrorism and global warming, but also to the contradictions that exist within the practice of New Public Management. This new form of Strategic Government has become the paradigm of choice for governments representing the traditions of both left and right, but it suits the instincts of the former more than the latter, particularly when linked to a commitment to the principles of sustainability associated with the economic, social and environmental triple bottom line.

But this is to move ahead of myself. Some definition and description is required. If we turn to political terminology again, subtle but important shifts can be discerned.

Concepts like "strategic planning", "joined-up government", "collaboration", "partnerships", "sustainability" and "progress indicators" have been superimposed onto those associated with the New Public Management.

The idea of comprehensive social change is back on the agenda. However, rather than just defining this change in terms of the values and institutions said to be fundamental to human welfare, governments are increasingly describing change with reference to economic, social, environmental and governance indicators, such as levels of employment, standards of health and education, biodiversity, air quality and degrees of citizenship. The argument is simple: if there is such a thing as "the good society", then surely it will display these features.

In some cases, most notably in Tasmania under the leadership of the late Jim Bacon, the community has been consulted about these objectives and what would measure their achievement. This has given renewed currency to the concepts of "citizenship" and "political engagement".[6]

What is also encouraging about the development is its problem-solving approach to public policy and administration. Achieving targets requires focus, co-operation across government and collaboration with the community. It is all about results rather than just inputs and outputs, and the results being referred to are "whole-of-society" results.

Public management is being localised ("place management") and personalised ("case management") as it is recognised that both locational and individual factors are at work in issues like poverty and social exclusion. It is not just a case of taking services to people, but of involving people themselves in problem-solving and capacity-building. People are seen, then, not just as citizens and subjects, customers and clients, but as "co-producers" in the new rights-and-responsibilities mix of modern politics.

Nor are these ideas only relevant to areas like welfare and health. We also see them at work in transport, crime prevention, water and energy policy. The view that "the personal is the political" is now established wisdom with respect to meaningful social change and the conservation of scarce resources.

All in all, what we see is a more comprehensive definition of the objectives of public policy and management, the setting of society-wide targets, the involvement of the people in the setting of these targets and the implementation of policy, and more co-operation and co-ordination across government and with the private sector and community.

None of this represents a radical overturning of the changes of the last decades of the twentieth century. Rather, it is a response to the contradictions created by that new contract and managerial state and a recognition of its limitations in the face of new issues and challenges.

## Efficiency or Effectiveness?

There was always a tension at the heart of New Public Management practice. Whilst it spoke of the three "E"s of public administration — economy, efficiency and effectiveness — the position and importance of the last objective — effectiveness — was always somewhat problematical. Here we can see the tension between public and private values fully exposed. Was the aim of the exercise to lift the productivity of the public sector or was it to create public value? Was it to serve the interests of citizens as taxpayers or the interests of citizens as clients, customers, or residents? Was it about public good or private choice?

In this battle of ideas and interests, "efficiency" was a winner. It was straightforward: the number of inputs required for a product or service. It was associated with an economic theory of resource allocation via markets. Different jurisdictions could be compared and benchmarks established. Public-sector agencies could be compared with their private-sector equivalents and put to the test through outsourcing. Governments saw themselves as corporations looking to maximise the efficiency of their operations in the interests of their owners — the taxpayers.

In many cases, this led governments, both federal and state, to conclude that some of their operations should be restructured and sold off to the private sector. In this respect, Australia was no different from many other jurisdictions.

This is not to say that New Public Management didn't produce some very innovative and useful methodologies for determining public-sector effectiveness, including citizens' charters, the use of consultation techniques, satisfaction surveys and, of course, room for direct choice by the individual. The problem was that the whole notion of effectiveness was framed narrowly around the work of the agencies themselves and not on the overall performance of the public sector and the society it served.

Of course, some government agencies are like businesses, and governments need to be businesslike, but governments are *not* businesses. The sum total of individual interests expressed through the market can never produce the public interest except via the logic of utopia. Considerations related to the long term as well as the short term, minorities as well as majorities, social relationships as well as efficiency, and environmental amenity as well as economic well-being all need to be taken into account.

For centre-left parties, the concept of sustainability became a powerful organising principle and methodology for policy analysis. Economic strength, social relationships and environmental amenity all became important. Rather than see government as organised to deliver each separately, it was redefined to become a means by which each was tackled together in the search for balanced and therefore sustainable outcomes. Indeed, to treat them separately ignored the obvious tensions that existed between them.

Even conservatives came to see the narrowness of the market morality and New Public Management agenda. This was reflected in their rediscovery of "values" related to family, community and nation. The state had a role to play to protect and promote these values in the market-place of modern ideas.

Strategic planning in government has brought all of these issues to the surface for proper investigation and resolution. Indeed, I would argue that a new sense of purpose has been injected into public sector politics and management as common purposes are clarified and *tests of* and *strategies for* achievement are developed in consultation with the public.

What is different about this version of planning is that it is not just about command and control. Issues related to individual motivation and community endeavour as seen as just as important as legislation, regulation and public provision. Consider, for example, the deeper understanding we now have of the complexities of tackling social exclusion, poverty and long-term unemployment. These complexities — and those related to the search for the triple bottom line generally — are brought to the surface, not as "determining structures", but as "problems to be tackled".

New Public Management was always going to have some difficulty with complex issues like poverty, long-term unemployment and social exclusion. Its vision of functionally separate and independently managed units of government delivering standardised services to customers or clients worked well for the "average" citizen. When it came to the differences associated with a multicultural society, the history associated with Indigenous disadvantage, the psychology associated with poverty, and the culture associated with long-term unemployment, it was bereft of solutions.

Thus commenced a range of initiatives in the way public services are delivered, such as partnerships with community and business, localised and individualised management and co-production. These initiatives were designed to fill in the gaps between the silos and re-establish the all-important enabling functions of government.

## Citizens or Consumers?

The truth is there is a range of contradictions with respect to the way we participate in society as voters or consumers. In the former, we decide as members of a community deliberating on the range and limits of collective provision. In the latter, we make decisions for ourselves and our families: which gas company? Which school? What form of health insurance?

There is a tension here that was not fully appreciated as the move to market solutions took hold. The point of public policy was defined as liberating the individual from the straitjacket of collective discipline except in the most basic areas of government provision such as national security, community safety and commercial regulation. Just as the adherents of this approach to government were uncomfortable in the face of politics with all its complexity, confusion, and compromise, so too were the public uncomfortable with the limitations the market model placed on the meaning of public purpose and participation.

By the early years of the twenty-first century, both major parties in Australia were being urged by their supporters to ask harder questions about these matters, particularly privatisation. Even the open-investment policies of the nation were put to the test when Shell made its unsuccessful bid to take over Woodside.

As a wider range of policies re-emerged as matters for public debate, a level of choice returned with the ALP generally opposed to privatisation (if not to competition) and the Liberal Party generally, but not always, in favour of privatisation. The role played by state Labor governments in facilitating this broader debate about "ends" and "means" was particularly important.

It has been the state governments who have pioneered a strategic approach to government in Australia. All of the states have a strategic plan or are, in the case of New South Wales, in the process of developing one: Victoria's *Growing Victoria Together*, Queensland's *Smart State Strategy*, Western Australia's *Better Planning: Better Services* and *State Sustainability Strategy*, South Australia's *Strategic Plan*, Tasmania's *Tasmania Together 2020*, and New South Wales' *A New Direction for the Future*.

They all involve developing major themes for government, priority setting around sustainability-type objectives, the setting of targets or strategic outcomes, the involvement of the people and the monitoring of performance. Under the umbrella of such planning, some major structural changes have been implemented and new means of public engagement introduced, not just around particular policy issues like water, but also through Regional Cabinets and Regional Parliaments.[7]

## A New Policy Agenda

The move to strategic planning, joined up government and public–private collaboration was not just a response to the contradictions of New Public Management. Yes, it provided for more legitimacy in an age of distrust. Yes, it provided for a sense of purpose within government. Yes, it provided for a more sophisticated debate about the ends and means of contemporary government. Yes, it allowed for a more pragmatic mix of public and private endeavour. It represented the working through of a series of problems that had developed with the implementation of New Public Management.

However, what is as important as these factors is the emergence of new issues on the political agenda that require strong and more strategic government.

In the first place, there have been important changes in priority for the big three areas of state government service provision: health, education and community safety. In health, it has become clear that policy needs to move beyond the treatment of illness to the prevention of illness. In education, the community requires a range of outcomes to be realised as well as the teaching of a particular curriculum. In matters relating to policing, there has been recognition of the need not just to fight crime but also to deal with the causes of crime.

At the federal level there has also been a recognition of the need to move beyond income support in welfare to capacity-building and personal responsibility. Issues seen as welfare issues have become employment-and-training issues, just as those traditionally seen as economic (such as human capital) have become personal, social and cultural issues as well.

Traditional models of service delivery — the provision of hospital care and medicine, the unexamined teaching of curriculum, the policing of the streets, and the welfare safety net — are simply insufficient if we are to deal with these broader issues. They are particularly inadequate if we are serious about creating a better way of life generally and for *all*, no matter what their background or circumstances.

No wonder, then, that joined-up government, early-intervention strategies, public-community partnerships, place and case management and concepts of co-production, personal responsibility, and community policing have all emerged as major influences on public-sector policy and management and the education and training programs associated with them.

## Global Warming and Terrorism

In the second place, we have seen the new issues of global warming and terrorism having a significant impact on government priorities and their delivery.

Global warming is an issue that requires strategic planning, not just within nations, but between nations. It is a truly global matter. Not only that, but it requires integration across the traditional boundaries that have separated environmental and economic considerations. It also means integrating longer-term concerns into policy-making today. It challenges not just our mainstream technologies but our culture of consumption.

Because of its importance it has become the policy province for political leaders with central-agency involvement in priority setting, policy-making and co-ordination across government.

Strategic planning is also required to deal with the reality and potentiality of natural disasters associated with global warming. Co-ordination across all government agencies with an interest in crisis management has become a necessity, and is recognised as a contemporary budget and administrative priority.

The same goes for counter-terrorism initiatives within government. Like global warming, terrorism has helped facilitate a comeback by state power and government initiative. Attention can be drawn to a number of themes.

Firstly, the co-ordination of government agencies with respect to surveillance through to incident management. Indeed, there are not many parts of government that haven't been mobilised in the planning process and all levels of government have been affected — local, state and federal.

Secondly, legislation-restricting rights and freedoms and extending police powers "in the public interest" has become commonplace.

Thirdly, matters relating to religion and political difference have become more controversial as governments look to define the contours of citizenship and better integrate minorities into the mainstream. From being a regulator and a facilitator, the state is also drifting into the role of "educator".

In many ways, the terminology of a "War on Terror" tells us a good deal about the increased role of the state as the important separations of political and military and politics and policing are blurred. Governments say that they must plan to avoid terrorism and deal with the eventuality should it occur. Laissez-faire is no longer an option.

## The Re-Birth of the State

Planning, then, is on the march as governments define their objectives on the basis of the triple bottom line and the new threats posed by global warming and terrorism. In working to achieve these objectives a renewed emphasis on the role of the state, increased co-ordination across government and partnerships with the community have become part and parcel of public management.

The belief that public concerns could be contracted out or left to the market for resolution by way of "the cunning of reason" has experienced a significant defeat at the hands of democratic logic and the needs produced by contemporary history. Governments are simply not in a position to deflect responsibility when it comes to matters of life and death, and matters about which the public wants real rather than rhetorical solutions.

There are, of course, different versions of strategic government, depending upon the political colours of the parties involved. For conservatives, planning with respect to the new terrorism is given priority. For centre-left governments, planning to cover the field of economic, social and environmental concerns is given equal weight. For left liberals the planning involved in countering terrorism is seen as counter-productive and authoritarian beyond the limits of acceptability. It is the case, however, that all have moved beyond the era of New Public Management. The state is no longer being hollowed out. It is being given a new sense of purpose and a new content with the wider planning, co-ordinating and facilitating roles being developed.

It is not, however, like the state of old. At the very heart of the politics of Strategic Government is a recognition of complexity, the inevitable clash of values, and the importance of civil society. There is an understanding that not all knowledge lies within government and that engaging the public is not an optional extra but an essential ingredient of good government.

The over-arching theme is one of government alongside the community, working with it to solve problems. This means more collaboration between levels of government, within governments themselves and between governments and their communities. An enormous range of relationships are formed, within which there are complicated patterns of accountability.

## Accountability and Strategic Government
The fact that the different levels and functions of government are now overlapping raises important questions for our democracy. What does it mean for democratic accountability? What does it mean for ministerial responsibility? What does it mean for public-service practice?

One of the essential features of a good system of democracy is proper balance between the centre and the regions, and the regions and the localities. As governments join forces to solve problems there is a risk of too much centralisation and standardisation. This can undermine more localised accountabilities, reduce meaningful choice in elections, and stifle innovation in policy and practice.

In Australia, the link that is often drawn between national development, nationalism and commonwealth power makes this an ever-present threat to good government.

In order to respond to this potential threat to institutional autonomy, we would do well to incorporate into our debates and ultimately into our system the principle of subsidiarity. This aims to ensure that decisions are taken as closely as possible to the citizen and that serious questions should be asked as to whether action at higher levels is justified in light of the possibilities available at lower levels of government.[8]

The same principle applies when considering relations between the government and the non-government sectors. Sometimes the pressure of incorporation may come at a price that is too high, as various welfare agencies have determined in relation to the federal government's welfare-to-work policies.

When it comes to ministerial responsibility, Strategic Government has brought with it a degree of inevitable confusion. In this case, I believe it is a good thing because of the simplicities and impracticalities associated with both the Westminster doctrine and the New Public Management revision of that doctrine.

Whilst it was clear that the Westminster doctrine of ministerial responsibility was clearly deficient in the real world of public management, its reverse, most commonly described as "Let The Managers Manage", had a corresponding political deficiency.

Firstly, its radical separation of ministerial power and public-sector management was not feasible in a world of marginal seats, targeted lobbying and media aggression. To put it another way, there is often a tension between policy rationality and the inevitable messiness of democratic politics.

Secondly, its tendency to shift blame from politicians to public servants took some of the sting out of democratic accountability. Indeed, there was something implausible about reducing ministerial responsibility to effective communication of government policy and the setting of performance targets for which public servants were held accountable.

The changes that have come with Strategic Government see Ministers back into the managerial equation. Indeed, in some of the jurisdictions which have developed plans, lead Ministers have been created to chair collaborative initiatives and given strategy-setting, negotiating and monitoring roles. However, public servants are still very much in the seat of policy delivery and human-resource management, for which there will be clear accountabilities, but now we see more balance in the relationship itself and in our understanding of responsibility.

This takes me to my third question about public-service practice. It is no longer a case of delivering a particular service. It involves a set of relationships and situations of complexity and even ambiguity. New skills related to public engagement and consultation, project management, managing in a society of diversity, working in teams, developing a multi-disciplinary knowledge-base and planning for the future have all become indispensable, even though awkwardly placed alongside our current systems of performance management and public accountability.

The bigger question is whether or not the patterns of accountability and public-sector capabilities that are developing in this new era of Strategic Government will be enough. Not only is there a risk of too much centralisation in the system of government, there is the related risk of too much power going to government generally. New Public Management required governments to perform fewer functions but to be strong in the way it carried out those functions — what Andrew Gamble called in his book with the same title: *The Free Economy and the Strong State.*[9]

Strategic government, on the other hand, is requiring governments to do more and in different ways: facilitating, co-ordinating, partnering and enabling. That being said, it is still the state we are talking about and you can't have states without governments and politicians. Note also the new powers being taken on by the state to "protect" and to "educate". These are powers that can be abused in a society of diversity and robust debate. As a community we need to ask whether we have an adequate system of checks and balances to combat abuse.

In the A.C.T. and Victoria they have asked this question and answered it with new human-rights protections in their laws.[10] This is a sensible course of action in a world where the power and authority of the state is bound to expand.

## Notes

1    See http://www.strategy.gov.uk.

2    John Maynard Keynes, *The General Theory of Employment, Interest and Money* (1935), Ch. 24 "Concluding Notes".

3    John Alford and Deirdre O'Neill, *The Contract State: Public Management and the Kennett Government* (1994).

4    Francis Fukuyama, *The End of History and the Last Man* (1992).

5    In the Preface to his *Philosophy of Right* (1820) Hegel wrote:
     "One more word about giving instruction as to what the world ought to be. Philosophy in any case always comes on the scene too late to give it ... When philosophy paints its gray in gray, then has a shape of life grown old. By philosophy's gray in gray it cannot be rejuvenated but only understood. The owl of Minerva spreads its wings only with the falling of the dusk."

6    See http://www.tasmaniatogether.tas.gov.au. See also Government of Western Australia, *A Voice for All: Strengthening Democracy Western Australian Citizenship Strategy 2004–2009* (2004).

7    See John Wanna and Paul Williams (eds), *Yes, Premier: Labor Leadership in Australia's State and Territories* (2005).

8    Subsidiary was established in EU law by the Treaty of Maastricht, signed on 7 February 1992 and entered into force on 1 November 1993. The present formulation is contained in Article 5 of the Treaty Establishing the European

Community (consolidated version following the Treaty of Nice, which entered into force on 1 February 2003):

*"The Community shall act within the limits of the powers conferred upon it by this Treaty and of the objectives assigned to it therein.*

*In areas which do not fall within its exclusive competence, the Community shall take action, in accordance with the principle of subsidiarity, only if and in so far as the objectives of the proposed action cannot be sufficiently achieved by the Member States and can therefore, by reason of the scale or effects of the proposed action, be better achieved by the Community.*

*Any action by the Community shall not go beyond what is necessary to achieve the objectives of this Treaty."*

See http://en.wikipedia.org/wiki/Subsidiarity.

9   Andrew Gamble, *The Free Economy and the Strong State* (1988, Second Edition, 1994).

10  See A.C.T., *Human Rights Act 2004*, and Victoria, *Charter of Human Rights and Responsibilities Act 2006*.

# Putting the Public Back Into
# the Public Service

Speech delivered at
the Annual President's Address,
Institute of Public Administration Australia (Queensland)

Brisbane, 20 November 2008

I think you would agree with me that we are living in confusing and troubling times. I'm not just thinking of the Global Financial Crisis and what that is going to mean, let alone what it has already meant. We can now see the balance of the economic power in the world shifting to China and India. America remains a military superpower but the weakness of its economy is painfully obvious. There is now a consensus on the causes and consequences of climate change but no agreement on how to tackle it. Whichever way you look at it, energy costs are going to rise, as are the costs of health care with our ageing society. Some commentators[1] have concluded that we are moving from an "age of abundance" to an "age of austerity" and yet we still speak as if the current difficulties are temporary.

What is this all going to mean for a country like Australia — "the lucky country", as Donald Horne so brilliantly described us in his classic critique? What are the implications for the way we imagine ourselves, organise our lives and set our priorities? These are, of course, questions we will need to analyse and answer *as a community*. This takes me to the activity developed by humanity to deal with our collective destiny — politics.

Although politics can't be reduced just to its electoral and parliamentary manifestations, these arenas exist as the pinnacle for our collective endeavours, even if it is only to confirm in law what has become a social reality. It was to this world of politics that I devoted twenty years of my life. Given that it's now nearly three years since I retired from state politics, it is an opportune time to reflect on politics generally, and more particularly on the relationship between democracy, public policy and public administration. I am no longer subject to the heat of the daily battles, and my work with public servants has enabled me to see another point of view. Unfortunately, however, I am burdened with the knowledge that both the supporters and critics of modern politics have a point. Those who support and practice politics know how hard it is to win and maintain a majority. They know that compromise may be necessary and is not a sin. Those who criticise modern politics know that too much emphasis on short-term events management can insulate the body politic from much needed change. The truth is modern politics needs both its politicians and its prophets, and hopefully they will be working together rather than shouting at each other over a dividing fence.

Something I have concluded is that you can't have democracy without politics, you can't have politics without politicians, and you can't have politicians without public servants. Systems, people and ideas are all involved. For both politicians and the public service it is a world of pressure — from people to government and from government to the public service. What matters is not just efficiency in performance but clearly demonstrated improvements in community well-being, what our public policy practitioners call "outcomes".

It's also a world with its own version of "the blame game". Quite often we see politicians (and their private-sector advisors) criticising the public servants for their failure to fully embrace managerialism, public relations and the market. On the other hand, we often hear from public servants and academics about the "politicisation" of the service arising from political appointments, a lack of employment security and the growing power of ministerial staffers.

This battle between the "mandarins" and the "managers" has been played out for some time now. It is symptomatic of a wider problem in our system and that relates to the gaps that have opened up between the people and the government ("lack of trust"), and between the government and its public sector ("lack of purpose").

Tonight I would like to attempt a resolution of some of these issues by focusing on the concept of the public interest and look to the potential that exists in current thinking and practice around strategic government. The working assumption behind my discussion is that ideas and values matter. Not only is this a legal fact in our system of government, but it is a key factor in understanding how our public sector operates and what we expect from our public servants. I will use history and contemporary issues to illustrate my argument that there is a way forward. Such a way forward is all about putting the public back into the public service.

## The Many Faces of Public Service

However, before moving to my central argument I would like to make a general point about the way we imagine and talk about the public sector. Too much commentary is based on the assumption that we are dealing with an undifferentiated whole. Too often we define and analyse "public service" by focusing on just one aspect at the expense of others. I'm not talking here about the different activities in which government takes an interest and which is reflected in the wide range of departments and agencies, but about the different aspects of the government function itself: law and policy making, service delivery, monitoring and law enforcement, and the general management functions needed to allow the system to work, such as financial, human resources and information management.

Each of these is quite different in its implications for public administration and public management. How often do we find, however, that proposals for public sector reform generalise from one of these functions to the sector as a whole? Compare, for example, the role of a customs officer or a corporate regulator with that of a social worker or place manager. The former are there to apply the law without fear or favour, and the concept of responsiveness doesn't really have much relevance to what they do. The social worker and place manager, on the other hand, have to address the specific and special needs of their clients, which in one case is an individual or family, and in the other, a defined community. Responsiveness is at the core of what they do.

For some public servants, the "client" or "customer" is the public service itself. They may be IT managers or human-resource managers performing clearly defined administrative functions. In other cases, public-sector agencies may be required to monitor and regulate the public sector itself. Because of this they need a significant degree of political and operational independence. I refer here to agencies like the Corruption Commission, the Ombudsman and the Auditor-General.

I trust these examples illustrate the point that the public sector performs a range of different functions, each of which will require different skills and capacities, and each of which needs to be understood within a different framework. At any time of the day we would see public servants advising the government, engaging with citizens, enforcing the law, monitoring suspicious behaviour or introducing new technologies or systems. Sometimes public servants need to "listen", sometimes to "think and plan" and sometimes to "enforce". More often than not, they are going to have to join up with other parts of government or the community to achieve the goals being set for them by the politicians.

How, then, do we make sense of this range of activities and functions that make up the public sector? Is it possible to bring some order and clarity to the complexity and confusion? Are there over-arching themes that make sense of the sector as a whole, and what it is to be a public servant? Are there principles that speak to all the public sector's activities and functions?

## The Principles of Public Service

I would argue that there is both a political and constitutional answer to these questions. The political answer has been provided by Mark Moore in his classic text *Creating Public Value* (1995). He refers to the "authorising environment" which mandates the work of the public servant. Such environments, he says, "sustain the managers' efforts in a particular form, at a particular scale, and on particular objectives".[2] As the political tides change, so do the authorising environments. This is a world largely, but not totally, driven along by the government of the day and the philosophies they embrace. Later in my talk I will fill in the details here by describing three comprehensive theories for the public sector that have been developed since the end of World War 2.

What follows is the first rule of public service. Woodrow Wilson put it this way: "Steady, hearty allegiance to the policy of the government they serve will constitute good behaviour".[3] It is a democratic principle that helps define the special nature of the work and the disciplines that flow from it. It is part of what it means to be a "public" servant.

However, this is not and cannot be the end of the story. There is another aspect of the issue that is all-too-often ignored by commentators and practitioners alike. This is the principle of the public interest. The Western Australian Royal Commission into the Commercial Activities of Government put it this way:

*The institutions of government and the officials and agencies of government exist for the public, to serve the interests of the public.*[4]

This was said to be one of two fundamental principles upon which our system of representative and responsible government was based, the other being: "It is for the people of the state to determine by whom they are to be represented and governed".[5] One is the "trust" principle, the other the "democratic" principle.

In saying this, the Royal Commissioners were echoing statements made by the NSW Supreme Court, Court of Appeal and by the High Court of Australia to the effect that governments are constitutionally required to act in the public interest.[6] There are a range of implications that flow from this and which relate to both "objectives and outcomes" and "processes and procedures". Amongst the best attempts at a definition that I have seen has been made by the Deputy NSW Ombudsman Chris Wheeler:

> *The public interest is best seen as the objective of, or the approach to be adopted, in decision-making rather than a specific and immutable outcome to be achieved. The meaning of the term, or the approach indicated by the use of the term, is to direct consideration and action away from private, personal, parochial or partisan interests towards matters of broader (ie. more "public") concern.*
>
> *The application of the concept is a separate issue and the answer to the question "what is in the public interest?" will vary depending on the particular circumstances in which the question arises.*
>
> *There are two separate components of the public interest — the process/procedure component and the objectives/outcomes component. In relation to the objectives/outcome component, identifying what is in the public interest in any given situation is a primary obligation on public officials who are exercising discretionary powers. This is no simple task and in practice involves:*
>
> - *Who should be considered to be the relevant public?*
> - *What are the relevant public interest issues that apply?*
> - *What relative weightings should be given to various identified public interests and how should conflicting or competing public interests be addressed?*

*While in many cases there will be no clear answer to each of the questions, what is important is that a conscientious attempt is made to find appropriate answers, and that the decision-maker is able to demonstrate that the appropriate approach was followed and all relevant matters were considered.*[7]

To meet the public-interest test with respect to process and procedure requires a range of commitments. Wheeler[8] has listed them as follows:

- Complying with applicable law (both its letter and spirit)
- Carrying out functions fairly and impartially, with integrity and professionalism
- Complying with the principles of procedural fairness/natural justice
- Acting reasonably
- Ensuring proper accountability and transparency
- Exposing corrupt conduct or serious maladministration
- Avoiding or properly managing situations where their private interests conflict or might reasonably be perceived to conflict with the impartial fulfilment of their official duties, and acting apolitically in the performance of their official functions (not applicable to elected public officials).

These issues are, of course, the matters for consideration when developing Codes of Conduct for Ministers, Members of Parliament and public servants.

In some ways we return to the concept of the public interest simply to remind us that we could do better in our decision-making processes. It provides a checklist of potential considerations for the public servant and, in a different way, for the politician. Sometimes we use the concept to assess whether or not a public servant (or politician) has acted improperly in the way he or she has discharged the responsibilities. Such impropriety might also add up to illegality. Whichever way you look at it, it is an over-arching concept of great significance.

Those who take a cynical view because of the conceptual complexity and practical difficulties of applying the public interest feed the credibility gap around "trust" and "purpose" that I mentioned earlier.

However, as the quotation from Chris Wheeler reveals, the use of the public interest is more useful in helping us to frame the "approach to be adopted" rather than defining the "specific and immutable outcome to be achieved".[9] Just what is the type and nature of the public sector that is in the public interest is heavily contested territory. This takes us back to Moore's authorising environment and the philosophies that guide it.

## From Post-War Mandarins to New Public Managers

If we return to the world that had emerged from the Great Depression and the Second World War there was a powerful consensus about the role of the public sector in a democratic society. It was the era of Keynesian economics and the Welfare State. The public sector had a powerful role to play as an economic regulator, investor in health, education and infrastructure and provider in times of need. This was the era of the "mixed economy" or "democratic capitalism" in which the government was seen as central to the resolution of the contradictions in free-market capitalism. In a sense, capitalism was saved from itself by the power and authority of democratic politics. The world's major ideological battle wasn't between plan and market, but between welfare capitalism and authoritarian socialism as exemplified in the Soviet Union.

The sense of social purpose inherent within public sector work was a powerful motivator. State enterprise was encouraged to ensure the provision of infrastructure, to provide a benchmark for competition and to ensure equality of access to good housing, health and education. Keen to avoid the instability and inequality of the past, politicians were happy to delegate significant power, status and authority to their public servants. This was indeed the era of the mandarins.

As time marched on, systems began to atrophy, new competitors emerged and communism collapsed. Change was inevitable and it came with what we now call the New Public Management revolution. It came first in the form of managerialism, and evolved into a fully fledged commitment to the market. This meant privatisation, commercialisation and contracting out. Increasingly, the private sector and non-government sectors were given a role in the delivery of services with the concepts of a "level-playing field" and "competitive neutrality" introduced to legitimise the shift away from the post-war balance of power between the government and private sector. In theory at least, New Public Management may have reduced the functions of government to defence, regulation and contract management. Indeed some of its protagonists argued as much.

Public–sector institutions were disaggregated and the bits benchmarked and managers expected to achieve efficiency targets. More reliance was placed on user charges and public–private partnerships. Cabinet was pictured as a board of directors representing taxpayers and the public sector was seen as a collection of corporations delivering to clients and customers. All in all, then, government was to be more businesslike in philosophy and practice. To back this up, the security of employment traditionally associated with the public sector was scaled back and regimes of performance management established.

I don't think any of us can underestimate the powerful impact this new approach to public management has had. The state was seen less as a vehicle for security and equality and more as a constraint on progress and innovation. The dominant paradigm was that provided by neo-classical economics and public-choice theory. It was believed that more good would come from less rather than more government intervention. Public servants were seen to represent an "interest" that thwarted the market. The "good" that was being referred to was primarily economic, in particular economic efficiency and economic growth.

This was a philosophy that fitted perfectly in the era of globalisation that followed the collapse of communism. It was all about competition and the market, both between and within nations. That special quality of the public service as a carrier of higher values remained intact, but with a much narrower frame of reference. The primary role of government was to facilitate economic growth by allowing the market to work. Even with respect to its other more supportive functions in health, education and welfare, the market was given a more expansive role to play, and new lines were drawn to shift the balance between collective and individual responsibilities in the direction of the individual.

## Towards Strategic Government

Once again, however, time and circumstances have necessitated a change of approach.[10] New challenges, such as terrorism, climate change and the Global Financial Crisis, point to the need for more action by government, better systems of regulation and more co-ordination across government. Complex issues, like social and economic disadvantage due to ill-health and low education standards, have not been solved by the so-called trickle-down effects of economic growth. Indeed, the strong focus on economic efficiency and growth has created its own problems for family functioning and social relationships generally. At the same time, recognition of the importance of the environment has necessitated a more broadly-based, sustainable basis for decision-making. Slowly but surely, society is rediscovering the power that can come from collective purpose and collective action. It means a more strategic approach to government generally, more concern for the long-term and for social and environment factors in the sustainability equation. It means a focus on results and outcomes as well as outputs and efficiency. It means joined-up government and new partnerships with the private and community sectors to tackle seemingly intractable problems in health and education. John Benington has put it this way:

*The challenges facing government and public services therefore include how to complement improvement of basic services for individuals with strategies also to improve the context and culture within which individuals live and work; to strengthen longer-term preventive measures as well as short-term remedial services; to create the pre-condition for the development of communal and shared responses to needs; and to support and promote the development of citizenship, the "community" and the public sphere.*[11]

This is all a long way from the market-driven solutions of the 1980s and 1990s. As Benington notes, this new model of public-sector management involves the command and control hierarchies of the state, competitive markets *and* the collaborative networks of civil society. In this sense it is a model of governance that goes beyond both the mixed economy of the 1950s and 1960s and the market-management model of the 1980s and 1990s. It recognises the importance of trust, subsidiarity and social inclusion to the achievement of the wider goods envisaged.

There are a number of ways of looking at this transformation in thinking about the role of the government and new approaches to public-sector management. Firstly, and importantly, we can see a new sense of social purpose. Indeed, in many ways there was a type of complacency in New Public Management. It wasn't a complacency manifested by inaction — quite the opposite — reform and change were not just slogans but guides to action. Indeed, plenty was done in Australia under the umbrella of the National Competition Policy of the 1990s. However, there was a reluctance to tackle bigger and more complex problems, particularly social problems. Concepts like social justice were questioned, and efforts to equalise opportunities described as counter-productive. The reform agenda was an economic reform agenda. There was always a sense of moral emptiness associated with this economically focused program. After all, we are not just consumers but also citizens with rights and responsibilities. Guaranteeing those rights may mean accepting responsibility to support individuals and communities with case and place management, for example.

Secondly, it is clear that it is a vision for the public sector that requires a new kind of political leadership that looks to act for minorities as well as majorities, the future as well as the present and the environment as well as the economy. The authorisation to act will need to come "not just from electoral mandates, but has to be won and constantly replenished from a wide variety of different stakeholders, from different levels of government, and from different parts of the public, private, voluntary and informal sectors".[12] Partnerships are crucial to its success. It also means elevated focus on the politics of inter-governmental relations at the global and national levels. This has been recognised in Australia's National Reform Agenda which has focused on a wide range of reforms, including those necessary for social inclusion.

Thirdly, it means public servants empowered to do more than just delivering the service and balancing the books. It means strong government, personalised services, tougher regulation where it really matters, new partnerships for community development and healthier lives, and more citizen engagement generally. It will need, of course, recognition by the elected arm of government that the market, even if embellished with a healthy dose of corporate social responsibility, simply can't deliver on social inclusion, a lower carbon imprint, and longer-term change based on early intervention. As a recent report from the UK put it:

> No country in the world offers excellent public services to all its citizens without active, enabling government.[13]

## Concluding Remarks

What, then, can we conclude about putting the public back into the public service? Firstly, we need to recognise the importance of the public interest as a governing principle for individual office holders and for the system as a whole. Secondly, we need to recognise the potential in the developing philosophy of Strategic Government to re-ignite our commitment to collective endeavours and to re-energise the public service as an agent of social change.

For the individual public servant we have the obligation to serve the government of the day within the legal framework provided by the public interest. It is more than mere administration. The "science of administration", as Woodrow Wilson explained, should "seek to straighten the paths of government, to make its business less unbusinesslike, to strengthen and purify its organisation, and to crown its duties with dutifulness".[14] Public servants act for governments but can add value to what they do. It is a calling of significance that can make a difference, whether we are talking about a fireman, a policy advisor or a public-health official. It is the ongoing work of government whose diversity and whose importance we devalue at our peril.

For the system as a whole, the public-interest test is less prescriptive but just as important, as it keeps us alert to the requirements of "the bigger picture". This bigger picture involves not just the depth of the participation and engagement associated with our democracy, but the range of objectives we bring to the political process and the timeframes we use to consider them. It is a powerful call to arms in a less-than-perfect world. Have we properly involved the public? Are we respecting the rights and interests of all our citizens? Have the solutions we propose been properly researched and adequately consulted? Are we protecting or undermining the environmental foundations of our existence? How sustainable are our policies and practices?[15]

However, to put the public back into the public service is not just to ask these questions. It should involve a stronger and more co-ordinated effort to provide answers. That will have to mean governments willing and able to go beyond the comfort zone of events management and into the dangerous territory of long-term planning and change.

We can now say, however, that our knowledge base about what needs to be done is strong and that there is a growing sentiment in the community that change is required. The time is ripe for investing a much greater proportion of our hopes for the future in the assets we share — our environment, our public institutions, our rules and regulations for commerce, and our democratic heritage. For too long they have been treated as optional extras to the market rather than foundation stones for a fair and decent society.

## Notes

1    For two examples see David Marquand, "The Scapegoat", *New Statesman*, 22 September 2008, pp. 32–34, and Robert J Samuelson, "Obama and the End of an Economic Era", *Australian Financial Review*, November 8–9, 2008, pp. 24–25.

2    Mark Moore, *Creating Public Value: Strategic Management in Government* (Harvard University Press, 1995), p. 130.

3    Woodrow Wilson, "The Study of Administration", *Political Science Quarterly*, Vol. 2 (June 1887), p. 216.

4    *Western Australian Royal Commission into the Commercial Activities of Government*, Part ii, 12 November 1992, 1.2.5.

5    ibid., 1.2.3.

6    See Chris Wheeler, "The public interest: we know it's important but do we know what it means", *AIAL Forum*, vol. 48, p. 13.

7    ibid., p. 24.

8    ibid., p. 13–14.

9    ibid., p. 24.

10   See my two essays "Towards a New Era of Strategic Government", in John Wanna (ed.), *A Passion for Policy: Essays in Public Sector Reform* (ANU E Press, 2007), pp. 75–89, and "Strategic Planning: is it the new model?", *Public Administration Today*, Issue 10, January–March 2007, pp. 28–33.

11   John Benington, "From Private Choice to Public Value" http://www. centrefor   excellence.org.uk/UsersDoc/John%20Benington%20-%20 From%20Private%20Choice%20to%20Public%20Value.pdf.

12   Benington, p. 32.

13   UK Cabinet Office, *Excellence and fairness: achieving world class public services* (2008), p. 35.

14   Wilson, "The Study of Administration", p. 201

15   I have developed some of these themes in "What is the Public Interest?", *Public Administration Today*, July–September 2007, pp. 44–48.

# 8.

# Federalism and Inter-Governmental Relations

# How Healthy is Australian Federalism?

Speech delivered at
Senate Occasional Lecture

Canberra, 25 February 2011

In today's lecture I will summarise the various issues we take up in examining Australian federalism; look at the politics of the federal idea throughout Australian history, noting how the Commonwealth has been the consistent winner; state my own position that federalism is a good idea whose benefits are clearly established by the evidence; look to how the states have tried to rescue their position in recent years through the embrace of the National Reform Agenda and Co-operative Federalism; provide an overview of the tensions that remain in the system established by the Rudd/Gillard government; make a case for addressing vertical fiscal imbalance (VFI) through income-tax sharing; and conclude, despairingly, that this is likely leaving Australia, at its best, with a second-best system.

There are so many issues related to a discussion of Australian federalism it's hard to know where to begin. In saying this, I'm always reminded of the story told by Gary Sturgess about a United Nations Committee commissioning international studies on the elephant:

*There were a variety of contributions. Each nation giving its own unique insights and expertise. Germany submitted a paper on the training and discipline of elephants. France questioned the existence of elephants. United Kingdom submitted a paper on the role of the elephant in colonial expansion. There were two papers from the US, one from the east coast ("Taking over elephants — economies of scale and synergetic benefits") and one from the west coast ("The joy of elephants"). And Australia submitted a paper, "Elephants — federal or state responsibility".[1]*

Indeed, when discussing federalism in Australia, this issue of commonwealth and state roles and responsibilities usually comes first. What does the Constitution say and how has that changed over the years, either through referenda or interpretation by the High Court? In recent years, the notion that we have a Convention to consider roles and responsibilities has been mooted but not realised in practice.

Linked to such a discussion is the question of inter-governmental relations and how they are managed, including in relation to overseas treaties and trade agreements. Under this heading is an assessment of the role and functioning of the range of institutions set up to facilitate co-operation between the levels of government, most importantly but not only the Council of Australian Governments.

Thirdly, there is the matter of commonwealth–state financial relations and the taxing powers of each level of government. In Australia this takes debate into the territory of vertical fiscal imbalance, the situation where the revenue-raising powers and expenditure responsibilities of each level of government are mismatched. A distinguishing feature of our federation is the very high level of VFI, with the commonwealth in the dominant position.

Fourthly, there has been substantial analysis of the govern-mental institutions that reflect the commitment to federalism, most notably the High Court, the Senate and, of course, the states themselves. Contrasting the way the constitutionally protected states and the federally constituted territories operate assists us in understanding the difference between a federal system and a unitary one with regions.

Inevitably, any discussion of proposals for significant change, such as the republic or a Bill or Charter of Rights, is caught up in an argument about these institutions, most particularly the states.

Fifthly, we examine how each of these issues come together to create an Australian model. Is it a case of "managerial" federalism, "intelligent" federalism, "opportunistic" federalism or "co-operative" federalism? On the other hand, some say we should recognise it for what it is, a case of "creeping centralism".

In discussing this issue, there is usually a prescriptive as well as a descriptive element, in particular analysis of the public policy implications of different ways to distribute powers, raise taxes, co-operate in matters of mutual concern and manage differences when there is disagreement.

It is at this point that ideology enters the equation. Federalism is a subject about which politicians and commentators have a view: for or against, change or no change? Such views aren't necessarily evidence-based but are often a mixture of pride and prejudice. In other words, is the advocate speaking from Canberra or from the states? Is the advocate a state or federal politician? Is the advocate a state or commonwealth public servant? We all have pride in what we do and the institutions we serve, and this can blind us to the bigger picture.

This leads me to a sixth and final way in which the issue can be analysed. What is the politics of federalism in Australia? Who are the participants in the debate? What power and influence do they have in determining outcomes? How do they mobilise and shape opinion? What is the attitude of the public to these matters? Do they care who delivers services or is it just a case of the outcomes? As John Howard put it in a speech on 20 August 2007:

*So much of the debates about commonwealth–state relations concerns the respective roles of the two levels of government, as if an appropriate balance were an end in itself. To me, that misses the point. We should be neither centralist, nor slavish adherents to states' rights. We should be focused on outcomes, not systems.*[2]

These matters are important for reformers because they help in determining what may or may not be possible by way of change. At any time there are forces working either for change or against change. They win or lose, not just on the basis of their political strength and argument, but also on how politics plays out in the circumstances that prevail. For example, Labor's proposals to build a co-operative federalism put to the people at the 2007 election may not have been so well received if John Howard's authority had not been so badly dented by complacency on climate change and aggressiveness on industrial relations.

When looking at the politics of Australian Federalism from the vantage point of twentieth-century history, it is clear that the commonwealth rather than the states has been the winner. Not only is it the case that a mixture of wartime necessity and constitutional interpretation have pushed the balance of power in the direction of the commonwealth, there has always been an ideological current favouring centralisation as better for economic planning, economic efficiency and good public policy. Not surprisingly, such a view has strong roots in Canberra and has often been associated with the assumed requirements of national sovereignty in a competitive world.

In earlier times it was also linked with a democratic socialist view that the will of the majority should prevail when confronted with the checks and balances we associate with liberalism, such as Upper Houses and the High Court, or with conservatism, such as a propertied franchise or malapportionment. In this mix, federalism was seen as an enemy of the creation of a united nation with one set of laws applying to all, noting, of course, that it took some time before "all" actually meant that and not just the white population.

In more recent times it has been linked to a conservative view that uniformity is better for business and our more mobile population. So too is centralisation seen as better to protect our geographical and cultural borders against minorities intent on undermining traditional Australian values with their post-modern curricula and libertarian attitudes.

Whilst this development of the right-wing side of Australian politics has opened up space for Labor to embrace federalism, there remains a strong residue of centralism within the Federal Caucus. This is partly a case of position (that is to say being in the Commonwealth Parliament) but also of ideology (that is to say, being committed to a "streamlined" system of regulation for the nation).

On how state Labor has responded to this new institution I will have something to say later in my lecture.

The first point I wish to make today, then, is that there has always been a heavily values-based opposition to the federal principle within Australian politics, firstly from the left and more recently from the right. Taking turns, they have lined up with the federal bureaucracy to seek more power for the commonwealth. This mixture of ideology and brute power, particularly over finance, has proved very effective in outflanking and when necessary overriding the states and territories. Both Labor and Liberal governments at the commonwealth level have been involved in this power shift.

It was the commonwealth seeking power to exclude state-based conciliation and arbitration and consolidate Work Choices that precipitated the challenge by New South Wales and the other states in the High Court. This resulted in a very expansive definition of the Corporations Power in S51(xx) of the Constitution.

Try as they might, the states were unable to convince the Court that there were clear limits to the exercise of this power.

Only Kirby and Callinan JJ pointed to the need to read the Constitution as a whole and to be mindful of preserving a balance between the two levels of government. One would have thought that this was the intention of those who framed the Constitution but, as has so often been the case, each head of power in the Constitution has been accorded full scope on the basis of its language rather than any theory of "balanced government".

The commonwealth knows, then, that it can push the boundaries in its law-making functions. Whatever the political colouring of the commonwealth government of the day it is being tempted to do this and urged to do it by a public service proud of its status and openly contemptuous of the "lower" levels of government. Usually it starts out as an aspiration for a "national" solution involving all levels of government, but more often than not finishes up as a commonwealth-controlled program.

Having said this, now let me draw your attention to the recently published analysis of Australian Federalism by Ann Twomey and Glen Withers: "Australia's Federal Future" (April 2007). In a methodical and empirical way, they demonstrate the economic, social and political benefits of a federal system of government. Of the debates about federalism in Australia they have this to say in their covering letter to the Council of the Australian Federation:

> It became apparent to us in writing this report that Australian attitudes towards federalism are out of step with those in the rest of the world. In Australia, it is often asserted that federalism is an old fashioned, cumbersome and inefficient system. Yet internationally, federalism is regarded as a modern, flexible and efficient structure that is ideal for meeting the needs of local communities while responding to the pressures of globalisation. The difference between these two views is stark.
>
> In this report we have used political, legal and economic analysis and international comparisons to highlight that, far from being a burden, Australia's federal system provides us with many economic and social benefits. For example, federalism:

- *Divides and limits power, protecting the individual;*
- *Gives Australians a wider range of choices and allows policies and services to be tailored to meet the needs of communities; and*
- *Spurs all Australian governments to be more innovative and responsive.*

*Compared to centralised, unitary governments, federal nations such as Australia have:*
- *More efficient governments; and*
- *Higher rates of economic growth and higher per capita GDP.*

*These benefits deliver significant economic and social advantages to all Australians. However, increasing centralisation in Australia threatens these benefits.*[3]

The truth about government is that no one level can be expected to get it right all the time. There are good and bad commonwealth governments, good and bad state and territory governments and good and bad local governments.

Somehow or other a range of commentators seem to think that increasing the power of the commonwealth will automatically mean a lesser involvement of vested interests in decision-making. Unfortunately, however, it is not the case that rationality resides in a particular level of government. All levels of government are subject to political pressure on issues like economic and environmental reform. This is clearly demonstrated in the debate currently going on within the commonwealth over the meaning of the words in the Murray–Darling legislation.

In recent times we have seen failures in public administration, some very serious, in all levels of government. At the same time, we have seen innovation and reform, some coming from above and some from below. Much of this has come from state governments. In a recently published speech, Helen Silver, Secretary of the Department of Premier and Cabinet in Victoria, has listed the following examples:

- Case-mix funding for public hospitals (Victoria)
- State-based greenhouse gas certification and abatement (NSW)
- Early anti-discrimination legislation (SA)
- Health care call centres (WA)

About such innovation she notes:

*There are tremendous benefits to be gained from vigorous competition between the states and territories, as proven strategies in one jurisdiction are taken up in others.*[4]

More controversial, and not yet universalised, are the Charters of Rights in the A.C.T. and Victoria and the Medically Supervised Injecting Centre in NSW. They sit in contrast to the euthanasia legislation in the Northern Territory and the civil partnerships legislation in the A.C.T. These were territories whose work could be easily overturned by the commonwealth.

This leads me to my second point for the day. Even though the position of the states has weakened constitutionally and financially they still play an important role in Australian politics. They provide important services and advocate for the communities within their boundaries and, however limited it may be, they still have important tax-raising powers. They are facilitators of development within a national and global context. Note, too, that they allow for displays of difference, perhaps best illustrated by the absence of poker machines in hotels and clubs throughout Western Australia.

We still have a complex system of power relations, unlike those that apply in a unitary system. A very good illustration of this complexity comes from the National Reform Agenda, for which a good deal of the political and intellectual work was done by Victoria during the Premiership of Steve Bracks, backed up as he was then by Terry Moran, head of Premier and Cabinet.

In many ways, we could see this proposal as a pragmatic but principled response by the states to the depressing reality of "creeping centralism". I say pragmatic because there was a recognition that vertical fiscal imbalance was a nut too hard to crack. It was to be a partnership approach to governance and financing directed to promoting competition and participation in the interests of productivity.

In proposing this approach, Victoria had drawn on the experience of the National Competition Policy of the 1990s. This had seen the commonwealth and the states agree on the changes required to improve productivity. However, each state was left free to determine the rate and range of change. Should their performance be assessed as acceptable by the National Competition Council they would receive payments from the commonwealth. This mixture of national purpose, state delivery and commonwealth incentives produced significant reform.

As Australia entered the new century it had become clear that the economic challenge was also a social challenge, particularly in health, education and social welfare generally. A healthier, more skilled and better motivated population was needed to bring about further productivity improvement. Given that both commonwealth and state governments had responsibilities in these areas it was clear that a new partnership would be required.

About the new financial and operational arrangements which have emerged from the Council of Australian Governments to facilitate this partnership let me say a member of things.

Firstly, that the "model" is very coherent in construction and intellectually sound in conception. Outcomes are distinguished from outputs, roles and responsibilities are to be agreed, performance indicators and benchmarks set to judge performance and the COAG Reform Council (CRC) created to monitor and assess that performance. At the heart of this model is the idea that agreement over objectives doesn't have to mean uniformity over the means to achieve them. Indeed, the whole idea of the program was to move away from the input-controlled Special Purpose Payments to a system that allowed for local flexibility. What mattered was whether the outcomes were being achieved not *how* that was to be done. From this emerged the new National Agreements in Education, Skills and Workforce Development, Health Care, Disability Services, Affordable Housing and Indigenous Reform.

The states loved it — guaranteed revenue, devolution of responsibility and transparency to drive performance by way of the public reporting of results across the nation. Added to this was a new system of National Partnership Payments (NPPs) to facilitate or reward reforms of national importance.

This leads to my second observation about the system that has emerged following the election of 2007. The NPPs are paid to the states to deliver discrete projects or outputs. They are to have a limited time horizon and with respect to reward payments, they are only to be paid following a favourable assessment of performance by the CRC. In relation to facilitation payments, they are only paid if certain things are done, deemed to be reforms of national significance.

There is a massive number of such partnership agreements, ranging from preventative health to early-childhood education, to homelessness and productivity places. Also in the mix is the NPP to deliver a seamless national economy which builds on the competition agenda of the 1990s. It contains thirty-six streams of regulation and competition reform.

In assessing what all this means for Australian Federalism we need to go below the surface and look at the real dynamics at play. Despite an aspiration to see a change in the culture of inter-governmental relations required to make this co-operative system work, the players at both levels are reverting to type. For its part, the commonwealth is finding it hard to accept the notion of federal balance and the diversity it brings, and the states can't resist the temptation to take the money at any cost, despite misgivings about what is being required when it is spent.

Once again, highly restrictive requirements and controls are emerging in relation to the NPPs.

Even in the Health and Education Agreements, the Commonwealth has moved beyond an outcome agenda to an output agenda with its push for hospital networks and a national curriculum. The very distinction between national agreements on outcomes and local delivery of outputs is being whittled away in the name of "implementation".

The concept of subsidiarity which requires decisions to be handled by the least-centralised authority and not handed up to a higher level unless the task cannot be properly undertaken from below, such as the defence of the nation, is as alien to the commonwealth as socialism has become for the Labor Party. Nor is it necessarily understood by the states and, if understood, often breached in dealings with localities and sacrificed in the search for money from the commonwealth.

We saw how some of these stresses and strains are playing out in the recent revision of the Health Agreement. Only deft footwork by Julia Gillard rescued the package. Note, however, that it is still an agreement which is yet to be finalised and there is sure to be more conflict over the detail.

However, what the health issue demonstrated was the potential that still exists for the states to push their agenda, should they so decide. They have power in the system. The federal Labor government couldn't afford continuing conflict with the states, particularly over the future of the GST.

Whilst it is clear, then, that co-operative federalism along the lines developed in recent years is the best way forward for the states, it remains doubtful whether it can be fully institutionalised in a way that protects their long-term interests and autonomy. Attitudes and values within the commonwealth may have moderated but it is hard to see that they have changed fundamentally. Unless they do, co-operative federalism will be a good idea that didn't realise its potential to renew federalism in Australia.

The reality here is that VFI continues to exert its influence. Resources mean power, power leads to temptation, and, more often than not, temptation leads to coercion and control. The only known remedy to this illness comes from checks and balances and a more equal distribution of resources. Is this possible in Australia today?

As I noted earlier, the states still have power and influence, even if limited and declining, compared to other nations. They provide a check and important balance to the system. The model of co-operative federalism could work if a genuine effort at addressing VFI was added to the equation and tax raising powers more evenly spread.

The distribution of the GST to the states and territories was never going to be a successful resolution of this matter. In the first place, it is a commonwealth tax and, as we saw last year, the temptation to claw some of the money back from the states is strong. In the second place, it replaced a range of state taxes which were not as efficient or growth sensitive but nevertheless they did raise revenue for state governments.

The only lasting solution to this state of affairs would be to allow the states back into the field of income tax. For this to occur, the commonwealth would need to cut income taxes across the board, thus making room for the states to apply their own rate. The tax would still be administered and collected by the commonwealth.

Should such as issue be put on the table it would require a further examination of commonwealth and state roles and responsibilities. Note also that it would open up a discussion of further tax reform and simplification at the state level, something the business community have been advocating for some time.

In saying all of this, however, I am reminded of what I concluded earlier in the lecture about the politics of federalism. Why would the commonwealth agree to such changes and give up power in the process? For this to happen they would need to be convinced that it is a good thing. Even if some on both sides of politics in Canberra saw that it was, they would meet strong opposition from colleagues. Remember the headline for an article by Mike Skeketee in the *Sydney Morning Herald* on Saturday 16 November 1991: "KEATING WRECKS CHANCES OF A SANER FEDERATION". He was referring to Paul Keating's scuttling of the then attempts by Australian governments to better fit taxing and spending powers throughout the levels of government. He did this by campaigning on behalf of commonwealth power within the Labor Caucus. It would be safe to assume similar conflict would occur today if a Prime Minister advocated radical change that returned financial power to the states.

For their part the states could — and should — advocate for such a change. However, they have no means under our constitutional arrangements to make it happen. As Darryl Kerrigan said in *The Castle*: "Tell 'em they're dreaming!"

Australia seems destined to have a federal system that at its best is second best. Our responsibilities in such a situation are to make that second-best system work as best as we can. That means the states being more forceful in pursuing their interests and the commonwealth more understanding of complexity and the benefits of diversity. Is that going to be possible in the adversarial system that has developed in our nation?

**Notes**

1    Gary Sturgess, 'The progress towards Commonwealth/state rationalisation', *Royal Australian Institute of Public Administration National Newsletter*, vol. 1, no. 2, June 1991, p. 12.

2    John Howard, Address to the Millennium Forum, Four Seasons Hotel, Sydney, 20 August 2007, http://pandora.nla.gov.au/pan/10052/20070823-1732/www.pm.gov.au/media/Speech/2007/Speech24507.html

3    A. Twomey and G. Withers, *Australia's Federal Future: Delivering Growth and Prosperity*, 2007, www.dpc.vic.gov.au/.

4    Helen Silver, 'Getting the best out of federalism – the role of the Productivity Commission and the limits of national approaches', *Australian Journal of Public Administration*, vol. 69, no. 3, September 2010, p. 327.

# New Partnerships and Social Compacts to Enhance Federalism

Speech delivered at an address to the
Australian and New Zealand School of Government
Annual Conference 2008

Melbourne, 11 September 2008

In my talk today I will start by making a general point about how we ought to approach questions related to governance and our federal system. I will contrast what I will call the pragmatic and philosophical outlooks and link this to an assessment of federalism.

In the second place, I will examine the way our federal system dealt with the microeconomic reform agenda which emerged as a dominant theme in the 1990s. Using the lessons from that era, I will look at the problem and prospects associated with the Rudd government's productivity and participation reform agenda. I will argue that there are important differences in context and policy that will make partnerships with the community and a stronger commitment to fairness vital ingredients in the reform effort.

## Pragmatism and Philosophy
However, let me begin with the distinction between pragmatism and philosophy. The pragmatist in these matters will ask:

"What works today?" The former Prime Minister John Howard provided us with a case study in pragmatism in his speech to the Millenium Forum in 2007:

> *So much of the debates about commonwealth–state relations concerns the respective roles of the two levels of government, as if an balance were an end in itself. To me, that misses the point. We should be neither centralist nor slavish adherents to states' rights. We should be focused on outcomes, not systems.*[1]

Such an approach begs the question as to whether federalism — and the balance that comes with it — is conducive of good outcomes. Indeed, the very study of government is about this question: what systems best survive the test of time and circumstance? And, surely, we should be concerned with accountabilities as well as outcomes.

This takes me to the philosophical approach. It encourages us to talk about means as well as ends and about process as well as outcomes. Good political philosophy — as practised, for example, by the founding fathers of the Australian Constitution — is both idealistic and realistic. It makes judgements about what works and what doesn't work, but in the context of time and circumstance. Our system needs to work today but it also needs to be able to sustain success. What may be a fix today may prevent a solution tomorrow.

## The Case for Federalism

Good systems need to be able to allow for change and to be able to manage change. They need to provide a framework that allows the creative and liberating aspects of politics to work. This means creating multiple centres of power and proper mechanisms of democratic accountability. A good federal system provides for this and that was recognised by the founding fathers when they took elements from the American Constitution and grafted them onto an English system of parliamentary government. Yes, it is true that favourable interpretations of the Constitution by the High Court and enormous financial strength has seen the power and reach of the commonwealth expand, but the states still play a major role in our system — as service providers, law-makers, advocates, facilitators, innovators and partners in a range of national initiatives.[2]

All too often, however, the debate about these matters is treated in a narrowly utilitarian and economistic manner, as if the nation is a giant factory. This manufacturing analogy is taken even further with the view that the sole aim of government is economic efficiency as defined by the neo-classicals. In such a view, government itself and the number of governments need to be limited. In its most extreme manifestation, such a view leads to the conclusion that politics itself is dysfunctional. Not surprisingly, then, the application of such an ideology has the unfortunate habit of breeding its opposite — populism — which as we know has the potential to develop in a particularly nasty way.

We need a philosophy of government that incorporates the values of liberty, equality and community. The federalist principle and its twin sister, subsidiarity, gives room for each of these principles. It gives choice to electors, fosters competition and innovation in policy, provides for checks and balances by creating multiple centres of power and allows for a healthy diversity to emerge in the way things are done throughout the nation. It is a system that is and has been successful in a range of ways, including economic.[3]

The implication of all of this is clear: we need to evaluate public-policy proposals not only on the basis of their short-term outcomes, but also on the basis of their longer-term system effects. We need to acknowledge that there will be pressures on the commonwealth to take up a range of issues deemed to be of national significance such as productivity, social and economic disadvantage, climate change, water and security. Inevitably this will take them into areas of state government responsibility. Just how this intersection is handled becomes a crucial issue.

## The Microeconomic Reform Agenda

In the last decade of the twentieth century, inter-governmental issues became crucial for a nation which had been constructed on the basis of protectionism and public-sector monopolies. With the intensification of global competition and technological change, a less risk-averse and more flexible economy was deemed necessary for national prosperity. It was agreed by the commonwealth and the states that a more open and competitive economy was required, and this meant less regulation generally and more contestability for the public sector. The microeconomic reforms that followed were far-reaching in their implications and generally regarded to have been successful in promoting productivity.

The federal system came into play because most of the reforms needed had to come from within the states. The model designed to facilitate change involved a commonwealth–state agreement, incentive payments from the commonwealth in the event of successful implementation of reform, autonomy for the states with respect to the reform process and independent monitoring to determine outcomes.

The states all agreed on the need for reform and accepted the responsibility to pursue it. However, they were not forced to make changes, simply given payments in the event of successful implementation. In each of the states the reform process had to be debated in the community and in the Parliament. In all the states except Queensland this meant winning the support of the Upper House as well as the Lower House of Parliament, never an easy affair in today's world of proportional representation. Indeed, the existence of these State Parliaments ensured that each of the reform items was given a thorough working over as one would wish to see in a properly functioning democracy.[4]

This model of commonwealth–state co-operation has provided the template for the Rudd government's productivity and participation agenda. However, before looking at this new agenda and its implications for federalism, let me note two important features of the successful microeconomic reform agenda.

Firstly, there was clarity with respect to the problem and what needed to be done to solve it. What we now call the neo-liberal or new public management ideology became established wisdom. Its policy prescriptions were straightforward: review legislative restrictions on trade and commerce and open up the public sector to competition and the level playing field. These "outputs" were seen to be necessary to achieve the desired "outcomes", that is, improved productivity.

Secondly, and importantly, only the government itself, on its own or acting through the Parliament, was involved in the change process. That is not to say that there was no community debate and controversy, but rather that the end of the process — as determined by the independent monitor — was a particular act or decision by the Cabinet and/or the Parliament.

## The Third Wave of National Reform

With these two points in mind, let me now move to the latest version of national reform. The focus of this so-called "third wave of reform" is on productivity and participation.[5] It differs from the earlier phase of reform with its incorporation of human capital and social inclusion, alongside regulatory and competition reform from the earlier era, as forces for productivity growth.

The argument behind the addition of these elements is simple — a healthier and more skilled population is a more productive one. So too is productivity enhanced when those previously incapable or unwilling to participate in the labour market begin to play their part.

Although the focus is still very much on productivity — necessitated by the continuing and growing pressures of international competition and an ageing society — the terms and conditions of the debate have been widened significantly. It is as if the economic radicals became serious about health, education and social inclusion and the social radicals became serious about the labour market and employment policy. Paul Smyth has described the two converging policy fronts that have taken us to social inclusion as a policy objective:

> *The first was more welfare related. State governments in particular have picked up on the point that poverty is more about an absence of money and that it is as much about a lack of skills, mental health, trust, social capital etc.*
>
> *The second front has opened up in economic policy. Increasingly the economic value of our human capital is being linked to its social foundation. If children, for example, grow up in a family without adequate income and without universal high quality childcare and pre-school then their future economic participation will be poor.*[6]

Whilst some of the policy prescriptions to promote social inclusion and better health and education speak for themselves, not all do. This is an area of policy disagreement. However, what is not a matter for disagreement is the life-cycle approach that has been embraced to further this economic and social reform program. What it means is the development of specific interventions to deal with the key transition points in a person's life, such as the all-important early years, schooling, the move from school to work and from work to retirement. The early years are seen as particularly crucial. As the government's own Budget Papers put it:

> *Over the longer-term, early childhood education generates substantial cost savings from improved health and productivity and reduced expenditure on social services.*[7]

What we have, then, is a description of the problem and a general understanding of what needs to be done to fix it. As was the case in the 1990s, many of the initiatives that would need to be taken to address the problem are the province of the states. This takes us to the model of co-operative federalism that has been designed to engineer change today.

## Kevin Rudd's Co-operative Federalism

There is little doubt that the Rudd model of co-operative federalism is the most sophisticated to have occupied this space for some time.[8] It is designed not just to facilitate the new reform agenda with its proposed National Partnership Payments to support the delivery of specified projects or facilitate or reward nationally significant reforms, it also involves a major reform of the Specific Purpose Payments system of commonwealth support for the states. In 2007–08 there were $22 billion worth of SPPs, equivalent to 2 per cent of the Gross Domestic Product.[9] They account for about one in six dollars of total state revenue and are many and complicated.

The aim of the reform exercise is to reduce the number of Specific Purpose Payments to five or six, backed up by new national agreements in the areas of health, early childhood development, schools, vocational education and training, disabilities services and housing. Rather than dictating how things should be done, it is intended that the new arrangements focus on agreed objectives and outcomes. Part of the agreement process will also be the clear identification of commonwealth and state roles and responsibilities with only high-level strategic outputs critical to clarifying outcomes being specified. The agreements will be ongoing, with independent assessment of performance to be undertaken by the COAG Reform Council. Such independent assessment is vital if there is to be accountability for performance.

The theme for this new system is simple and straightforward — unity over the objectives and significant autonomy for the states with respect to the means to achieve these outcomes. The current system of input controls will come to an end, being replaced by objectives, outcomes and strategic outputs.

It has also been agreed that each Statement of Objectives and Outcomes attached to a Specific Purpose Payment will need to address the issues of social inclusion, including responding to Indigenous social and economic disadvantage. In other words, social inclusion is not to be treated as an "add-on", but is to be integrated with mainstream policy objectives.

The National Partnership Payments to facilitate or reward reforms deemed to be of national significance will be an addition to the system of Specific Purpose Payments. Reform facilitation payments will be paid in advance of implementation in recognition of the costs involved in reform. Reform reward payments will not be paid to a state unless the COAG Reform Council certifies that certain performance benchmarks have been achieved. Some payments will also be made to the states to assist with discrete infrastructure projects. Indeed, one feature of the proposed model is that capital as well as recurrent expenditure is involved, the former via the proposed infrastructure funds (Building Australia Fund, Education Investment Fund, and Health and Hospital Fund).

One can see how some of the ideas associated with the microeconomic reform agenda of the 1990s have been incorporated into the new model. Firstly, there is agreement between the commonwealth and the states to tackle the human capital and social inclusion issues related to productivity enhancement. Secondly, there is a recognition of the need for flexibility in the delivery of change. Thirdly, there is a system of incentive payments designed to encourage change. Fourthly, there is a process of independent monitoring by the COAG Reform Council.

## Some Contemporary Challenges

However, there are a number of differences that need to be acknowledged and their implications examined. The first relates to the relationship between outputs and outcomes. With respect to the economic reform agenda of the 1990s, it was agreed that microeconomic reform measures by state governments and state parliaments would promote productivity by way of increased competition and a greater reliance on market signals. In other words, it was enough for all sides to agree on certain policy initiatives (or outputs) as it was assumed they would lead to the desired outcomes (increased productivity).

With respect to the current agenda, the agreement is to be on the outcomes and perhaps some high-level strategic outputs seen as necessary for those outcomes. However, regarding the specific policies and programs that will lift and extend education standards, improve health outcomes and promote labour market participation, there is not the same level of agreement. We have already seen this illustrated in the debate over education and schooling. We know that the model is designed to allow for flexibility and diversity in policy and service delivery. However, the temptation will always be there for the Commonwealth to move away from a purely outcomes-based accountability. It has the financial power and, of course, history has taught it that the High Court will generally accommodate its point of view on constitutional interpretation.

One should also note that the level of transparency that will be created by this new regime will put the states on the spot with respect to their policy and implementation credentials. Indeed, by clarifying roles and responsibilities in the context of a new financial agreement the states will be clearly accountable for their performance. They will be under pressure to perform.

In order for federalism to be the winner from these arrangements the commonwealth will need to resist temptation and the states will need to improve their policy making and policy delivery mechanisms.

The second difference from the 1990s also relates to the question of outputs and outcomes, and raises a major issue regarding reform implementation. The competition reforms of the 1990s required action by governments and parliaments alone — introducing a purchaser–provider split, disaggregating and corporatising or privatising government utilities, removing restrictions on free trade and commerce and ensuring a level playing field between the government and private sectors. The financial incentives that were provided were to governments *to do certain things*. In an important sense it was a top-down government.

The third wave of national reform is quite different in that it seeks improved outcomes in health, education and employment. Not only is there the desire to lift standards generally, but also to tackle social exclusion. Issues like the incidence of chronic disease, the prevalence of common risk factors that contribute to disease, preventable morbidity and mortality, obesity and diabetes, literacy and numeracy, retention rates in education and the culture and capacities associated with work have become central to the productivity and participation agenda. And as noted earlier, early-childhood services have been elevated up the ladder of public policy priorities.

What is interesting about these issues is not just that there is fierce debate about what works and what doesn't work; none of them can be properly addressed without the engagement of the community and without recognising that a "one-size-fits-all" approach is doomed to fail. In fact, when we speak of the community we need to acknowledge that we are really speaking about the many communities, some urban, some rural and some remote, that makes up each state. If the outcomes being sought are to be achieved, engagement and specificity will be crucial. We are talking here about case and place management as well as the engagement of the private and non-government sectors at the national, state and local levels. It is an agenda that involves capacity-building as well as community involvement over agenda setting and service delivery.[10]

In other words, what is going to matter is not just the structure of inter-government relations and the funding model that will back it up, but also the ability of governments to involve the community, including business in its health, education and labour market agendas. Reform is going to involve partnerships between governments, individuals and communities, particularly regarding social inclusion. Indeed, if the outcomes are going to be achieved, the ability of the states to create and manage such partnerships is going to be crucial. They will need to be facilitators in the way they deliver their services throughout their jurisdictions. In other words, the governance aspects of the new reform agenda don't just involve inter-governmental agreements but will also require partnership agreements at the regional and local levels within each state.

I think we need to acknowledge that whilst Australian public institutions have been generally effective they have not been able to produce the same "equalising" efforts as those of other nations.[11] Of course, the social and economic backgrounds we have will have a strong influence on outcomes (such as levels of educational achievement), but the whole point of publicly funded services is to even these differences out as much as possible. Reversing some of these statistics, and the inequalities they represent, won't be possible with a continuation of the status quo. This is where the National Partnership Payments become crucial — they will need to be designed to promote the sorts of changes that will make the system more responsive to the needs and interests of the most disadvantaged in the community.

## Managing the Politics of Change

This leads me to another observation about the problems attached to the social-inclusion agenda. Very rarely is it the case that complex agenda like this are given a free run within government. Usually they compete for time and resources with other agenda, in this case the more narrowly defined microeconomic reform agenda, a broader national security agenda which will come at significant cost, and, of course, the most diabolical of issues climate change. We know how microeconomic reform impacts on power and distribution, and Professor Garnaut has been reminding us of how a reduction of our carbon imprint will have differential impacts through society. Perhaps it will be necessary to see social inclusion less as a means to greater productivity and more as a part of a broader fairness agenda designed to hold society together in a time of change. This means toughening up the equity elements of the new reform agenda.

I say this in the context of experience of the first and second waves of economic reform. At that time there was a clearly defined reform narrative and a major effort to involve not just the levels of government but also the major economic interests in the reform process. Indeed, the Accord with the trade union movement and the articulation of the idea of a Social Wage for working families was important glue. However, even then it was difficult to contain the discontent that surrounded a change process dedicated to more fully exposing the economy to market risks. Significant interests, particularly in rural and regional Australia, felt they had no stake in the reform process and a sense of grievance emerged which remains a powerful force today. The point I am making here is that the Rudd model of co-operative federalism faces the sort of risks associated with any model of top-down performance management. Yes, there are clearly defined objectives, the precise measures of performance, the incentives for all levels of government to participate and an independent assessor to report to the nation on the achievement of the targets. However, not only will the achievement of the particular goals themselves require the engagement of individuals and the community (as I noted earlier in my talk), but so too will the success or otherwise of the project itself. It will require a justifying narrative that is widely understood and deft political management from the commonwealth. Recognition of the institutions, interests and sentiments involved, in particular the states, whatever their political colour, will be required. And, of course, society is *always* more restless and less rational than is assumed in the best of the change management texts. Thus I'm afraid it will remain unless we broaden and deepen the terms and conditions of the contract between government and people to strongly reflect the equality element of our commitment to liberty, equality and community.

## Notes

1    John Howard, Speech to the Millenium Forum, Sydney, 20 August 2007.

2    See Geoff Gallop, "A Radical Legacy", *Griffith Review*, Autumn 2008, pp. 55–62.

3    On the case for federalism, see especially Ann Twomey and Glenn Withers, *Australia's Federal Future* (Australian Council for the Federation, 2007).

4    See Geoff Gallop, "The future of federalism", Keynote address, Institute of Public Administration Australia, Perth, 19 September 2007.

5    See Victorian Department of Premier and Cabinet, *The History of the National Reform Agenda* (n.d.) for a list of the major documents developed in support of the third wave of reform.

6    Paul Smyth, "Business should seize its role in promoting social inclusion", *The Age: Business Day*, 11 October 2007, p. 4.

7    Australian Government, "Ministerial Statement — Education Revolution", in *Budget 2008–09*.

8    For a summary, see Australian Government, *Budget Paper No. 3*, 2008–09.

9    Robert Carling, "Fixing Australian Federalism", *Policy*, vol. 24, no. 1, Autumn 2008, p. 32.

10   See Tony Nicholson, "Social Inclusion the path to prosperity", *The Australian: Opinion*, 23 November 2007, p. 16.

11   See Kevin Rudd, "Quality Education", Address to the national Press Club, 27 August 2008.

# Planning and Levels of Governance

Speech delivered at
an address to the 2007 Planning Conference,
NSW Department of Planning

Sydney, 14 August 2007

I appreciate the opportunity to talk to you today about my views on planning and the role it can play in helping us create a better future. It was certainly my view in government that the planning portfolio was not just one that simply needed to be "managed" but was one that needed to be a "driver" within government. It is clearly one of those areas of government that can make a discernible difference to the standard of life we enjoy.

In making this observation I note that the parameters of planning have expanded. While the regulation of land use is still central to the system, it is seen in relation to all the factors that influence community well-being. The Planning Institute of Australia has put it this way:

As well as assessing development proposals and devising policy to guide future development, planners... specialise in areas of planning that include:
- Urban planning
- Regional and rural planning

- Development assessment and land use
- Social- and community-based planning
- Urban design
- Environmental planning and natural resources management
- Transport planning
- Heritage and conservation
- Place, project and major events planning.[1]

This is a mind-numbing range of disciplines that is indicative of the extent to which the profession has developed since the early days of "town and country planning". More importantly, though, it is indicative of the new concerns that have been taken to the system courtesy of successful political and social movements for change. What I am concerned with today is the way these issues are dealt with within our system of government. In particular, we need to ask: How do we manage the local, regional, state and national dimensions of the planning process?

## The Western Australian Experience

Let me begin with some comments on my experience as Premier of Western Australia.

Western Australia is fortunate in that it has possessed a centrally based statutory planning scheme for the metropolitan area for over fifty years. The Western Australian Planning Commission exercises control over subdivisions and supervises local planning. It also established a levy on land taxpayers to fund metropolitan improvement.

It is remarkable how the 1955 Stephenson–Hepburn *Plan for the Perth Metropolitan Region: Perth and Fremantle* has paid off in terms of setting aside land for parks and reserves, protecting transport corridors and ensuring we have centres for commerce and industry. It is a good case study in the importance of incorporating the long term into our thinking and practice today.

This being said the very concept of planning and the range of policy instruments to make it work is forever developing.

For one thing, it had become clear in 2001 that we needed to better integrate the work being done within government, in both policy development and implementation, if contemporary needs were to be met. To this end, we amalgamated the land use and transport planning functions of government in a new Department for Planning and Infrastructure.

Ministerial responsibility for this department, Main Roads, the Public Transport Authority, the Port Authorities, the WA Land Authority and the urban redevelopment authorities went to one Minister — the Hon. Alannah MacTiernan — who is still in the job today.

Minister MacTiernan not only oversaw these structural changes but introduced a philosophy of community engagement to the work of her agencies. This involved government acting as a facilitator to bring divergent voices and interests together. It also meant the proper involvement of the public in the planning process. This was no better illustrated than in the *Dialogue with the City*, a community engagement exercise, that led to a new metropolitan plan *Network City*.

What emerged from the consultation process was a desire for a city that was more differentiated and supported local communities. Sensible urban consolidation and the revitalisation of older suburbs were supported or, as the Minister put it in a speech here in Sydney last year:

*We want to move away from the fried egg planning of a small number of mega-centres surrounded by a sea of suburbs toward a complex, interactive network of local community centres.*[2]

I want to say two other things about Western Australia's experience. Firstly, Perth's redevelopment authorities — Subiaco, East Perth, Midland and, more recently, Armadale — have been success stories. Two are inner city and two are on the metropolitan fringe. With their combination of planning and development powers they have been able to regenerate town centres and facilitate public and private investment. Local governments have been fully involved in the work of the authorities and they have seen the political and economic leverage they can bring.

Secondly, Western Australia has a unique system of nine appointed Regional Development Commissions covering the non-metropolitan area. Although they don't have the degree of legislated power possessed by the urban redevelopment authorities, they have been able to provide a regional leadership and planning function for their communities and local authorities, who have representation, and with whom the levels of co-operation have been good.

The regions have been able to engage in sustainability planning, form partnerships with private and public agencies, and invest in infrastructure. Land-use issues are important in their work, often necessitating regionally facilitated consultation processes. They also exercise an important voice in Cabinet through their responsible Minister. Indeed, it was my view that the regional dimension needed to be represented in the decision-making process as well as the traditional functional interests like health and education.

I mention these urban and regional agencies of government as institutions that lie in that important space between the local and the state systems. They are needed and will work well if they are given the appropriate levels of status, power and resources and if they involve and co-operate with local government.

I trust that the comments I have made on the Western Australian experience give you some idea of where I am coming from in the planning domain. What matters is how we manage that territory where the state, regional and local agencies and interests meet. Where partnerships can be formed and shared responsibilities agreed, real progress is possible.

## Planning Principles Today

However, this is to jump the gun with what I want to say. First and foremost we need to ask: What is being expected of government today? I would answer this question by referring to three concepts: sustainability planning, strategic government and democratic engagement.

Put simply, we are being asked to ensure that social and environmental factors are given equal consideration to economic factors, to set long-term objectives for government along with strategies, programs and policies for their achievement, and to more fully involve the public in both the planning and implementation phases of the process. It means accepting that changes today are necessary and that the proper management of those changes through the engagement of the people is now the vital ingredient of good government.

New South Wales has acknowledged this up front with its *State Plan*. What it means is that partnerships around the priorities set by the *Plan* will be the order of the day. The partnerships may be between state government agencies, they may be between government and the community or they may be between the different levels of government.

I note that the Department of Planning is the lead agency for two of the *Plan's* priority areas: ensuring jobs are closer to home and that there is an appropriate supply of land and housing to meet demand. I note also that the community feedback pointed to water supply and public transport as two areas where improvements were "most clearly wanted".

The values associated with local community and the important role being played by Catchment Management Authorities indicated what can be called respect for the "bottom-up" approach to government. Reference is also made to the role that regional managers within state government are to play in partnering with local governments and communities to ensure existing regional plans, including regional land use plans, are linked to delivery of the *State Plan*.

Also relevant to our considerations today is priority P1: increased business investment. To this end, the Cabinet Office (now Premier and Cabinet) has been given the task of cutting red tape, reducing turnaround times and increasing the certainty of expected timeframes for major development-assessment approvals.

## From Theory to Practice

This takes us to the contentious issue of performance and its connection to power and responsibility. How is performance measured and assessed? Who does the measuring? Who is responsible should improvements be needed? This has put the processes of both state and local government in the spotlight and comes on top of a trend towards the "panelisation" of planning and the adoption of various forms of private certification for building work, subdivisions and simple development applications.

It is in this context that Peter Williams from the University of New South Wales has written recently:

> *Achieving a balance between crucial public policy outcomes and the public consultation and participation processes that ideally should accompany them is therefore likely to be an ongoing challenge for both governance and planning in Australia.*[3]

Just as state governments are under pressure to perform, so too are local governments, and ensuring that improved "performance" is not at the expense of the wider public interest is never easy.

It is an issue that needs to be treated realistically. Amateurism and cavalier behaviour in planning matters can have a disastrous effect on timelines. Planning is not beyond politics but it is an area where basic knowledge of planning law and policy has become necessary if responsibilities are to be exercised efficiently. A serious discussion of this issue, along with the proper resource base for the planning function within local and state government, ought to be a priority if the required balance between process and outcome is to be found.

The public good is a slippery concept. It is not a given, but a work-in-progress. When it comes to exercising delegated powers we ought to ensure all issues are properly canvassed.

Educating decision-makers about their responsibilities under the law would be my first priority.

I know the jurisdiction is quite different in both size and political culture, but I always felt that the late Jim Bacon was on the right track with his partnership agreements between Tasmania's state and local governments. It allowed the two levels of government to put on the agenda matters of concern for which solutions would be sought, and it made the relationship between state and locality *an ongoing concern*. Adding a regional dimension to this equation of dialogue around the detail would be an added advantage.

There is a strong "localisation" as well as "globalisation" at work today. It is more than mere sentiment and can act as a substantial value around which interests coalesce. It means that changes to the system of local government will always be contentious — and potentially counter-productive. Indeed, in order to deliver some outcomes, state governments require the involvement and support of local communities and their local governments, a classic example being crime prevention and community safety. Such partnerships require trust and stability.

When it comes to strategic planning at the state or regional level, there are always going to be conflicts that have to be managed, whether the councils that face the state government are small or large. It follows that local government amalgamations are best treated on their local merits and cannot be expected to deliver a ready-made solution for planning conflicts. Somehow we need to ensure the state, regional and local domains all have a voice in the system. Radical reductions in the influence of any of these levels carry dangers for the public interest.

One area where size may be an issue is that of resource availability and its impact on planning capability. However, even here we have learnt that service-sharing arrangements across the boundaries can be more effective than amalgamation.

Whichever way we choose to look at it, the big picture is always going to be the "Big Picture", represented most often by the state government. It means planning for the future, identifying transport corridors and growth areas and, in today's world, reducing the overall carbon imprint. Conflict with local and regional interests is a permanent possibility, if not an inevitability. The key to success in all these areas will be "trust" and "politics". Is the government believed when it says its plans are necessary and unavoidable? Is the government prepared to engage and involve the people and any relevant stakeholders in the changes required?

This is where the art and science of community engagement enter the picture. I say "science" because many methodologies are available: consensus forums, citizens' juries, multi-criteria analysis conferences, enquiry-by-design dialogues, deliberative surveys and twenty-first century town meetings. If such methodologies are to succeed there will need to be a sharing of information, a willingness to listen and seek common ground, and shared ownership of the outcomes. None of this is easy, but given the complexity of many of the issues and the high probability that there could be debilitating conflict and delay, community engagement is not just a good idea but a political and administrative necessity.

## Commonwealth Involvement

You may have noted but I have yet to mention the commonwealth government. They, too, develop big pictures, not just about Australia's position in the world, but also about human settlement and how it should be planned. We saw significant commonwealth involvement in urban and regional planning issues in the Whitlam years and then again in the early 1990s with the *Building Better Cities* program. Australia today has been described as "one of the few advanced Western nations lacking a sustained commitment to a national spatial policy".[4]

This is true, but in respect of environmental protection generally, and land management and sustainability in our regions, there has been a regeneration of interest. The proposed takeover of the management of the Murray–Darling Basin provides an illustration of this, as does the National Water Initiative and the National Heritage Trust. Significant commonwealth funding has been devoted to these initiatives.

Where properly negotiated and planned, such national initiatives can assist in the production of good outcomes for states and their regions and localities, just as *Better Cities* did in the early 1990s. However, it remains to be seen whether the commonwealth will ensure that a properly considered framework is in place not only for the development of such nationwide agreement, but also in relation to the funding decisions made in connection to them. Two points are worth noting here. Many of the current areas of commonwealth interest do not involve them on a day-to-day basis — as they do in the states — and given the financial strength of the commonwealth, the temptation to pork-barrel is always strong. We should want commonwealth involvement that is appropriate and which can add value. The competition reform agenda of the 1990s was an example: the states preserved their autonomy but were given an incentive to bring about change.

There is room in the Australian federal system for a national planning process around a sustainability agenda for both urban and regional communities. This I would contrast with an ideologically driven centralism that attempts to avoid or undermine the established processes of inter-governmental co-operation.

The challenge will come when the nation gets serious about its responsibilities to tackle climate change. The system will be tested at the various points where interests clash and inter- and intra-government co-operation is required. Thus it is, always.

## Conclusion

I would like to conclude my comments by focusing on what I see to be the three major requirements for good governance in the planning area.

Firstly, co-ordination and co-operation across the levels of government should be given a high priority. We need to ask of ourselves: What amount of time and resources is being devoted to the relationship aspects of the planning function? This is not an area of government that should only be activated in the event of crisis or conflict, it should be an area of ongoing concern and attention.

Secondly, state and local government support for regional institutions within the cities as well as outside them is very important if plans and their implementation are to be meaningful. Planning is about new development and re-development. For both, regional considerations are vital.

Thirdly, the art and science of community engagement and the proper management of conflict is a major asset for modern governments. Plans inevitably create what the media provocatively, but probably accurately, call "winners" and "losers". This needs to be recognised upfront when plans are being developed and when they are being implemented.

## Notes

1 Quoted in Susan Thompson, *Planning Australia: An Overview of Urban and Regional Planning* (Cambridge University Press, Melbourne, 2007), p. 23.

2 Alannah MacTiernan, "Learning from the Western Australian example — the new rail line and collaborative network city program", Metropolitan Planning Summit, Sydney, 29 June 2006.

3 Peter Williams, "Government, People and Politics", in *Planning Australia*, p. 46.

4 Susan Thompson, "Introduction", in *Planning Australia*, p. 3.

# 9.

# A Fair Society

# Is Australia Advancing Fairly?

Speech delivered at
New Agenda for Prosperity Conference

Melbourne, 27 March 2008

Is Australia advancing fairly?

In seeking to answer this question it is important that we go to the heart of the matter and ask: What do we mean by fairness?

This is important because there is a school of thought which holds that fairness cannot be defined and shouldn't be the focus of public policy. Even as an aspiration, so the argument goes, it inevitably leads to more harm than good.

Counter to this point of view, I believe fairness can be defined as a general principle and as a working principle for government. The American political philosopher John Rawls provides an excellent starting point with his concept of "justice as fairness".[1]

Rawls asked us to imagine a situation in which we come together to agree to a set of rules for our common life. However, none of us is to know our race, gender, social class, talents, capacities, religious beliefs or conception of the good life. We are, as it were, placed behind a "veil of ignorance".

In such a situation, Rawls believes individuals will choose a state which will give each the most extensive liberties compatible with like liberties for others and which ensures that any social and economic inequalities are to be arranged so that they are to the greatest benefit of the least advantaged and attached to positions open to all. In other words, we would always seek to have the *highest* minimum level of freedom, wealth and opportunity. It is the least-risk strategy and, I would add, what it means to live in a community as opposed to a tribe or a completely commercialised society.

What I like about Rawls' theory is that he forces us to ask hard questions about restrictions on liberty rather as John Stuart Mill did in his classic *On Liberty* (1859). However, he also forces us to ask hard questions about social and economic inequalities rather than being swept along by the view that they are inevitable and unchangeable. The onus of proof is on those who enjoy such privileges to demonstrate their relevance to those without them. I am reminded here of the Christian concept of a "preferential option for the poor", defined and analysed so well by Father Gerry Arbuckle in a publication commissioned by Catholic Health Australia earlier this year.[2]

That Australian policy makers have sought to counterbalance market realities with the fairness principle has been a recurring theme in our history. Both government and non-government organisations have been involved in this enterprise. Despite these efforts, I doubt whether any of us could say that we have achieved the *highest* possible minimums in freedom, wealth and opportunity. As Professor Tony Vinson has observed recently, "Pockets of concentrated and severe social disadvantage have become entrenched across rural and remote as well as suburban Australia".[3] None of us, peering in from behind the veil of ignorance, would accept these conditions as adequate for ourselves or our families.

The fact is the fairness principle has always been — and still is — heavily contested and even more so in recent years than was the case, for example, in the first two decades that followed the Second World War. Not only does it come up against the free market principle, but also the realities of contemporary democratic politics and its bias towards the interests of those with numbers and voice. The politically inspired policies promoting what is well described as "middle class welfare" are a case in point. Once entrenched, such benefits are difficult to remove.

The fairness agenda has had to battle not only on the ground where it confronts political and market realism, but also in the world of ideas where personal behaviour has become *the* issue rather than one half of a rights-and-responsibilities equation. Economic thinking narrowed and social policy was transformed into its handmaiden.

There are, however, some grounds for political and public policy optimism. Regarding the first, it is important to note the defeat of Workchoices. For the electorate, this was a deregulation that went too far. It tells us that at least fairness in the workplace is still part of the all-important middle-ground of politics. This was certainly one cultural battle that the Howard government didn't win.

With respect to public policy, more generally considered, we can note a number of developments. First and foremost is the recognition in contemporary economic theory of the impor-tance of human capital and a healthy society for growth and productivity. This forms the basis for the third wave of national reform agreed between the commonwealth and the states and territories.[4] It should mean a greater effort to tackle the factors that cause ill-health and low school attainment.

This accommodation between social and economic policy has also arisen with respect to the debate over skills shortages. Local-level partnerships between business, government and the community have been recognised as potential levers for the creation of skilled and available labour, particularly, but not exclusively, in rural and remote Australia.

A better union between economics and fairness is coupled with a more realistic understanding of the effort that is going to be needed to tackle social exclusion. The concept of income support is a necessary but hardly a sufficient condition for social inclusion. We are talking here of culture and capacity — a culture of self-respect and the capacity to participate. The context may be an individual or a community making both case and place management — both expensive options if applied properly — a requirement for good policy.

All of this suggests, as Frank Stilwell and Kirrily Jordon have noted, "the need for a more tailored approach to the eradication of poverty and recognises the diverse character of the problems of economic and social marginalisation".[5] Recognition of diversity sits uneasily alongside the ideology of mainstreaming and would almost certainly imply that we need a range of service providers — government and non-government — if positive results are to be forthcoming. It also means that change will need to be "bottom-up" as well as "top-down"; it is to be owned and thereby sustainable. None of this will be easy, and all of it will require a long-term commitment rather than short-term enthusiasms.

Maintaining such a commitment in the face of opposition from free-market economics and the temptations of political realism is never easy but will be complicated even further by the emergence of climate change as a major political issue. As Ross Garnaut has noted, climate change and the policies designed to address it will have important distributional implications which cannot be ignored by those committed to a fairness agenda.[6] Indeed, it may be the case that the extent of the efforts required to tackle climate change will necessitate a new politics of fairness, just as we saw during and after the Second World War.

To help make fairness a reality, the government, non-government sector and individuals all have a role to play. Governments can't do it all and they will require special skills in managing a process that will need to ensure that taxes and expenditures are better targeted in the interests of equality of opportunity rather than in the interests of those already privileged. However, the private and non-government sectors will need to play their part in supporting innovation and providing opportunities for the poor. Indeed, social inclusion can't just mean self-respect and individual capacity, it must also mean social and economic opportunity. For too long we have allowed these collective and community foundations of our individual freedoms to wither on the vine. Restoring the balance brings hope to those currently disenfranchised and is a worthy object of our national attention.

**Notes**

1   See John Rawls, *A Theory of Justice* (Harvard University Press, 1971).

2   Gerald Arbuckle, "A Preferential Option for the Poor", *Application to Catholic Health and Aged Care Ministries in Australia* (Catholic Health Australia, 2008).

3   Quoted in John Langmore, *To Firmer Ground: Restoring Hope in Australia* (UNSW Press, 2007), p. 13.

4   See in particular the Victorian Premier, *Governments Working Together: A Third Wave of National Reform* (August 2005).

5   Frank Stilwell and Kirrily Jordan, *Who Gets What? Analysing Economic Inequality in Australia* (Cambridge University Press, 2007).

6   See Garnaut Climate Change Review, *Media Release*, 20 March 2008.

# In Defence of Multiculturalism

Speech delivered at
2011 Barton Lecture, Newcastle University

Newcastle, 30 March 2011

May I begin by thanking the University of Newcastle for the invitation to deliver the Barton Lecture. It is indeed a great privilege.

I'm sure you will have noted the irony in the fact that my topic is multiculturalism and it was Edmund Barton who took the *Immigration Restriction Bill* and the *Pacific Islands Labourers' Bill* to the Parliament, thus establishing Australia as "White Australia", a position it maintained until well into the twentieth century. It has been Barton's views on federalism and judicial review that have been of more interest to me, and I'm not sure the centralising changes we have seen in those domains have always been for the good.[1]

Still, that is another story. What about White Australia and multiculturalism?

The headline on ABC Radio's website on 17 February this year said it all: "Multiculturalism is Back".[2]

This followed the speech Immigration Minister Chris Bowen had given the night before and important speeches given by Angela Merkel and David Cameron on the subject from a German and a British perspective.

Merkel said that Germany's attempt to create a multicultural society had "utterly failed". Why? Because not enough attention was given to the need for integration into German society. Germans, she said, had encouraged foreign workers to come, but kidded themselves into thinking they would not stay. For their part, migrants had not done enough to learn the language and accept Germany's cultural norms.[3]

David Cameron ran a similar theme. "Under the doctrine of state multiculturalism", he said, "different cultures have been encouraged to live separate lives". More dangerous, though, was the toleration of behaviour that ran counter to "our values" which he listed as freedom of speech, freedom of worship, democracy, the rule of law and equal rights regardless of race, sex or sexuality.[4]

Chris Bowen, on the other hand, was quite happy to embrace the term "multiculturalism". The Australian version of the doctrine, he said, had worked well, avoiding the sorts of problems we have seen in Europe.

For the critics, however, Bowen's defence was not digestible. Gary Hardgrave, who had been Minister for Citizenship and Multicultural Affairs in the Howard government from 2001 to 2004, said the term has "passed its use-by date". He continued:

> *I think they're now trying to create the same sorts of schisms that they created while they were in office between '83 and '96, the kind of different treatments, separate treatments...*
>
> *And the big danger is if you use multiculturalism as an excuse to treat people differently and separately then you're going to get the sort of schisms we're seeing in Europe and in England where there's been no investment in bringing people together.*[5]

In tonight's lecture I want to seek clarity in the debate about the term and its application to public policy. I would like to go deeper than the usual-but-not-unimportant discussions about the role multiculturalism has played in creating new perspectives on lifestyle issues like food, fashion and design, and, indeed, the impact it has had on our broader understanding of human history and what can lead it to unravel. Indeed, it is not often the case that one nation can carry enough experience to deal with all the contradictions and complexities that come with human life. For example, the fact that we became home to some who survived the Holocaust has added to our understanding of the sources and dynamics of human evil, and our Jewish community has been consistent in its campaigning against racism.

In doing so, I'm sure you will observe that my support for multiculturalism is not half-hearted or compromised. I will argue that the discussion needs to be situated in the broader debate about "living with difference" and that multiculturalism is not the antithesis of, but rather is an expression of liberal values such as tolerance, respect for the person, freedom, equality and the rule of law. By defending multiculturalism we defend and strengthen our society rather than attack and weaken it as some have argued.

Let me also declare an interest. From 2001 to 2005, I was not only the Premier of Western Australia but also the Minister for Citizenship and Multicultural Interests. During this first term of government I chaired the community-based Anti Racism Steering Committee from which emerged the WA Charter of Multiculturalism (WA Charter) and the Substantive Equality Unit in the Equal Opportunity Commission. We also increased the penalties attached to crimes for which there was a racial element.

It was the dialogue and debate within the Steering Committee that helped frame my views on the subject. It took me beyond intellectual argument, as important as that is, to the felt experience of people with different backgrounds and ideas to what we might label "mainstream Australia". It's always important to remember how significant are the day-to-day experiences of migrants, what is said to them and how they are treated in the wide range of situations that none of us can avoid. These day-to-day experiences can range on the positive side, from lending an ear through to comprehensive and unqualified support, and on the negative side, from unintended offensiveness through to systematic discrimination. Think about your own life and I'm sure you will agree with me that such experiences matter.

Work as a politician also allows you to witness the enthusiasm displayed when migrants become Australian citizens by uttering the words: "From this time forward, I pledge my loyalty to Australia and its people, whose democratic beliefs I share, whose rights and liberties I respect, and whose laws I will uphold."

For those of a religious disposition, the words "under God" can also be used.

I would go so far as to say that the vast majority of people who come to live here do so because they want to share in the Australian story and the rights and responsibilities that have been built into it. They come, as Chris Bowen put it so well, "not to change our values but because of them".

I say these things about the motivations of migrants and their experience of our nation not to close off the debate but to remind us all of some facts that ought to be taken into account when considering all of the questions posed in a discussion of multiculturalism. Multiculturalism involves an outlook on living in a diverse society as well as public policy.

Note, too, that we cannot properly consider these matters without incorporating the First Australians — the Aborigines and Torres Strait Islanders. Debating the meaning and consequences of diversity and difference is not just about migration but also about Indigenous rights and interests, particularly but not only as they relate to land and language. Although some say this diminishes the historical and political significance of the Indigenous question, I'm pleased to see that the recently released *The People of Australia: Australia's Multicultural Policy* (February 2011) has done just that.

One might also ask: Is multiculturalism only about Indigenous and migrant Australians? Is it just about the seven million people who have migrated here since 1945? Is it just about those migrants and the 517,200 people of Aboriginal or Torres Strait Islander descent?

In fact, multiculturalism is a public policy developed in response to the presence of differences in society. Such differences may be based upon language and place of birth, race and ethnicity, ideas and religion, or history and culture. Even long-established communities with little or no immigration will need policies to deal with the differences in their midst. Belgium and Switzerland immediately come to mind, at least before the new wave of migration beginning in the 1960s when new issues of difference were added to those of old.

Multiculturalism as public policy is one option amongst others.

What, then, is multiculturalism? In the WA Charter, a multicultural society is defined as follows:

*A society in which respect for mutual difference is accompanied by equality of opportunity within a framework of democratic citizenship.*[6]

Contained within its ambit are three ideas: mutual respect, equality of opportunity and democratic citizenship.

In analysing these ideas further, let's be reminded of the great liberal project of the last three, some might say four, centuries. In essence, it was designed to tackle religious, and later racial, intolerance and discrimination. Rather than support one religion or one group, the state would guarantee the rights and interests of all. Freedom of expression and lifestyle were to be protected so long as their exercise did not infringe the rights of others. It became known as the "Harm Principle". "The only purpose for which power can be rightfully exercised over any member of a civilised community against his will", said John Stuart Mill, "is to prevent harm to others".[7]

Not only would freedom replace authoritarianism through the protection of civil liberty, but also through political liberty and the establishment of democratic government. It took many years, indeed centuries, but step-by-step the franchise was extended to all and governments made properly accountable to the people.

It soon became clear that the development of political liberty alongside civil liberty created a new challenge, recognised only too well by the same John Stuart Mill. He called it the tyranny of "prevailing opinion and feeling" or "the tyranny of the majority". Today it is recognisable as populism.[8]

The argument went like this: if the majority rules, what is to stop them imposing their will on the minority? What price is individual and group freedom in a democracy? What about individuality in a mass society? One of the answers given to these questions was simple but powerful: the power of government should be limited, with plenty of space provided for freedom of expression and lifestyle.

Over the years, many institutions have been developed to back up the Harm Principle and ensure limited government in a democracy — bicameralism, bills and charters of rights and judicial review. It is worth noting that, from time to time, each of these has been the subject of populist attack.

In the liberal world view, individuals were free but only up to a point, and laws and regulations were needed, but only up to a point. On just where these "points" should lie is the subject of much contention in our society. Some, like the radical libertarians, and the radical communitarians question whether or not such accommodation is feasible and acceptable. They see freedom and community as mutually inconsistent objectives. It follows that you have to believe in one or the other.

Whichever way you look at it, it is not an issue for which there is a technical solution, it is a political issue requiring political resolution and it is highly improbable that there will ever be unanimous and sustained agreement on policies for appropriate regulation and equal opportunity.

The school of thought from which multiculturalism has been born, left liberalism, sees the best route to social harmony as the guarantee of freedom and the provision of opportunity. This means taking positive steps to tackle discrimination whatever its base: gender, sexual orientation, class or geography. It says we should seek liberty and equality, not one or the other.

Multiculturalism is all about tackling racism and discrimination, promoting mutual respect across the religions and taking steps to help newly arrived migrants adjust and become involved in their new society (for example, through English language training). It has also meant the provision of opportunities to protect and promote other languages and cultures, as well as services to allow non-English speaking people to go about their daily lives (for example, through translator services ).

Multiculturalists see no contradiction between the objectives of integration and diversity. As Professor Duncan Ivison from the University of Sydney has put it:

> The multicultural polices of the 1970s in Canada (and later Australia) were an attempt to make the integration process for migrants less racially charged and discriminatory as well as to incorporate newly emerging forms of non-discrimination and human rights into public policy.[9]

They were all about recognising a new reality and finding the means to ensure it worked for all and not just some.

When it comes to the use of taxpayers' money for some, if not all of these initiatives, disagreements inevitably follow. Opponents of multiculturalism tend to see these things as the responsibility of the individual rather than the obligation of the state. They see much that is spent on integration and the protection of diversity as wasted expenditure because it privileges some at the expense of others. Indeed, by advocating for equality of opportunity as well as formal equality under the law, multiculturalists raise the hackles of those who see these extra steps to promote equality as discriminatory and unnecessary in a free society and market economy. They don't like the use of "difference" as the basis for policy in that it creates group rights rather than individual rights. That is, why they are highly critical of affirmative action, powerful unions and many social benefits, at least when they are given in the absence of mutual obligation.

What we see here is a debate within the liberal tradition about how far to extend the principle of equality. Multiculturalism is controversial because it is on the left-liberal side and takes equality and difference seriously, the former as a spur to government initiative and the latter as a reminder of the need for case and place management when it comes to service delivery. As the WA Charter puts it:

> *In pursuing the goals of democratic citizenship the government recognises the need to individualise service delivery if it is to guarantee equitable treatment for all. It recognises that universalist provision of services in the public sector may obscure the distinctive needs of minority communities and cultures.*[10]

To me this idea of taking both liberty and equality seriously seems commonsense. We have seen it work effectively in the aftermath of the Great Depression and in relation to the challenges to democracy that came with fascism and communism. By compromising with its critics and taking on board policies for equal opportunity, capitalism saved itself from the extremes that circled it. So too, have we seen multiculturalism operating as an example of this outlook work effectively in countries like Australia and Canada. It means offering friendship rather than hostility, and support rather than empty rhetoric. It's not perfect. Nor does it absolve us of the responsibility to examine carefully programs proposed in its name. Times change but often policy is slow to catch up.

If opponents of multiculturalism don't see equality of opportunity as the key to social cohesion, what is it that can do the job?

It is when you probe deeply into this question that you can see the other objection to multiculturalism. It is, they say, not prescriptive enough when it comes to the values needed to hold society together. It is true, they acknowledge, that liberty and democracy help, but in the absence of national values, which are understood, propagated, and widely supported social harmony is always at risk.

When critics use the term "integration" they mean integration into a particular way of life which privileges aspects of our Judeo-Christian religious tradition and promotes particular values like "mateship" and particular institutions like the British Monarchy and the "Westminster System" of parliamentary government. Undermine these, they say, and the stability we have enjoyed is under threat. The arguments used in the republic debate are a case in point.

It is pretty obvious why this is a bone of contention for those who don't understand and/or share such values. To become an Australian citizen means to become a particular type of Australian citizen rather than just a law-abiding citizen respecting of the rights and liberties of others. Is it really sameness of politics, spirituality, culture and aspiration that defines an Australian citizen?

Defenders of multiculturalism often attempt to overcome this nationalist objection by claiming that they are the true carriers of the Australian tradition. In *The People of Australia* it is put this way: "The multicultural character of Australia is central to the Australian story. Governments should tell this story".

Others would say that the concepts of a "fair go" or "mateship" are consistent with multiculturalism.

It is true that Australian history has always involved differences, in the first instance between settler and Aboriginal, between Catholic and Protestant and between convict and freeborn Englishman. These differences have been played out in different ways at different times and are an important resource for learning about society and what holds it together and what pulls it apart.

In this sense, it helps frame the discussion of the topic of living with difference. However, like all nations, Australia's history is full of contradiction and ethical ambiguity. To romanticise or demonise the past as a basis for contemporary argument adds little to the acceptability or otherwise of the case being made.

What I think we can establish is that the implementation of multiculturalism and a new approach to immigration as an alternative to White Australia and the discriminatory practices embedded in it came at a good time for Australia. Globalisation and the benefits it can bring, most notably a larger market, was a reality that didn't intimidate or frighten many Australians. Diversity was not only good in that it opened us up to new and interesting lifestyles but also because it connected us to the global economy, particularly in the Asian region. There was a productive fit between the opening up of our economy and the opening up of our society, with trade and investment not just having a commercial dimension, but also a political and personal one.

Remember, though, that none of this happened without politics. What we now describe as the move into an open and global future was — and still is — contested.

The real argument is not that multiculturalists are relativists, as some critics say, but that they are idealists who believe that our system built on liberty and equality should form the basis of our shared culture rather than the necessarily limited and limiting values we have inherited from the past. What is different about multiculturalism is that its shared values are more culture-neutral, more open-ended and more egalitarian. It is quite wrong, however, to say that multiculturalists do not draw lines in the sand.

Multiculturalism does have a concept of shared values that can form the basis for political education and the regulation of civil society. It is the case, for example, that some practices deemed acceptable in other places, such as female genital mutilation, are not deemed acceptable in Australia because they infringe the rights of women. Multiculturalism only works if its liberal principles are applied without fear or favour.

However, on where to draw the line between what is acceptable and what is unacceptable when it comes to deeply held convictions is never easy. We recognise the significance of Christmas and Easter. We say the Lord's Prayer in Parliament. We allow Muslim women to wear the burqa, despite some feminist objection. In fact, Australia's Churches have successfully argued that the nation's anti-discrimination laws should not apply to them because of their religious position on issues like women priests, divorce and same-sex relationships. Here we see a political accommodation between state and religion that reflects the power and influence of tradition in Australian society. I'd call this a case study in pragmatic multiculturalism rather than a principled application of the doctrine.

It is ironic that the very people who defend these compromises are quite often the same people who oppose multi-culturalism as creating different categories of Australian. In fact, it is multiculturalism that creates just one category, that is to say, people with rights and interests as human beings, the traditional liberal approach. Indeed, the whole point of liberalism was to break down the "them" and "us" view of the world, at least up to the point where the society which defended political and civil liberty is itself under threat. On this question of liberty versus tyranny, there is clearly "them" and "us"!

In saying all of this, I'm well aware that logical consistency isn't always a good basis for understanding or judging human behaviour. I know society runs on emotion as well as reason, and that nationalism is a powerful current within any society. I know that there will always be tension between different religions and different religious denominations. So too is it highly unlikely that we could ever see a society without collective sentiments and the pressures they create.

When it comes to changing the world we need political judgement as well as idealistic aspirations. Multiculturalism is as challenged as it is challenging. That has always been the case for those who have pushed the boundaries of change. It spends money on and protects the rights of minorities. It asks us to be compassionate when faced with the request for asylum. It urges reason when emotions are running high, as they were following the September 11 and Bali bombings.

It's the same with the argument for a Charter of Rights or the argument for same-sex marriage. Liberalism and tradition have always been uncomfortable bedfellows and will continue to be so as long as tradition seeks to legislate on the basis of questionable logic; some might call it prejudice.

Liberalism, particularly left liberalism, has never found the going easy in modern democratic societies. It is critical. It challenges us to set higher standards rather like Jesus did in The Parable of the Good Samaritan.

This is the problem for multiculturalism. It doesn't give us a simple formula for government, but it forces us to think more carefully about the way we deliver government services. It encourages us to examine our own assumptions and biases and what they mean for others. It gives real content to concepts like tolerance and mutual respect. It encourages us to occupy the shoes of "the other" in our midst and address the special needs of minorities and newcomers. It is most important to use it as a guiding light in a migrant society like ours, and it forces us to ask the question: Is it sustainable to bring society together on the basis of a shared religion and culture, or should we see our rights and responsibilities as human beings as the real and lasting cement for society?

Just as importantly, it imposes on minorities — as well as the majority — the obligation to join in this exercise in rights and responsibilities. This, of course, is an ongoing process that often involves varying degrees of acceptance and sometimes resistance. Intolerance, oppression and bigotry are what multiculturalism is designed to counter, not to encourage. Both the civil society as well as the state may be its targets.

We need multiculturalism, not because it is without the dilemmas associated with all grand narratives or because it is easy to apply given the real world of established traditions, but because it offers hope for a better society in a necessarily global but also troubled and uncertain world. Living with difference is the contemporary challenge, and multiculturalism is its best friend.

**Notes**

1    See Geoff Gallop, *A State of Reform: Essays for a Better Future*. (Helm Wood Publishers, 1998), pp. 54–60.

2    http://www.abc.net.au/am/content/2011/s3141073.htm

3    See "Multiculturalism makes a return", http://www.abc.net.au/worldtoday/content/2011/s3141369.htm

4    See "State multiculturalism has failed, says David Cameron", http://www.bbc.co.uk/news/uk-politics-12371994?print=true

5    See "Multiculturalism makes a return".

6    *WA Charter of Multiculturalism* (November 2004).

7    Quoted in Richard Reeves, *John Stuart Mill: Victorian Firebrand* (Atlantic, London, 2007), p. 264.

8    See Reeves, *John Stuart Mill: Victorian Firebrand*, pp.294–298.

9    *"Multiculturalism"*, Human Rights and Democracy Forum, HREOC and Sydney Democracy Forum, August 2007.

10   *WA Charter* (2004).

11   *The People of Australia: The Australian Multicultural Advisory Council's statement on cultural diversity*. (April 2010), p. 17.

# 10.

# A Deeper Reality

# The Well-Being Agenda

Speech delivered at
the 2009 Grace Groom Lecture

Canberra, 14 May 2009

I very much appreciate the opportunity to deliver the Grace Groom Lecture today. In doing so, I acknowledge the contribution Grace made to the Mental Health Council of Australia as Chief Executive from 2002 to 2005. When it announced the establishment of the Grace Groom Lecture to pay tribute to Grace (who died in 2006), the Council noted her "capacity to marry strategic understanding with an appreciation of the practical issues involved in reform". This is exactly the mixture of elements we require if we are to meet the health challenges of the future.

It is not as an expert on the many issues surrounding mental health that I address you. Rather it is as a citizen whose own interest in the subject is both personal and political: personal because of my own experience of depression, and political because of my passionate commitment to the role of public policy as an instrument for human improvement.

## National Health and Hospitals Reform Commission

Let me begin by commending to you the Interim Report of the National Health and Hospitals Reform Commission of which I am a member, along with the Chair of the Mental Health Council, Rob Knowles. You may have noticed that we have discussed mental illness in a section of the report entitled "Facing Inequalities".

We did this for a number of reasons. Firstly, we pointed to the fact that whilst mental disorders (including problems and illnesses) represented 13.3 per cent of the total burden of disease (coming third after cancers and cardiovascular diseases), expenditure in this area is only 7 per cent of total health expenditure, and only 12 per cent of this funding is allocated to supporting people with mental illness who are living in the community.

Secondly, we referred to estimates that a majority, perhaps over two-thirds, of people with a mental disorder do not receive any treatment in any twelve-month period. Adolescents and young adults are particularly reluctant to seek treatment or assistance.

Thirdly, we pointed to recent studies that show less than 30 per cent of Australians with a disability due to mental illness participate in the workforce. This is *less than half* the rate of comparable OECD countries.

Along with dental care, the health of Aboriginal and Torres Strait Islander peoples and those living in rural and remote communities, mental illness is an equality issue. Or to put it another way, it is a social justice issue. As the World Health Organisation Commission on Social Determinants of Health put it: "Where systematic differences in health are judged to be unavoidable by reasonable action they are quite simply unfair."[1]

## Mental Health: Politics and Culture

What we see, then, is a society with a significant burden of mental illness and an inadequate approach to dealing with it. When I reflect upon my own experience and that of the community as a whole, I am led to ask: Why don't we treat mental health as seriously as we ought? In seeking an answer to this question I am led to consider two factors, the first political and the second cultural.

Politics, as we all know, is partly, if not wholly, about "the numbers", and despite the size of the problem, mental illness hasn't generated the same degree of political momentum as, say, elective surgery waiting times and hospital care more generally.

This may have been the case, but in more recent times one would have to conclude that mental health has been more successful. Consider, for example, the depth and breadth of the commitments entered into through the 2006 National Action Plan on Mental Health. This Plan and those that preceded it were prepared and agreed upon following a massive lobbying campaign by a range of organisations, including the Mental Health Council.

However, the truth is that the difficulty of creating momentum in this area has been, and still is, as much a cultural issue as it has been a numbers issue.

Let me use depression as an example.

Not talking about illnesses like depression is part of their definition. We hold it in and this can mean individuals locked up inside themselves, their minds hammering away 24 hours a day. All too often we treat it as a condition that can be "wished away". However, the evidence tells us that the bottling up and internalising of our feelings and emotions in a private struggle for liberation can be counter-productive.

Prejudices like this, and the anxieties and illnesses they conceal, feed off each other like psychological twins. The more the concealment, the more the depression. It is all the more tragic because we know that effective treatments are available. When it comes to those who don't seek treatment we need to remind ourselves that stigma — and its twin, the fear of exposure — are still active ingredients in today's environment.

So too is ignorance.

Looking at the way organisations manage depression and related illnesses, including anxiety and substance abuse, beyondblue concluded:

> *Depression and mental illness... are not managed well across organisations. In fact many current management practices, such as recommending taking time off work or a holiday may only compound the problem and make the situation worse.*[2]

The reality is that taking time off may simply give the mind more time to stalk its victim. As Tessa Wigney, Kerrie Eyers and Gordon Parker from the Black Dog Institute have concluded: "Depression infiltrates your thoughts and takes over your mind. It distorts your senses as well as your perceptions of the past and future. It is a state of excruciating isolation."[3] It is the depth and intensity of the suffering associated with depression that renders worthless many of the homespun remedies for tits treatment.

## Stigma, Ignorance and Avoidance

Stigma encourages repression and ignorance produces avoidance. As the Buddhist scholar and teacher Stephen Batchelor has put it:

> *How much of our life is spent in avoiding what we really are? Yet in a quiet corner of ourselves, do we not secretly recognise the deceptive strategies of such avoidance? How often do we find ourselves happily indulging in some trivial pursuit, even though a deeper awareness is whispering to us of its futility?*[4]

In reading this quotation I am reminded of Leonard Cohen's "Everybody Knows"

> *Everybody knows that the boat is leaking...*
> *Everybody knows, everybody knows,*
> *That's how it goes, everybody knows...*
> *Everybody got this broken feeling.*

This is powerful language. These are powerful insights. What is this "deeper awareness" about which Batchelor speaks? Is it something that can be defined and translated into fuel for thought and action? We know the truth of this avoidance but why do we practice it?

In asking this question I am reminded of a distressing and haunting image produced by Richard Eckersley in a speech delivered to the Australian Institute of Family Studies in 1998. In that speech he described young people as "the miners' canaries of our society, acutely vulnerable to the peculiar hazards of our times". The young, says Eckersley, have picked up on the failure of modern society to offer meaning for today and hope for the future.[5]

This is a bold claim. Perhaps it is too bold. Indeed, Eckersley has his critics who point out that modern science, market economics and accountable governments have produced vast improvements in the quality of life for that portion of humanity fortunate enough to enjoy them. Not only that, but the economic base is now strong enough to allow for the provision of quality health (including mental health) services for those in need.

All of this is, of course, quite true. But is it the whole story? To my mind, Eckersley has captured an aspect of modern life which resonates with the actual experience of people and the felt quality of their relationships. He takes us below the surface to where our feelings and emotions come into play.

Indeed, it is interesting to reflect upon our models of thinking about politics and economics and what they imply.

## Our Model of Politics and Economics

Consider the basic model of political theory that has underpinned our thinking about legitimacy and government. It starts with natural or God-given rights to life, liberty and property. The role of government is to provide a framework that protects these rights. At the heart of politics is a social contract between the people and the government.

The Americans provided a broader framework for thinking about politics with their inalienable right to "the pursuit of happiness". What they seemed to have in mind were issues like the freedom to marry, to enjoy privacy and to pursue a business or occupation of one's choice so long as it was not inconsistent with the rights of others. It was good, solid liberal philosophy.

Coming with a political theory was an economic theory of growth and the free market. This gave a dynamic and progressive element to the social contract between government and the people, and even if qualified by welfare and social justice considerations in the twentieth century, it still proposed Gross Domestic Product (GDP) as the best measure of community success.

The problem, of course is that whilst these formulations were crucial foundation stones for the creation of a better world, they became a form of religion, claiming to disclose all we need to know about the human condition. We still see this today in the debates around complex issues like environmental amenity, climate change, economic regulation, substance abuse and mental health. It is a clear case of the arrogance of ideology riding roughshod over the reality of complexity.

As I have noted earlier, this ideology impacts at the level of the individual as well as the level of the community. What we assume to be the case and what is the case are two different things. This takes me back to my comments about stigma and ignorance. The psychological sciences expose the social and biological limits of our apparent freedom, but doesn't society tell us we have "freedom of will"? Self-awareness brings to the surface issues we may prefer to see repressed. And repress them we do. We take our first steps to freedom when we realise we are not "free". I suspect, however, that awareness of all the forces — social and biological — that influence our behaviour is challenging in a society that values freedom so highly.

At the level of our community life we are the victims of our own success. Despite the advice of a long list of philosophers and theologians, both ancient and modern, we continue to treat material wealth as the badge of progress. Linked to all of this is our consumer society. We define ourselves by what we can produce collectively and what we can consume individually. This has had enormous implications for how we approach work, how we arrange our family lives and how we treat ourselves and our environment.

## The Search for Sustainability

Life is full of contradictions and the sources of anxiety are many. We worry about the meaning of existence in the face of our inevitable death. We worry about ourselves and our place in the world. We worry about the future and what it will bring. Each of us, then, has to live with the pain of existence, the struggles of life and the uncertainties of the future. We are all different and some of us are predisposed to depression and other serious mental illness. Sometimes the mix of biochemistry and social existence sends people to the edge. Psychotic episodes become part of their daily reality.

Why, then, do we complicate matters with intellectual abstractions, dysfunctional social relationships and unrealisable aspirations? We know community well-being and our environment matter, but have difficulty according them equal status with economic growth. The problem, of course, is that what we might call a sustainability approach that integrates economic, social and environmental factors is complex and challenging.

We know there is a deeper reality to our make up as individuals, but its complexity frightens us. As a community we know of the limitations of material wealth as a measure of true value but we seem incapable of breaking its grip on our imagination.

Indeed, just to prove how powerful it is, modern consumer society has created its own version of the well-being agenda or happiness agenda. Happiness has become another consumer item to be purchased in a pre-packaged form like any other.

What we see is a cult of self-improvement, which Barry Magid has correctly described in his excellent book *Ending the Pursuit of Happiness*, as the "compulsive pursuit of happiness". He continues:

> *Deep down we don't want to be a human being, because being human means being subject to all the inevitable pain and suffering of being human. Our bodies are subject to change. We grow and develop and we exercise and become strong and fit. But all of us will eventually grow weak and sick and helpless, some sooner than others, for reasons that may not be under the control of the best of our diets, exercises or fitness programs. What then? Have we somehow failed? Sadly, many people would rather treat the inevitable consequences of being human as a failure of their project of perfection in one of its many guises than admit that the most basic things about life are not and never have been under our control.*[6]

As individuals, then, we prefer the illusion of freedom rather than the complexity of self-awareness and all that it means for coming to grips with our emotional and spiritual as well as our material and intellectual needs. As communities we prefer the simplicity of economic growth and personal consumption rather than the complexity of sustainability and community well-being. We might like to assume away our emotional hinterland and our biochemical make up, but this will not make it so.

## Moving Forward

To move forward we need to achieve four things: a continuing campaign to combat the stigma and ignorance; a stronger emphasis on early intervention and prevention; better access to treatment where it matters, in the community; and more concern for the social, environmental and economic forces that affect our well-being. It is all about culture and context, long-term preventative measures as well as short-term remediation and, most importantly, it is about citizenship and solidarity.

We need more discussion and debate around the question: What does it mean to live in a healthy society? It is not as if we don't have mountains of evidence about the factors that can create a better context for life. Indeed, what we call the well-being agenda has made significant progress in recent years by sharpening its definitions, placing a stronger focus on the social and economic determinants of health (rather than the subjective and individualised emphasis in some of the earlier work), and developing relevant indicators for researchers and governments. Living in a democratic and stable society that provides for its material needs is one of those factors. So too is having supportive friends and family, having rewarding and engaging work with adequate income, being free of violence and abuse, and being part of a community that cares for the health of *all* of its citizens. New thinking and practice is going to be needed around the 'balance' questions — the work/life balance, the liberty/equality balance, the regulation/deregulation, and growth/environment balance. These are legitimate issues for governments as well as individuals to ponder when considering policy options, including urban and environmental planning. As Hugh Mackay put it recently:

> *If we believe in the benefits that flow from being part of a functioning community, the real challenge is to find more ways of bringing people together again.*[7]

Refocusing our collective efforts in these ways is not going to be easy. Government is all about priorities, and I have already noted the powerful forces in modern society and modern thought which devalue a wider commitment to well-being. Already we can see how the global economic downturn is feeding this reductionist view of human circumstances. This is not the time, many are saying, to focus on anything but the state of the economy. However, if we are entering a period of constrained growth, as I believe we are, the level of sophistication in our thought and in our politics is going to have to improve. I predict a battle of ideas in which the simplicities of an economically charged populism will fight hard for preservation against the alternative concepts of fairness, sustainability and community well-being.

## Notes

1. *Commission on Social Determinants of Health, Final Report – Executive Summary* (WHO, 2008).
2. *The beyond blue depression in the workplace initiative*, p. 2.
3. *Journeys with the Black Dog* (Allen and Unwin, Sydney, 2007), p. 3.
4. *An Existential Conception of Buddhism* (Wheel Publications, Kandy, 1984), p. 1.
5. "Redefining progress – shaping the future to human needs", 6th Australian Institute of Family Studies Conference, Melbourne, 25–27 November 1998.
6. Wisdom Publications, 2008, p.46.
7. "We must find ways of bringing people back together", *Sydney Morning Herald*, 25 April 2009.

# Essential Ingredients of a Healthy Community

Keynote address delivered at
the Western Australian Community Foundation
Annual Summit

Perth, 9 June 2006

I'd like to begin my address today by quoting from the political novel *Primary Colours*, published in 1996. As you know, the novel is about the Democratic Party Primaries and involves a Governor from a small southern state.

At one point in the campaign a stunning speech is delivered by one of his opponents. Contained in this speech is an extraordinary description of contemporary politics and what we should do to re-make it.

> *This is really a terrific country, but we get a little crazy sometimes... I guess the craziness is part of what makes us great, it's part of our freedom. But we have to watch out. We have to be careful about it. There's no guarantee we'll be able to continue this — this highwire act, this democracy. If we don't calm down, it all may just spin out of control. I mean, the world keeps getting more complicated and we keep having to explain it to you in simpler terms, so we can get our little oversimplified explanations on the evening news. Eventually, instead of even trying to explain it, we just give up and sling mud at each other — and it's a show,*

*it keeps you watching, like you watch a car wreck or maybe wrestling.
That's right. The kind of posturing and hair-pulling you see us do in
thirty-second advertisements and on podiums like this one is exactly like
professional wrestling: it's fake, it's staged, it doesn't mean anything. Most
of us don't hate our opponents; hell, we don't even know 'em. We don't
have the fierce kind of ideological differences we used to have, back when
the war in Vietnam was on. We just put on the show because we don't
know what else to do. We don't know any other way to get you all riled
up, to get you out to vote. But there are some serious things we have to
talk about now. There are some decisions we have to make, as a people,
together. And it's gonna be hard to make them if we don't slow this thing
down a little, calm it down, have a conversation amongst ourselves.*

He concluded by saying:

*And I guess that's what I want to do with this campaign: sort of calm
things down a little, and see if we can start having a conversation about
the sort of place we want America to be in the next century.*[1]

Although it is clear that there is much more substance to
the party-political debate in the United States today, with the
Iraq War playing a similar role to Vietnam, the contrast drawn
in the speech between politics as adversarialism and soundbites
and politics as a serious conversation about the future stands the
test of time.

Let's take his advice and calm things down so we can think
clearly and rationally about what needs to be done to produce a
healthy community.

## How to Approach the Subject

There are a number of ways we could tackle the issue of a
healthy community.

We could focus on the sorts of values we would like to see
incorporated into the social, economic and political institutions
and practices.

This would be a useful exercise in that it would make transparent our most fundamental beliefs in values such as freedom and democracy, equity and justice, and rights and responsibilities. At the same time we could explore principles like accountability, sustainability and reconciliation.

The problem, however, is that it is how we apply these values and principles, most of which are in constant tension, if not conflict with each other, that is most important.

Another approach would be to describe in as much detail as we could what a healthy community would look like.

By doing this we would be getting closer to that which would be useful. However, there is a danger that we would simply build an idea-type utopia in our mind and not come to grips with the practical issues and constraints involved in its realisation.

I will endeavour, then, to approach the subject from the point of view of what the evidence tells me — either from personal experience or academic research — about the ways and means by which we can produce better outcomes in today's world.

I certainly hold the view that we can aim higher than a politics based simply on the pursuit of economic growth and the management of the conflicts that result with a divide-and-rule form of populism.

The alternative is more complex; it requires more discipline within government and it requires the support of the community to work, but it offers that much-needed and all-too-often missing element in modern life — hope.

## Indicators of a Healthy Community

In speaking of a healthy community, are we simply referring to one with a strong and growing Gross Domestic Product per capita? Or, to put it another way, is material wealth the basis of health and happiness?

This takes me to the important and growing literature on "Indicators of Well-being" produced in Australia by the Australia Institute, in the United Kingdom by the New Economics

Foundation and in the United States by Redefining Progress.[2] They are all working within a framework provided by the ongoing debate about sustainability.

The central point made in this literature is that we can't simply rely upon the Gross Domestic Product as an indicator. It works within the realm of monetised exchange, it doesn't distinguish between productive and unproductive activities (or, indeed, between costs and benefits) and it ignores the distribution of income throughout the community. Nor does it take account of household labour, a major contributor to our well-being.

Its reference points are totally economic, and we all know that the quality of our society and the environment is equally important. Issues like crime and violence, antisocial behaviour, family and relationship breakdown, urban amenity, air pollution, resource depletion, climate warming as well as the quality of health provision and education all play a role in determining not just our individual life chances, but the quality of our life more generally.

There are two ways to deal with this analysis — either develop a new indicator which takes these factors into account or develop a set of indicators and benchmarks for the range of economic, social and environmental factors deemed relevant to well-being.

My preference would be for the latter, although the work associated with the development of an indicator is most helpful. However, one wonders whether it is possible to bring together measures for these various factors into the one framework. Some of the measures are qualitative and some are quantitative. To reduce the former to the latter is a cause for concern. Indeed, it is doubtful whether there can be one measure of progress that would satisfy any human community as to its overall relevance. For one thing, technological change is constantly altering the terms of the debate about progress.

However, the development of indicators in connection with these factors is very important and should be a feature of modern government.

In the first place, they provide a very useful checklist of what to look for in determining the health of a community. For example, they will find any imbalances that may result from the priorities set by the government or by the community itself.

In the second place, they bring discipline and a sense of purpose to government itself.

## Purpose in Government

Even if the government doesn't set specific targets, the development of goals towards which it directs its efforts and attached to which are indicators of progress has the potential to bring that much-needed purpose and priority to government activity. This represents a strategic approach to government.

There is no doubt that much of government today is short-term and reactive. The development of a sense of purpose is a much-needed corrective to this phenomenon. Some jurisdictions have gone so far as to involve the community itself in the setting of objectives, benchmarks and targets. The highly successful *Tasmania Together* program initiated by Premier Jim Bacon was an example of this.[3]

*Tasmania Together* has 24 goals and 212 benchmarks by which progress is measured. Attached to each benchmark is a goal, a standard, an indicator and a target. The goals relate to Community, Culture, Democracy, Economy, and Environment.

In the Western Australian government's strategic plan of 2003, goals were set in relation to five areas — People and Communities, The Economy, The Environment, The Regions and Governance — attached to which were seventy-two strategic outcomes.[4]

When you look at the range and type of indicators you can start to get a feel for what modern democracies are seeking — the provision of jobs in a competitive economy, a fair distribution of the benefits of growth in a society that promotes equal opportunity, freedom for the people to pursue their ideas and interests, and protection and conservation of the natural and cultural heritage. In the national context you would add protection from external and terrorist attack. To feel threatened or uncertain in the face of world events can undermine all efforts to realise a healthy economy.

Note how both of the plans — Tasmania's and Western Australia's — incorporate governance arrangements. All too often we simply look at government as a means to an end. The truth is that the quality of our governance arrangements is itself an issue that ought to be incorporated into any account of our quality of life.[5] Nor is it just a case of improving the efficiency and effectiveness of public administration and public services generally. It also means improving our democracy and the way we engage the public in decision-making.

In our society, politics provides the link between government and the people. There is no reason that this ought to be restricted to elections every four years. Proper methods of consultation can make a real difference in providing for more efficiency in government (particularly financial efficiency, as potentially costly and time-consuming delays are avoided by dealing with community issues upfront and preferably in the planning stages of decision) and in ensuring relevance in service delivery. It should not be an afterthought but a process built into decision-making at the earliest possible stage.[6]

There are, of course, different levels of government — national, state and local. The ideas being developed here today would apply whichever level one was referring to. Indeed, I would argue that state and local governments have been more innovative in their approach to government than has the commonwealth government in recent years.

## Diversity and Balance in Society, Economy and Polity
This leads one to make the obvious point that there are communities as well as a community. When we refer to a healthy community we may mean the nation, a state or a locality. We may mean a region, a town or a suburb. We may mean

an association of like-minded individuals brought together by interest or aspiration in almost all areas of life. We may mean a religious community, a political community, an ethnic community, an occupational community, a sporting community or a cultural community.

I would argue that one of the ingredients of a healthy community is the existence of lots of communities within its boundaries. As Robert Putnam has written in his study of the Italian regional governments:

> *The correlation between civic engagement and effective government is virtually perfect.*[7]

In the regions of north-central Italy, rich networks of community associations, organised horizontally, have created richer economics, better governments and more social and intellectual progress generally.

I believe Putnam's argument about social capital and civic engagement can also be applied to our multicultural society and our market economy. Social harmony doesn't require social or religious control in the interests of one culture or one religion. In the real world of diversity, harmony comes from mutual respect and tolerance. Our democratic processes and liberal culture are needed to allow people the freedom to express themselves within the minimum limits deemed necessary.

It is important that we encourage exchange, dialogue and co-operation between people of different backgrounds, cultures and religions. As Putnam has noted, there is a difference between "bonding" and "bridging" social capital. The former involves connections that link people to others like themselves. The latter involves connections that link people to others unlike themselves.[8]

If we have only bonding social capital there is a danger that differences may degenerate into division and conflict. Bridging social capital, on the other hand, brings together different races, ethnic groups, generations and social classes. It is harder to build, but especially important in democratic societies. When you see bridging social capital at work in sporting and service clubs you can appreciate the role it plays in bringing people together.

A rich mosaic of bonding and bridging communities is both a means to and an end of a healthy community. It's not just a case of a healthy community, it also means healthier people generally. Epidemiological studies in the United States have shown that social involvement and social cohesion are positively linked to public health.[9]

Just as you can't straitjacket human society within one culture or one religion, so too you can't straitjacket the economy within one system of ownership and control. A healthy economy will involve government and private-sector enterprises as well as other economic forms, such as co-operatives and mutual societies. This is important, not just for reasons of choice and efficiency, but also for reasons of balance. As Henry Mintzberg has put it so well:

> *Above all, we need balance among the different sectors of society. This applies to attitudes no less than to institutions. Private-sector values are now pervading all of society. But government and other sectors should be careful about what they take from business.*[10]

By having a genuine mixed economy that involves government, private and communitarian elements we are best placed to achieve public interest outcomes.

This case for balance can also be made in respect of our federal system of government. There are locational and historical elements in Australia's pluralism that energise our democracy and allow for more choice and innovation.[11]

It is important, then, that each of our levels of government be treated seriously and given the constitutional, political and financial autonomy to be able to make a contribution to national progress. The link that has often been drawn between "the

Nation" and "the Commonwealth" and between "Nationalism" and "Centralisation" needs constant challenge. We need strong and innovative governments at all levels.

In and of itself, a market economy and the economic rationalist approach to policy associated with it are incapable of creating a healthy community. That's why the range and diversity of community associations, cultural capital, economic forms and centres of political power are so important to our health as a community.

Let me summarise my arguments so far:

- A healthy community will involve strategic government around the achievement of important objectives in relation to the economic, social and environmental indicators of well-being
- Good government is not just a means to an end, it is an end in itself
- A healthy community will require a wide range of healthy communities that develop social capital and bring people together in the public sphere, mutual respect amongst the diverse cultural and religious traditions, a balanced market involving government, non-government, co-operative and private-sector organisations, and strong, autonomous and innovative governments at all levels.

## Tackling Poverty

In talking of a healthy community we cannot ignore the question of distribution — how are the burdens and benefits distributed throughout the community? Can we guarantee that our citizens have equal opportunity to participate in social, economic, and political life? Do we have pockets of poverty holding people back from realising their capacities?

These are not just abstract distributional questions but important questions of public health. Empirical research has shown that "income distribution plays a greater role in the quality of public health than more traditional indices do".[12] It follows that a community which provides equal access to a good education, quality health care, security and amenity is one that will have higher levels of trust and social cohesion. Once again, it is government that has a key role in ensuring that this is the case.

In many ways we could characterise the Australia of today as strong on market economics, better on the environment than it was before, but still battling to deal with the wider social consequences of the type of economy and lifestyle that has emerged in recent years.

So too are we battling to find solutions to the problem of persistent poverty in our cities, regions and isolated communities. Even if the overall performance of our nation, state or locality was good in economic, social and environmental terms, the reality of poverty and what it means for individuals and families should never be let to slip off the radar screen of community concern.

One thing is clear — whilst the issue is not only a responsibility for governments there is little doubt that without concerted and co-ordinated action from governments such persistent poverty will remain. In order to achieve their objectives, Governments will need partners from the non-government sector and social entrepreneurs within communities, but they will have to provide significant resources and focus if the problem is to be tackled. In this respect, there are two challenges facing governments.

Firstly, to adopt a strategic, life-cycle perspective to social policy that aims to prevent the emergence of problems in the first place.

The Brotherhood of St. Laurence has come up with a strategic direction for its own work that focuses on the "at risk" years: the early years (both at home and into school), the years from school to work and further education, the periods in and out of work (whether voluntary or involuntary), and the retirement years.[13] This is the type of holistic approach we need, backed up by properly joined-up government and case and place management for individuals and localities. The more that service delivery can be localised and individualised the better. Indeed, "wherever possible people should have a direct personal relationship with government, rather than relying on one-size-fits-all principles which lead to crude, inefficient outcomes."[14]

We now have an enormous amount of research relating to these at-risk years (for example, from our own Telethon Institute for Child Health Research) that should become the basis for government and community-based initiatives, particularly in education and training, so that all our citizens have the capacity to participate in the mainstream social and economic life of the nation.

Secondly, to adopt more comprehensive interventions to address existing poverty, be it individual, family or community (or, as is most often the case, all three at once).

Here, issues related to passive welfare dependency, long-term unemployment, the Stolen Generation, disability, mental illness, drug and alcohol abuse, homelessness, family violence and child abuse make it a hard nut to crack. There is not one rule for all situations, and all too often the assumptions that lie behind our chosen interventions are themselves the problem.

This is also an area where there can be a complicated intersection between our social policy networks and programs and our criminal justice system. The encouragement of more co-operation across these sectors — particularly at a local level — which we are now seeing represents a positive step forward.

Certain factors are very clear if we are to make progress in tackling persistent poverty:

- it is resource intensive
- if change is to come, the individuals, families and communities themselves will have to be engaged in and committed to the process
- a one-size-fits-all approach will not work
- change agents are vital ingredients for success.

To say the issues related to persistent poverty are complex is an understatement. This is certainly not an area for right-wing intolerance or left-wing impatience. It requires hard work over a long period, particularly in respect of Indigenous poverty.

The unpalatable truth is that we have some communities in our nation that are completely dysfunctional. To talk of a healthy community means first and foremost establishing a proper system of law and order as recommended in our Gordon Inquiry.[15] Then the process of building can proceed through the provision of government infrastructure and support for social entrepreneurs and community leaders. However, without partnerships with the business community and engagement with the market economy that leads to employment and income, all the above will be incapable of producing lasting change. As Noel Pearson has observed:

> *No amount of resources and government and non-government service delivery will solve our social problems as long as our people are economically passive. This means work.*[16]

In tackling poverty, then, governments need strategies that go to the causes of poverty, particularly in the "at risk" years as well as strategies that address the complex reality of existing and persistent poverty.

A commitment of resources, community and business support, and new approaches to service delivery will all be needed if social exclusion is to be overcome and equal opportunity guaranteed.

## A Hierarchy of Needs?
This observation by Pearson raises the issue as to whether there is a hierarchy of needs — starting with the material and going through to the spiritual — around which priorities should be framed. What this would mean, for example, is that the economy ought to be given priority within the triple bottom line of economic, social and environmental factors.

The type of thinking involved in this approach would have it that we should abstract "the economy" from its social and environmental context and vigorously pursue its health independently of concern for community and the environment.

The fact is that the triple bottom line is a bottom line. Not only are there biological and ecological principles that have to be represented in order for human life to be sustained, there are also personal and social principles that have to be followed if economic development is to be possible: trust, for example.

Not only are there connections at this basic level. We should also refer to the costs of environmental decay and the benefits of a pristine environment for today's tourist economy. We should also note that when economic and social principles are applied in support of each other, nations are inevitably more productive and certainly happier.[17]

Yes, we do have to eat to live, but we also need to breathe and to feel. Nor is it just a question of "body and mind". It's also a matter of "soul". Life needs to be meaningful as well as productive and relational. If we don't provide space for human beings to seek meaning, our personal and collective lives will suffer.

All of these considerations make it harder for the decision-maker. There is no hierarchy of needs or naturally provided set of priorities. Everything is connected and dependent in one way or another. This makes for complexity in the pursuit of a strong economy, a good society and a clean environment.

It is not surprising, then, that instructive commentary on healthy communities today will use concepts like sustainability, balance, holistic government, rights and responsibilities and public–private partnerships. These are the sort of concepts that indicate seriousness with respect to the problems we face and the solutions we need. They reflect the complexity of real life and correctly focus on the public-policy intersections rather than the bureaucratic highways.

However, as our friend the Democratic candidate noted in my quotation at the start of this lecture, these are the sorts of concepts that cannot be easily converted into soundbites for the nightly news. It's not just a case of complexity of decision, it's also a case of complexity of vocabulary. There is an important communication challenge that faces all of us who wish to make a difference.

## Conclusion

How, then, can all these issues be brought together? What is essential for a healthy community?

Two factors stand out: strong and purposeful government, and active citizenship in all its forms.

If we are to create the balance necessary for a healthy community and incorporate economic, social and environmental factors into our thinking and practice, strong government is vital. It needs to be purposeful and strategic with respect to sustainability, to be tough and compromising in confronting violence, discrimination and prejudice, comprehensive in its assault on social exclusion, forward looking in its support for education and research, and clear and disciplined in its defence of diversity and competition in all areas of life, including government and politics.

At the same time, however, there needs to be active citizenship in all its forms, ranging from individual interest in public affairs to participation in community associations. It also means corporate citizenship and public–private partnerships in economic and community development. Indeed, the creation of a healthy community is not the responsibility of government alone — it requires all our efforts. Just as there needs to be balance within government, there needs to be balance between the community and the government.

Government and community are always connected, sometimes positively and sometimes negatively. We can predict good outcomes when they are connected via accountability and citizenship. We can predict less-than-good outcomes when they are connected by populism and cynicism. We can predict bad outcomes when connections are weak and a narrowly based government faces narrowly focused and privatised individuals. We need citizenship and politics, community and government. At their fulcrum may not be utopia but there may very well be a healthy community.

## Notes

1   Anonymous, *Primary Colours : A Novel of Politics* (1996), pp. 289–90.

2   www.tai.org.au, www.neweconomics.org, www.rprogress.org.

3   www.tasmaniatogether.tas.gov.au.

4   Department of Premier and Cabinet, Government of Western Australia, *Better Planning; Better Services* (2003).

5   Geoff Mulgan, "We need government and we need it to be boring", *The Spectator*, 13 May 2006, pp. 16–7.

6   See John Stewart, *Further Innovation in Democratic Practice* (1996) and *A Voice for All: Strengthening Democracy, Western Australian Government Citizenship Strategy 2004–2009*.

7   Robert Putnam "What Makes Democracy Work", *IPA Review*, vol. 47, no. 1, 1994, p. 32.

8   "Robert Putnam on Community", ABC Radio National Life Matters, 26 September 2001, http://www.abc.net.au/rn/talks/lm/stories/s373745.htm.

9   Ichiro Kawachi, Bruce P. Kennedy and Kimberley Lochner, "Long Live Community: Social Capital as Public Health", http://epn.org/prospect/35/35kawanf.html.

10  Henry Mintzberg, "Managing Government Governing Management", *Harvard Business Review*, May–June 1996, p. 83.

11  Greg Craven, *Conversations with the Constitution* (2004), ch. 3.

12  Kawachi, Kennedy and Lochner, *Long Live Community*.

13  Tony Nicholson, "Studying the Map and Plotting a Course", *Brotherhood Comment*, November 2005.

14  Geoff Mulgan, Perri 6 et al., *The British Spring: A Manifesto for the Election After Next* (1997), p. 49.

15  *Gordon Inquiry into Response by Government Agencies to Complaints of Family Violence and Child Abuse in Aboriginal Communities* (2002).

16  Noel Pearson, "What Cape York Communities can do to help themselves", *On Line Opinion*, 15 June 2001: www.onlineopinion.com.au.

17  See Robert Kuttner, *The Economic Illusion: False Choices Between Prosperity and Social Justice* (1987).

# 11.

# The Personal

# A Personal Journey of Healing

Speech delivered at
A Reason of Hope: Healing in a Chaotic World,
St Vincent's Hospital

Sydney, 22 October 2007

In introducing me today, Mark mentioned my friendship with Kim Beazley. That is a lead in to the first comment I want to make about my own religious affiliations. I was being pressed by the media on what my most basic beliefs were and answered in the following way: "I am a lapsed Methodist non-denominational sceptic who thinks Christianity is a good thing". On telling this story to Kim, he responded as quick as a flash: "That makes you a modern Anglican!"

Talk of religion takes me to the intellectual challenge posed by your conference theme "A Reason to Hope — Healing in a Chaotic World".

## Anxiety and the Human Condition

My interest today is with the human condition and the sources of anxiety therein.

A comprehensive analysis of this issue would involve three elements: what I would call the "spiritual", the "personal" and the "intellectual". For an individual they are overlapping issues, but for the purposes of analysis we often engage in the process of abstraction.

In my talk today the focus will be on the "the personal" dimension, but I note the limitations of this approach, as ideally each of the elements should be incorporated into the analysis and treated as a whole.

This being said, I will commence my talk with a summary of each of the elements and how they relate to a discussion of anxiety.

Let's start with the nature of existence itself and the questions that follow. Who are we? Why are we here? What is the meaning of life in the face of the inevitability of death?

I would call this "existential anxiety" and it has led to much spiritual and philosophical exploration over the years. The different religions all provide their own unique answer which becomes the basis for what is appropriately called "faith". However, even the most faithful often admit to doubt when confronted with human weakness and human failure or with natural calamity and natural disaster.

Next, we have the questions each of us ask about ourselves. Who am I? Where do I fit? These are questions asked by particular people in particular circumstances. They are personal questions that involve individual and society, psychology and sociology.

Sometimes everything is in balance, but all too often it isn't, and what we feel may have causes we find difficult or impossible to understand. For too many this can mean depression and melancholy.

Thirdly, we have the truly intellectual dimensions of human existence. Human beings are self-conscious, and language is a means to that end. They can reflect on the past and project into the future.

This can be an enormous source of anxiety as we see our failings from the past and find it difficult to imagine a better future. At the very minimum, we can never be sure about what the future holds.

Each of us, then, has to live with the pain of existence, the struggles of life and the uncertainties of the future. We need answers to the spiritual, personal and intellectual questions that follow.

## The Personal Dimension

Let me begin by telling you the story of the American business professor keen to educate his students in more than the laws of profitability. The professor came into the class and placed a glass jar on the desk. Then he brought out a bag full of stones and placed them one by one into the jar until no more could fit in.

"Is the jar full?" he asked. "Yes", replied his students.

Smiling the processor produced a second bag — this time full of gravel. He managed to shake the smaller stones into the spaces.

"Is the jar full?" he asked again. "No", said the students, a little wiser this time.

"You are right", he said, producing a bag of fine sand, which he coaxed into the spaces between the stones and the gravel.

"Is it full now?" The students were suspicious by now and said "Probably not, sir, knowing you".

They were right. He pulled out a small jug of water and poured it into the jar.

"Now", said the professor, "What does that teach us?"

Being a good business student and imbued with the White Anglo-Saxon Protestant ethic, one responded. "No matter how busy your schedule, you can always fit something more in."

"No", thundered the professor, "what it shows is that if you want to get the big stones in, you have to put them in first".

It was a lesson in priorities.[1]

"What are the most important priorities?" That was a question I couldn't avoid early in 2006 when a condition that had bothered me for sometime took over.

I was paralysed. I was trapped in my own mind. The past was the present and the future. I couldn't laugh and I couldn't feel.

With the help of family and close friends I made a decision to seek medical help and to change direction in my life. This was the turning point — an end to pointless resistance and the beginning of change. Medical advice and assistance followed.

This leads me to an important statistic: around one million adults and a hundred thousand young people live with depression every year. What lies behind these figures is the human reality of depression, individuals locked inside themselves, their minds hammering away twenty-four hours a day, forever in or on the edge of panic. They are vulnerable, needing help. They may be politicians. They may be tradespeople. They may be judges. They may be labourers. They may be "tough" sportsmen and sportswomen. They face the risk of self-harm or suicide as a release from pain is sought.

Understanding that depression is an illness is the first step a caring community can take.

## Stigma and Ignorance

Despite the increased understanding of issues related to mental health, stigma still remains the most significant challenge facing the field today.

Let me give you an image of how it works.

Prejudice and melancholy feed off each other like psychological twins. The more the concealment, the more the depression.

Not talking about depression is part of its definition. We hold it in. We treat it as a condition that can be "wished away". It follows that the first step in the recovery process is awareness that it is a treatable illness.

Consider the facts.[2]

Sixty to seventy per cent of patients with depression will respond to initial treatment with mono-drug therapy (usually twelve to twenty sessions, or about twelve weeks). Of the thirty per cent who do not respond to initial treatment, the majority will improve on an alternative approach, and upward of ninety per cent will eventually recover fully.

It's one thing to recognise that it is a treatable illness, another to explain why people need treatment today and why so many don't access it.

And note, as well, that despite enormous advances in treatment therapies there are still those for whom the answers cannot be found. That's why we need to continue the research effort in relation to this most complex of illnesses.

When it comes to those who don't seek treatment, we need to remind ourselves that stigma — and its twin, the fear of exposure — are still active ingredients in today's environment.

So too is ignorance. For example, we still have the "pull yourself together" school of thought and, of course, the "take some time off" school of thought.

Taking time off can be most beneficial — if coupled with treatment. However, all too often it may simply mean more time for the mind to stalk its victim.

In saying this I am reminded of the recently published *Journeys with the Black Dog*. It is a collection of stories from those who have experienced depression, put together by Tessa Wigney, Kerrie Eyers and Gordon Parker from The Black Dog Institute. Writing about these stories Wigney, Eyers and Parker note:

> *...what is not often understood about depression is that the suffering goes well beyond the physical realm of insomnia, loss of appetite and low energy. Depression infiltrates your thoughts and takes over your mind. It distorts your senses, as well as your perception of the past and future. It is a state of excruciating isolation.*[3]

It is the depth and intensity of the suffering associated with depression that renders worthless many of the homespun remedies such as taking time off.

This takes the discussion of depression to a deeper level: to the person himself or herself. We are all different in so many ways, and for so many different reasons, including genetic make up and life experience, particularly, but not only, in the early years. Studies show biochemical and genetic links to depression. They also show how a predisposition to depression may translate into illness itself because of life stressors such as relationship problems, family tragedy, financial crises or other medical conditions.

These are, of course, complex issues and all of us from time to time will experience mood swings and varying degrees of anxiety and melancholy.

## Mental Health and Well-being

This leads me to ask some fundamental questions: How seriously do we treat mental well-being as an object of personal and collective concern? Do we take our own well-being as an object of public policy and family concern as importantly as we should? Is well-being an issue we only confront in its absence? Why don't we put it forward as a major priority in our thinking and practice?

In looking at these questions I often turn to a quotation from the Buddhist scholar and teacher Stephen Batchelor:

> *How much of our life is spent in avoiding what we really are? Yet in a quiet corner of ourselves, do we not secretly recognise the deceptive strategies of such avoidance? How often do we find ourselves happily indulging in some trivial pursuit, even though a deeper awareness is whispering to us of its futility?*[4]

We know the truth of this avoidance, but why do we practice it?

I believe there is an answer to this question and it relates to the fact that self-awareness and community awareness bring to the surface issues we may prefer to see repressed. It exposes the limits of our apparent freedom: doesn't our society tell us we have freedom of will? It calls to account some of the illusions under which we live: aren't material living standards the best test of progress?

The other problem is that understanding and self-awareness create an imperative for change. Change is challenging. Even when we recognise the need to change,we all too often see it as the responsibility of others or something that can come from a part-time, half-hearted effort.

Recognition of this last point can be seen in Jennifer Wright's observation published in the Western Australian Law Society's journal *Brief*:

> *People seem to want to self-actualise before they attend to the foundation blocks of their lives.*[5]

Isn't modern consumer society powerful? It even has the capacity to absorb and co-opt that which seeks to transform it!

We have emotional needs, but how many of us care about that when looking within and exploring without?

Our emotional needs are not optional extras, they are integral to our being as humans. This was made clear to me by a nun who is working in aged care but had been an educator. She explained that teaching many in her classes was impossible because students came to school stretched and stressed from less-than-perfect and occasionally destructive family relationships. Add to this the noisiness of today's media saturated society. To make learning possible, she devised some prayers built around the ideas and practice of meditation. By calming the students down it became possible for them to learn.[6]

## The Social Dimension

This story not only demonstrates that our emotional needs are so important, but it also reminds us of the challenges that face the young, and indeed, the not so young, in our fast-moving and chaotic world.

People often develop anxiety disorders in their teenage years. For adolescents, the anxiety and fear associated with growing up, learning about life and looking to an uncertain and unknown future can be overwhelming, particularly given the competitive pressures in today's world. All too often, depression can become embedded to stalk and haunt an individual throughout life's journey. It stays within, like a secret for whom there is no story-teller.

It is concerning to find that 42 per cent of 11,300 young people surveyed by Mission Australia in December 2005 ranked suicide and self-harm in their top three issues of concern.

More priority needs to be given to supporting and encouraging our young people when considering the balance between family and work. More to the point, we have a responsibility to understand that the way society functions has an impact on the way young people think and feel. Indeed, it has been correctly observed that our young are the miners' canaries of modern society.

The research that has been done on the factors that lead to a positive outlook, engagement in life, meaning and satisfaction is an important starting-point for any way forward.

It is particularly pertinent if we are to help our youngsters meet the challenges of growing up. It is also important if we are to maximise the opportunities for well-being more generally. The research tells us that well-being is supported if we:

- Live in a democratic and stable society that provides material resources to meet needs
- Have supportive friends and family
- Have rewarding and engaging work and adequate income
- Be reasonably healthy and have treatment available in case of mental problems
- Have important goals related to one's values
- Have a philosophy or religion that provides guidance, purpose, and meaning to one's life.[7]

None of these things guarantees happiness and well-being, but they provide a healthier framework within which the individual can seek their own balance, free of the extraneous factors that can be so destructive. Life is full of contradictions anyway. Why would we complicate matters with dysfunctional social relationships and unrealisable aspirations?

I'm reminded of Peter Drucker's brilliant essay "Managing Oneself". In it he urges all of us to look at our strengths and weaknesses and how they relate to performance and happiness. Just as important are our values and how they relate to the work we are doing. "Organisations", he notes, "have to have values. But so do people. To be effective in an organisation, one's own values must be compatible with the organisation's values". What's more, values are not just operational, they also involve ethics and the "mirror test". "What kind of person do I want to see when I shave myself in the morning, or put on lipstick in the morning?"[8]

Not all jobs are appropriate for all people. Not all aspects of work are appropriate for all people. We are all different, but all the same regarding the need to find the right balance between our intellectual, emotional and spiritual needs.

All too often, the individual finds himself or herself in a situation of seemingly unmanageable stresses and strains. It is as if the imbalances within are being fed and nourished by the imbalances without. It is this complex inter-relationship between personality and environment which makes depression such a difficult issue to understand.

## Conclusion

Let me conclude by summarising the observations I have made as a result of my own experiences and further reflection on the subject:

- Priorities matter and the way we choose them is important.
- Depression is a treatable illness.
- Stigma and ignorance are the major barriers to its treatment.
- It's when individuals seek help that they are on the road to liberation, but that is the hardest step.

- It's one thing to tackle mental illness, another to promote mental well-being. All too often, well-being is treated as a peripheral or secondary issue.
- Our young are the miners' canaries of modern society, and it is especially important that we provide a caring environment for the transition to adulthood.
- Self-awareness is the key for individuals, families and communities, but we all too often prefer to live by myth and illusion: the myth of material welfare and the illusion of free will.
- The key to self-awareness is to understand the emotional as well as the intellectual and material needs we have.
- We live in a world of complexity and challenge, and it's not surprising that we put up enormous barriers to its proper and objective exploration.

This takes me to the story of the emperor who was not satisfied with the religions and philosophies of his day. He embarked on his own search for the truth and came up with three questions and three answers.

What were the questions?
- When is the most important time?
- Who is the most important person?
- What is the most important thing to do?

What were his answers?
- When is the most important time? Now — it is the only time we have.
- Who is the most important person? The person you are with (and if you are alone, that is you).
- What is the most important thing to do? To care.[9]

That's pretty good advice in a world that battles between the extremes of freedom as license and duty as repression.

**Notes**

1   Story is from Ajahn Brahm, *Opening the Door to Your Heart and Other Buddhist Tales of Happiness* (Lothian Books, Sydney, 2004), pp. 163–4.

2   From Mamta Gautam, "Depression and Anxiety" http://www.drgautam. com/gautam/article6.html

3   Tessa Wigney, Kerrie Eyers, and Gordon Parker (eds), *Journeys with the Black Dog* (Allen and Unwin, 2007), p. 3.

4   Stephen Batchelor, *An Existential Conception of Buddhism* (Wheel Publications, Kandy, 1984), p. 1.

5   Jennifer Wright, "Coping with the costs of success", *Brief*, October 2004, p. 11.

6   Sister Anthony, *To God on a Magic Carpet* (Spectrum Publications, 2004).

7   Ed Diener and Martin Seligman, "Beyond Money: Towards an Economy of Well-being", *Psychological Science in the Public Interest*, vol. 5, no. 1, 2004, p. 25.

8   Peter Drucker, *Management Challenges of the 21st Century* (Harper Business, New York, 1999), p. 178.

9   Sourced from *Opening the Door of Your Heart*, pp. 112–116.